The Experienced Soul

AKIBA HEBREW ACADEMY

Modern Hebrew Classics
David Patterson, Series Editor

This series presents formative works of lasting significance that have appeared in Hebrew, as well as more recent critical work. The series is designed to acquaint the English reader with the quality of modern Hebrew writing in its period of revival and renaissance and to reflect the cultural, religious, and social conditions and conflicts in Jewish life in the nineteenth and early twentieth centuries.

The Experienced Soul: Studies in Amichai, *edited by Glenda Abramson*

Joseph Perl's *Revealer of Secrets:* The First Hebrew Novel, *translated with an introduction and notes by Dov Taylor*

Tradition and Trauma: Studies in the Fiction of S. J. Agnon, *edited by David Patterson and Glenda Abramson*

The World of Israel Weissbrem, *translated by Alan D. Crown*

Out of the Depths, *Joseph Chaim Brenner, translated by David Patterson*

The Experienced Soul

Studies in Amichai

EDITED BY

Glenda Abramson

A Division of HarperCollins*Publishers*

Modern Hebrew Classics

Some material in the early part of the introduction was reprinted from Glenda Abramson, *The Writing of Yehuda Amichai: A Thematic Approach*, with permission of the State University of New York Press.

All rights reserved. Printed in the United States of America. No part of this publication may be reproduced or transmitted in any form or by any means, electronic or mechanical, including photocopy, recording, or any information storage and retrieval system, without permission in writing from the publisher.

Copyright © 1997 by Westview Press, A Division of HarperCollins Publishers, Inc.

Published in 1997 in the United States of America by Westview Press, 5500 Central Avenue, Boulder, Colorado 80301-2877, and in the United Kingdom by Westview Press, 12 Hid's Copse Road, Cumnor Hill, Oxford OX2 9JJ

Library of Congress Cataloging-in-Publication Data
The experienced soul : studies in Amichai / edited by Glenda Abramson.
  p. cm.—(Modern Hebrew classics)
 Includes bibliographical references and index.
 ISBN 0-8133-2730-X (hc)
 1. Amichai, Yehuda—Criticism and interpretation. I. Abramson, Glenda. II. Series.
PJ5054.A65Z64 1997
892.4'16—dc21   96-6694
                                                                                                        CIP

The paper used in this publication meets the requirements of the American National Standard for Permanence of Paper for Printed Library Materials Z39.48-1984.

10   9   8   7   6   5   4   3   2   1

*My soul is experienced and built
against erosion like mountain terraces. I'm a man who holds on
I'm a middle man, a buckle man.*
                     (Great Tranquillity—Questions and Answers)

Contents

Acknowledgments xi
Introduction, Glenda Abramson xiii

1 A Tribute to Yehuda Amichai: How Amichai is Regarded
  by Egyptian Intellectuals, *Abd El-Khalik Gobah* 1

Part One
Poetry

2 Towards a Comprehensive Study of Amichai's Poetry,
  Arnold J. Band 9

3 The Conceit as a Cardinal Style-Marker in
  Yehuda Amichai's Poetry, *Ziva Shamir* 17

4 On the Political Significance of Amichai's Poetry,
  Boaz Arpaly 27

5 Yehuda Halevi and Solomon Ibn Gabirol in
  the Early Poetry of Yehuda Amichai: Two Different
  Poems—Two Different Styles, *Masha Itzhaki* 51

6 Portrait of the Poet in a Landscape, *Glenda Abramson* 57

7 The Metaphor of the Persona, *Ziva Feldman* 71

8 The "Feminine" in Yehuda Amichai's Poetics,
  Nili Scharf Gold 77

9 Amichai and the *Likrat* Group: The Early Amichai and
  His Literary Reference Group, *Gershon Shaked* 93

Part Two
Drama

10 God, Jonah, and the Drama: The Actualization
    of a Myth, *Gabriella Moscati Steindler*   123

Part Three
Fiction

11 Home and Abroad: The Case of Amichai's
    Not of This Time, Not of This Place, Risa Domb   133

12 A Home Within: Place and Time in
    Amichai's Fiction, *Leon I. Yudkin*   141

13 Poetic and Dramatic Elements in the
    Children's Literature of Yehuda Amichai,
    Menucha Gilboa   149

About the Book   159
About the Editor and Contributors   161
Index   165

Acknowledgments

This volume is offered as a tribute to Yehuda Amichai on the occasion of his seventieth birthday, which was celebrated in Oxford in 1994 by an international conference devoted to his works. My most grateful thanks to the Oxford Centre for Hebrew and Jewish Studies, without whose support this book would not have been produced. Thanks also to Emma Muir, Alun Ward, and Melanie Sampson for their hard and unstinting work and to Stephen Ashworth for his patience and meticulous attention to detail.

Glenda Abramson

Introduction

Glenda Abramson

Yehuda Amichai was born in 1924 in Würzburg, Bavaria, to a family of Orthodox Jews. He received a traditional education and first encountered Hebrew through prayers at the age of four or five. In 1936 his family emigrated to Palestine, settling first in Petach Tikva and then in Jerusalem where he continued his religious education.

During the Second World War he joined the Jewish Brigade and served in Egypt. Later, in the *Palmah*, he smuggled arms and "illegal" immigrants into Palestine. At this time he began to read modern English poetry, particularly the works of W. H. Auden which, together with the poetry of the medieval Jewish warrior-poet Shmuel Hanagid, were to remain a major influence on his own writing. His encounter with Auden and, to a lesser extent, with the works of T. S. Eliot led to his exploration of the Hebrew language as a vehicle for expressing the postwar mood. When asked in an interview whether he viewed himself as a rebel against the tradition of Shlonsky and Alterman, Amichai denied any conscious attempt to initiate a new wave of poetry. However, he is frequently cited by critics as the forerunner of a school of poetry that celebrates the developing language by utilizing its colloquial richness. He is also credited with belonging to the "generation of the land", *dor baaretz*, the generation of writers born during the first quarter of the twentieth century, fondly termed the *Palmah* generation. This popular sobriquet is largely a generalization, for the generation to which it refers does not constitute a homogeneous artistic "school"; its nominal representatives fall into distinct categories determined by biographical circumstances, by cultural background, by their choice of themes, or by the poetics that distinguishes one literary convention from another. Amichai's work is a case in point: it constituted a departure from any previous or contemporary literary norm. In his extensive paper for this volume, Gershon Shaked discusses the relationship between Amichai's new "genotype" and that of his literary forebears.

During his adolescence Amichai abandoned formal religious practice, without relinquishing its spirit or his love of the poetry of the Jewish liturgical texts, which he exploits in his verse. His rebellion against the traditional Orthodoxy practised by his family to a very large extent conditions his writing. It is his language, "the stones of the past", that determines his position in relation to the religious vernacular associated with and represented by his father. The clear statement of this position is made within his language itself.

Amichai's first book of poetry, *Akhshav uvayamim haaherim* (Now and in other days), appeared in 1955 and was awarded the Shlonsky Prize in 1957. It was followed by *Bemerhak shtei tikvot* (Two hopes apart) in 1958, which set the tone for poetry that distilled the disillusionment of an entire generation. At the same time this poetry introduced the themes that were to characterize the remainder of his work: love, war, the passage of time, his spokesman's relationship with his father, and his confrontation of his own mortality. Amichai's linguistic innovations were marked by his incorporation of the most common elements of the vernacular, technological and military terms, snatches of popular lyrics, proverbs, idioms, and slogans, in addition to ironic wordplay, rich imagery, and the use in Hebrew of the conceit, a term which has been fashionably if not always accurately applied to his figuration. In one of the essays that follow, Ziva Shamir elucidates this figure, putting the record straight about Amichai's use of it.

In 1961 Amichai published a collection of short stories, *Baruah hanoraah hazot* (In this terrible wind), in which he recounted, among other topics, his wartime experiences in Egypt and Palestine and demonstrated his ability to write prose, albeit strongly laced with the imagery of his poetry. In 1959, at the age of 35, he returned to Würzburg for the first time, visiting the sites of his childhood which meanwhile had been destroyed by the war. The experience of return resulted in a novel, *Lo meakhshav, lo mikan*, 1963 (*Not of This Time, Not of This Place*), and the radio play *Paamonim verakavot*, 1963 (Bells and trains), which won the Kol Yisrael first prize for a radio play in that year. Amichai's memories of Würzburg (appearing in these works in the fictional guises of Weinburg and Zingburg respectively) create unexpected nostalgia and a dislocation of the idea of *place*, symbolized, as Risa Domb demonstrates, by the splitting of the novel's protagonist into two distinct personalities. Through this device the novel also contemplates the split personality of the modern Israeli: half in thrall to his birthplace, the other half grasping the future of redemption in Israel. At the same time it examines the post-Holocaust need to revisit, and then if possible reclaim a lost childhood.

After the Six-Day War in 1967 Amichai published *Akhshav baraash*, 1968 (Now in the noise), which contains two long works, *Yerushalayim 1967* (Jerusalem 1967) and the quasi-autobiographical *Masot benyamin haaharon mitudela* (The travels of the last Benjamin of Tudela), a confessional review of his life from the time of his departure from Germany in 1936, and, at the same time, a reflection on the human condition in the twentieth century. His second novel, *Mi yitneni malon*, 1971 (To have a dwelling place), was an unusual departure for Amichai and it confused and angered the critics and the reading public. It served his need to vent some of his disillusionment about the United States, on the one hand, and Zionism, on the other, and also to shatter a certain public image of himself which had been formed over the years, in his own words, that of a "holy cow, writing about beautiful things . . . ".[1]

In his later volumes Amichai abandons the careful prosodic structures of his earlier poetry and the classical forms of couplet, quatrain, and sonnet, and creates a more liberally constructed, less figured, open verse, suffused with elegiac and nostalgic lyricism. *Velo al menat lizkor*, 1975 (Not for the sake of remembering) employs a new poetics centred on brutal images of dryness, mourning, barrenness, and loss. The language is unadorned, with repeated instances of wordplay. This book contains little reference to his customary themes of war, Israeli society, or the Israeli landscape but is among the most emotionally, almost desperately, concentrated of Amichai's verse, equalling the "Benjamin" cycle in intensity.

Love in the season of truth

What blooms
what thinks
in this spring?

What of the night? You. You're of the night
signalling you.

And the sound, what? Blood
in your lucid body's canals.
They hear.

Washing hands, washing nails.
She'll cry out. A hard hairdo without water.
It hurts.
("What do you want of me?")

> *A speaker of truth*
> *yes, yes, be fruitful and multiply!*
> *Yes, yes.*
>
> *(p. 39)*

Subsequent books of verse moved Amichai's poetic discourse, not laterally into a broadening of thematics, but more deeply inwards, confirming it as a single, multivalent document of both personal and national significance. *Gam haegrof haya paam yad petuhah veetzbaot*, 1989 (The fist was once an open hand and fingers) broke new ground in linguistic sparseness and in its—sometimes bitterly—elegiac tonalities.

Biographical facts occupy a prominent place in Amichai's writing which is especially noted for its apparently personal and autobiographical flavour. By extension and implication they also illuminate his society and its particular preoccupations. In the address to the Writers' Convention in 1968 he expounded his notion of the role of the writer in Israeli society as one who shares the communal experience and writes about it, one who is at the same time engagé and isolated: "Out of three or four in a room / one is always standing at the window, / He must see the evil among thorns / and the fires on the hill . . . ".[2] A great deal of Israeli fiction is autobiographical, much of it dealing with the childhood of the protagonist in realistic detail, with particular emphasis on the relationship of the child to its natural environment. This allows the author to celebrate the Israeli landscapes and cityscapes and to chart their changes in response to altered circumstances. Childhood stories also express the author's nostalgia for an idealized past in which the child's innocence was shared by that of the landscape. Israeli poetry as a whole relies less heavily on autobiographical fact, concentrating instead on varieties of personal experience. Amichai's poetry falls somewhere between both possibilities, autobiographical in appearance and mood rather than in substance. He has declared that all poetry is to an extent autobiographical, meaning presumably that in its introspective intimacy it allows insight into the mind and heart of the writer, rather than rendering a life story. In this respect his own poetry is deceptive, for while its composite effect is that of a coherent life history, it consists more accurately of a selection of events from a life, which become the basic propositions upon which his entire literary output is based. His composite hero, the lyric "I" of his verse, the narrator of his fiction and Jonah of his full-length stage play *Masa leninveh* (Journey to Nineveh), is derived not only from his life events but also from certain mythic motifs: exile from a birthplace; the loss of a beloved and innocent girl who dies as a sacrificial victim, to be sought subsequently through the love of many women; war and the hero-as-warrior; the putative killing of the father through rejection of his teaching signifying also a rebellion against God. Ultimately, after many physical and spiritual journeys in search of understanding, the hero attains his own old age and the beginning of wisdom.

Despite the autobiographical truths and despite Amichai's contemporary settings and language, much of his poetry exists within a world that is closer to myth than to the realities of modern Israel. The people who populate his poetry, and the cities and landscapes in which they move, inhabit a plane somewhere between the real and the metaphysical: gods in the guise of angels and rabbis, and God himself, eat, drink, chastise, pray, and play games among the mortals—the speaker, "I", his parents, his children, and his loves. Between the dead and the living stands the vivifying mechanism of memory which, in the speaker's world, allows death to be denied, chronology to be distorted, past and present to lose their divide, and the interrupted colloquy with the father to be continued. At the centre of the poetry stands the ordinary man, once a soldier and lover, now a wily transmuter of the language of God into the language of man. He perceives the ambiguous ordinariness of events through which even language appears to be attenuated. Typical of his spokesman's ironic self-deflation is his comment, "I'm a poor prophet" ("poor" in the sense of "impoverished"):

> *I'm a poor prophet. Like a poor child*
> *who has only two crayons. I draw my life*
> *in war and love, noise and silence.*
>
> *The great prophets threw away half their prophecies*
> *like cigarettes half-smoked by a bad-tempered smoker.*
> *I collect them and make them into poor prophecies for me.*
>
> *Water is quiet in water-tanks,*
> *in empty pipes no-water wails and snores.*
>
> *Words absorb "blood, sweat and tears"*
> *and are thrown in the garbage. Words for one-time use*
> *like paper tissues. People for one-time use,*
> *this is their eternity.*
> *Words should have been empty*
> *and narrow and hard, like a watershed,*
> *despair and hope, joy and sadness, anger and tranquillity*

> should have streamed to both sides
> to a new course.
>
> I'm a poor prophet. I live in others' hopes
> like in a ray which is not meant to light me.
> I cast a shadow as my image, my likeness,
> with my body I block out a famous and beautiful sight.
> I come between the viewer and his vision.
>
> I'm a poor prophet who returns home at noon
> to eat and rest and to sleep in the evening.
> I have an annual holiday and a sabbatical
> and life insurance and an old age pension.
>
> I began my life from very low down.
> As I rise high with soul-intoxication,
> as I reach the peak of my fantasies,
> I find myself among ordinary people
> who have children and a job and family worries
> and domestic cares. These are my fantasies.
> I'm a poor prophet.
> **(Gam haegrof hayah paam yad petuhah veetzbaot, p. 62)**

Notwithstanding the argument about Amichai's contribution (or lack of it) to Israel's political debate, the *perception* of a contribution conditions much of the public and critical response to him. For example, Ziva Feldman rejects any ideological or political subtext in Amichai's poetry, attributing it to a "sole esoteric persona expressing his feelings". Boaz Arpaly, on the other hand, in common with many commentators, argues:

> [E]ven when poetry on the face of it contains nothing political or it is difficult to pinpoint any political stance in it, it may have a political effect and political importance in the specific circumstances in which it appears. In the right context, all poetry, no matter what its surface contents may be, can be accorded a political status and political significance.

Abd El-Khalik Gobah offers a succinct evaluation: "The Egyptian intelligentsia recognises Amichai as a man of his time. In addition to the feeling that his poems bestow a new mission on Israeli intellectuals during the era of peace, they also bestow on him a position of honour and obligation to take an active part in the efforts towards a stable and lasting peace amongst the nations." He quotes Amichai's line: "I am a racist for peace." Even in our day in Israel, whether they like it or not, poets are still prophets. Amichai may not allow himself an overtly political voice, but his work is certainly *politicized*, increasingly so over the past decade. For example, his frequent recalling of the period of the War of Independence has accreted strong political overtones.[3] It seems that the preservation of the early heroic stereotypes—throughout Amichai's poetry on war and in his short stories—implies the glorification of the origins of the present Israeli crisis. Yet whether or not the poetry sets out to provide a public voice, it is ultimately the reading public who decides. In great art every reader finds what he or she is seeking, and neither they nor the academics who purport to direct their thinking need necessarily agree.

Collected in this volume are essays by today's leading Amichai scholars in Europe, Israel, and the USA, essays covering the full generic range of Amichai's work: poetry, fiction, drama, and stories for children. The variety of essays reveals a variety of approaches to this work, some contradicting others, some oppositional almost to the point of conflict. Divergent points of view and opinions about it lead to a variety of interpretations, many of them representing particular interpretive schools of criticism. The conflict of interpretation subverts all earlier judgments of Amichai's work as being "simple" or "accessible". On the surface it indeed seems to be so. However, the diversity of approaches taken by scholars in this volume indicates, among other things, that Amichai's "accessibility" is deceptive: on the contrary, his work exposes layers of concealed meaning through his unique employment of a system of tropes, most notably metaphor and the conceit, in addition to his idiosyncratic use of intertexts and textual allusions. For example, the self-effacement of "I'm a poor prophet", its presentation of the simple, homely man's colloquial declarations, belies the poem's structural sophistication, its extended metaphors, ironic juxtapositions and reflections on language. Moreover, as Nili Gold effectively argues, Amichai's language sometimes incorporates linguistic and poetic structures which are more common to feminine discourse. Ultimately one realizes that Amichai's is a sustained method of verbal deception which can frequently mislead, even trick, the innocent reader.

Far from detracting from the value of his writing, the critical conflicts, divisions, and attributions merely illustrate the fact that this artwork which engages by its apparently unilateral simplicity, its attractiveness, its pseudo-ingenuous wit and playfulness is still able to rouse strong and partisan emotions in its interpreters. With all this, the inner reaches of Amichai's work remain untouched, only deceptively attainable. They lead the reader and the critic across layers of meaning and displacement, beyond masks and dissimulation into a profound, disquieting, and unique vision of twentieth-century urban life.

Amichai's poetic style, his subject matter, and his genuine anxiety expressed in richly textured verse have gained him a wide Israeli and international following. For two generations he has been the most well-loved Israeli poet, read by millions in a variety of languages and taught in schools and universities. He has received many prestigious prizes, among them the Bialik Prize (1975) and the Israel Prize (1982); his books have been translated into forty-seven languages, and a multitude of translations have appeared in English alone. He has lectured at universities throughout the United States, and in Europe and South America, and has participated in numerous international poetry festivals. In 1994 he celebrated his seventieth birthday which was marked (*inter alia*) by a conference about his work at the Oxford Centre for Hebrew and Jewish Studies in Oxford. Lines from his poetry have become part of common usage within Israel, as epigrams and aphorisms, cited in lawcourts, in the Knesset and other venues of public utterance, forming part of the fabric of Israeli public discourse. A number of full-length studies have been written about him, three of which are discussed in this volume by Arnold Band. A bibliography of Amichai's published work in translation alone numbers 622 pages.[4]

What clearly emerges from the papers in this volume is the sense that Amichai's innovation rests not only on what he has initiated but also what he has abandoned: national sentiment, excessive ornamentation, rhetoric, mannerism (although he is considered a mannerist by at least one of our writers), and high-flown artificial language. His influence on modern Hebrew literature is inestimable; at first he appeared to be no more than a part of an evolving literary movement (so intriguingly delineated by Gershon Shaked) but subsequently his new style, his language, his "countervalues", to use Professor Shaked's term, his poetics as a whole, have become a new literary norm in Israel.

Notes

1. Interview, London, August 1986.
2. *Shirim 1948–1962* (Poems 1948–1962) (Schocken Publishers, 1968), p. 76.
3. See Dalia Karpel, "Mekaveh lanobel" (Hoping for the Nobel Prize), *Ha'ir*, 3 November 1989.
4. Essi Kandelshein and Nava Duchovne (eds.), *To Commemorate the 70th Birthday of Yehuda Amichai: A Bibliography of His Work in Translation* (Institute for the Translation of Hebrew Literature, 1994).

1

A Tribute to Yehuda Amichai: How Amichai is Regarded by Egyptian Intellectuals

Abd El-Khalik Gobah

It is well known that intellectuals, in expressing their opinions, exercise an influential role in society. They have the ability to engage in debate and to offer criticism of cultural, social, and ethical shortcomings. In this regard it is worth noting the fact that the group of Egyptian intellectuals who are interested in Hebrew literature is not restricted to professors who teach Hebrew language and literature, or Hebrew linguists, or students of Semitic languages, of which there are many thousands. One must include those intellectuals interested in world literature, and hundreds of thousands of them read translations from Hebrew in Arabic or English.

Indeed, intellectuals of any society have a vital role in the crystallization of public opinion and even in influencing the course of public thought. This role is especially prominent in cases of national importance, in that the intelligentsia has a special ability to concretize what occurs in society and to emphasize currents of thought and the direction of various ideas. Thus, one can say that the writer—any writer—stands at the top of the ladder of priorities in the research and discourse of intellectuals. These see in their works a sort of mirror which faithfully reflects not only the emotions and thoughts of the writer but also the thoughts and ideas of the society as a whole. Indeed, the writer becomes quite renowned when his works presage what will occur in the future. Even if these works do not rank as clear prophecy, scholars are able to pinpoint their degree of vision after perhaps a few decades. This, in our opinion, is the case regarding Yehuda Amichai.

Egyptian intellectuals are aware, according to the above conventions, that the writer and poet Yehuda Amichai has earned a place for himself in the heart of the reader of modern Hebrew poetry. A following has developed because of the variety of his works, which include the short story, the novel, the play, and the radio script. But it is in poetry that he is most distinguished.

Amichai wrote his first collection of poems, entitled *Shirim* (Poems), in 1955. This collection included *Akhshav uvayamim haaherim* (Now and in other days), *Bemerhak shtei tikvot* (Two hopes apart), and *Baginah hatziburit* (In the public garden). In 1961, his collection of short stories, *Baruah hanoraah hazot* (In this terrible wind), was published.

In 1963, his novel *Not of This Time, Not of This Place* was published. This engaging and expansive lyrical novel describes a strange and desperate pursuit in a German country village, a deep and conquering love one summer in Jerusalem, and the crisis which the hero, Joel, experiences. The text is rich with lyrical *piyyutim* and gripping in its episodic descriptions which captivate the reader with the force of Amichai's enchanting poetic language. From the double persona of Joel, divided between Jerusalem and the German city of Weinburg, rises the total confusion of the generation which is still torn between two worlds.

In 1968 Amichai's *Paamonim verakavot* (Bells and trains: radio scripts and plays) was published. The book contained two radio scripts and two plays of which *Bells and Trains* was awarded the Kol Yisrael first prize in 1963. This radio play has been translated into many languages and broadcast in Italy, France, Sweden, Denmark, Switzerland, Hungary, Germany, and Finland. The second radio play, *Hayom shebo nikbar Martin Buber* (The day Martin Buber was buried), was awarded the Kol Yisrael first prize in 1968. *Shetah shel hefker* (No-man's-land), a one-act play, was performed by the Zavit Theatre in 1962, and *Journey to Nineveh* was staged at the Habimah Theatre in 1964.

In *Velo al menat lizkor* (Not for the sake of remembering), published in 1975, written during 1970–71, there is an intense but simple concentration of characters and metaphors. A more efficient use of words is discernible amidst a painful recognition of a world in which words are no longer able to express everything. One can also detect a growing maturity in this work.

In addition to Amichai's many other books of poetry, including *Shalvah gedolah, sheelot uteshuvot*, 1980 (Great tranquillity—questions and answers), and *Love Poems*, first published in 1978, in 1985 he published a book of philosophical poetry, *Meadam ata uleadam tashuv* (From man you are and to man you will return). As a whole, these books express a maturity of emotion, precise wording and images, with a first-person description of love and life which typifies Amichai's poetry.

I would like to emphasize that most of Amichai's poetry has been translated into other languages including English, French, Italian, Swedish, Danish, Hungarian, German, Finnish, and Arabic. I was one of the Egyptian writers who studied Amichai's writings after he won the 1982 Israel Poetry Prize. It was then that we began to correspond.

My book, based on my Master's thesis, was published in 1985 in Arabic and included many citations in Hebrew and Arabic. To my great regret, due to many factors and circumstances, it was not published by a popular press. I still have hope that this scientific work will be published soon. My book, *The Poetical Works of Yehuda Amichai*, contains three major sections. The first section treats the life of the poet. This section is divided into two parts: the political and social context of Amichai's era, which sheds light on the influence of conditions and social and political developments on his works and on his early years. The second section, "The poetic style of Amichai", is divided into three parts: "The development of Hebrew poetry in the modern era", "An overview of Amichai's works", and "The poet's motifs of style". The third section, "Directions in Amichai's poetry", contains three parts: "Issues and structures in Amichai's poetry", "His poetic direction", and "Religion and nationalism in his poetry". The summary includes the conclusions of the research, and a large appendix of examples translated into Arabic. At the end there are bibliographical notes in which are included publications in Hebrew, English, and Arabic.

This research is a strong indication that Yehuda Amichai has reached an esteemed position amongst Egyptian scholars, those interested in modern Hebrew literature, and its students in Egypt, and, in my opinion, in other Arab countries such as Lebanon, Jordan, and Syria. However, Amichai is most popular amongst Egyptian intellectuals. He himself understood this during his visit to Egypt in 1993, when he lectured at the Israel Academic Centre in Cairo. Here are a few of the many reactions attesting to Amichai's popularity amongst scholars of Hebrew literature in Egypt:

(a) Yehuda Amichai is considered one of the most prominent poets. The Egyptian intelligentsia recognises that he is a man of his time. In addition to the feeling that his poems bestow a new mission on Israeli intellectuals during the era of peace, they also bestow on him a position of honour, and an obligation to take an active part in the efforts towards a stable and lasting peace amongst the nations.

Certainly one must look at the poet's importance through the topics of his works. The pivotal elements in his thought that have brought him fame and typify his works are remembrance of the past, the threats of the future, time and the vicissitudes of consciousness, the lasting and the ephemeral, change and forgetfulness, war, death, love, and peace.

(b) There is debate amongst scholars of modern Hebrew literature in Egypt on the works of authors who have been awarded prizes for Hebrew literature. Yehuda Amichai is placed at the top of the ladder.

(c) The debate amongst scholars, Hebraists, and experts in modern Hebrew literature focuses on the differences of meaning, style, and registers in the poet's work. Indeed, there is a special character and a unique and powerful voice throughout all his themes, including the theme of peace, which has developed into an ideology. He writes:

> *I no longer care about dying alone*
> *But I want to die in my bed*
> **(Shirim, p. 83)**

> *But with hands, it is better that they be*
> *hands of a lover, and not the hands of war.*

(d) Amichai's poetry has a broader significance than its critical evaluation, since it may influence the readers' opinions regarding issues of peace and everyday life. These possibilities are increasingly developing, in our opinion, amongst the intellectuals on both the Arab and Israeli sides.

(e) The majority of Egyptian intellectuals interested in modern Hebrew literature agree that Amichai's works express an essential quality, namely, simple writing that does not cater only to professional readers, no demonstration of verbal muscle. The language is transparent and speaks for itself. In other words, the poet appeals directly to the reading public. However, the verbal simplicity does not restrict the poetry's profundity. A simple sentence such as "The two of us together and each one alone" (*Shirim*, p. 13) will remain as profound as life itself.

(f) Amichai has occupied a prominent place in the research of several Egyptian professors in terms of the feelings he expresses and in terms of his thought. In this regard, he is thought of as one of the authors who is sensitive to the changing voice of the cultural and educated milieu within which he lives and creates. Indeed, Amichai is exceptional in his close listening to this voice. For example, he writes in his poem "El male rahamim" (God full of mercy):

> *If God were not full of mercy*
> *There would be mercy in the world and not only in him.*
> . . . .
> *I who picked flowers on the mountain*
> *And looked in all the valleys,*
> *I who brought corpses down from the hills*
> *Know how to say that the world is empty of mercy . . .*
> **(Shirim, p. 69)**

And he writes:

> *Men adorned themselves with their first love*
> *And not with decorations from battle and war*
> **(Sonnet 23, Shirim, p. 58)**

> *The true abortion,*
> *those who fall in war:*
> *against this*
> *no one protests*
> . . . .
> *I am a racist of peace*
> **(She'at hahesed,**
> **The hour of grace,**
> **pp. 47–48)**

These are only a few of the many examples which are woven into Amichai's books of poetry and prose. One may say that the works of this poet demonstrate that he has integrated the trends and possibilities of peace and brotherhood while they were still unknown or only partially perceived by society. Therefore, his works have not infrequently become primary sources which form the basis of further studies. The variety of Amichai's work will continue to provide bounty for investigation by Egyptian researchers, from critical research to seminars on motifs and images, metre and grammatical usage. There is no doubt that Amichai's poetry is a great world from which enlightened Egyptian intellectuals derive much pleasure.

Part One
Poetry

2

Towards a Comprehensive Study of Amichai's Poetry

Arnold J. Band

The poetic career of Yehuda Amichai is clearly one of the longest and most productive in the history of modern Hebrew literature and has elicited a sizeable body of criticism, mostly favourable, at least until the early 1970s when some academic critics began to call attention to what they felt was repetitiousness in his poetics. Amichai, furthermore, is the most widely read Israeli poet, both in the original Hebrew and in translation, especially to English. These basic uncontestable facts must serve as a preface to any attempt to consider the *totality* of Amichai's poetry, a process which has begun during the past eight years. Since 1986, four book-length works which point in this direction have appeared: Boaz Arpaly's *Haperahim vehaargatel: shirat Amichai 1948–68* (Tel Aviv: Hakibutz Hameuchad, 1986); Yehudit Tzvik's *Yehuda Amichai: mivhar maamarei bikoret al yetsirato*, including a lengthy survey of Amichai criticism (Tel Aviv: Hakibutz Hameuchad, 1988); Glenda Abramson's *The Writing of Yehuda Amichai: A Thematic Approach* (Albany: State University of New York Press, 1989); and Nili Gold's *Lo kabrosh: gilgulei imagim vetavniyot beshirato shel Yehuda Amichai* (The transformation of images and structures in the poetry of Yehuda Amichai) (Tel Aviv and Jerusalem: Schocken, 1994).

The presence of these four works should move Amichai criticism to a new stage since they raise the basic problems which serious reading of the poetry must confront; while we should anticipate a continuation of enlightened readings of individual poems or journalistic rehearsing of the features of Amichai's poetry that were identified thirty years ago, responsible readings should begin to address the issues raised in these books. The three monographs (Arpaly, Abramson, Gold) are, in themselves, interesting exercises in reading, each reflecting the cultural milieu of their authors, thus inviting specific comment. And while I do not intend to present a critique of these three books, I shall address some of their achievements and limitations. What intrigues me are the respective methodological positions—explicit and implicit—of these three authors. I therefore concentrate on the act of reading, on the interaction betwen the critic and the texts of Amichai, an interaction mediated by certain critical suppositions. For a variety of reasons which shall become clear as we progress, I divide—however tentatively—Amichai's periods of creativity into two: an early Amichai, including the first five volumes of poetry through *Akhshav baraash* (1968), his novel, *Lo meakhshav lo mikan* (1963), most of his stories collected in *Baruah hanoraah hazot* (1961, 1973), and his play, *Paamonim verakavot* (1968).[1] Without this periodization, no progress can be made in the study of the considerable *oeuvre* of our poet.

Though the Tzvik anthology of essays is not central to my discussion here, it is my point of departure in that it provides a balanced assessment of the reception of Amichai's poetry over a period of more than three decades. The book documents the evolving reactions to Amichai's poetry, moving from the first volume, *Akhshav uvayamim haaherim* (1955), which signified a generational shift of taste and thus naturally elicited mixed reactions, to almost universal acceptance in the 1960s, and to the initial negative critique in the 1970s with the publication of *Velo al menat lizkor* (1971). There is, however, a marked incongruity between the coverage of critical positions summarized in the introduction and the articles collected and offered as representative since there is very little in the latter category dealing with the later Amichai, precisely when the criticism begins to turn somewhat against him. The reader cannot escape the impression that Amichai's greatest poetic achievement is to be found in his poetry of the 1948–68 period, a position which Gold contests vigorously, Abramson rejects, but Arpaly's study corroborates.

Though Arpaly's study, *Haperahim vehaagartel*, was published in 1988, it is an expansion of his doctoral dissertation submitted in 1977 and is thus close in origin and inspiration to the early Amichai. It deliberately limits its analysis to poems published between 1948 and 1968. Arpaly regards Amichai as one of Israel's leading poets whose poetry introduced a revolution in Hebrew poetics in the early years of the state, and who, because of his achievement and influence, earned the status of a modern Hebrew classic poet. His study aims to describe the poetry with two goals in mind: "[first,] the generation of the overall meaning by which many heterogeneous phenomena, which constitute the individual poems and [Amichai's] poetry in general, and the presentation of the central poetic features which these phenomena create when combined; and [second] the interpretation of the poetry, on the one hand, and the presentation of the central poetic principles embedded in it, on the other hand" (p. 7).

This declaration of purpose, well executed in the book, should alert the reader to the obvious fact that we are reading a critical study that derives from the Russian Formalist tradition, in this case in its Tel Aviv reincarnation. The basic concepts, the careful yet convoluted rhetoric, the obsession with poetics, the reference to Hrushovski and Lotman are unmistakable. The cautious presentation makes for difficult reading, but guarantees the production of an indispensible study of Amichai's poetics, at least as it is manifested in his early period.

The interpretations of the poems and the analysis of their poetics are dealt with either together or separately, since Arpaly believes that these two acts are inextricable in the process of proper, scientifically grounded reading, that while one must establish an interpretation before analyzing the poetics which generate it, that interpretation must be grounded in a rigorous descriptive poetics. The result is at times illuminating, at times obfuscating. In general, the book is detailed and fragmented because of both the dazzling variety of Amichai's poetic devices and the specific application of formalistic methods of analysis. The author obviously senses this problem since in addition to the regular table of contents, he appends to his study a nine-page detailed table of contents (pp. 317–325). If there is any example of what I have called elsewhere "the academization of Hebrew literary criticism", this is it.

Arpaly begins by posing the question: what organizing features generate meaning in the typical Amichai poem which often lacks traditional prosodic and syntactic structures? His highly qualified answer to this question is "the catalogue", a concept he pursues in minute detail from a variety of angles throughout the study. Along the way he deals with such items as the poetic "I", the poet's "fictive biography", the motif of God, the state, society, the lover, and so on, all treated more as compositional than representational items. In the process, he produces dozens of significant interpretations of individual poems. On page 223 Arpaly reaches the point where he can begin to make major comparisons between the poetics of Amichai and that of major Hebrew poets who preceded him: Bialik, Tchernichowski, Greenberg, Shlonsky, and Alterman. Amichai's—and Zach's—revolt against the Alterman model of poetics is treated in some detail, as it should be, but mostly on the level of poetics. The possible nexus between poetics and ideology involved in the shift in poetic norms and tastes in the early 1950s comprises the final twelve-page chapter (pp.

288–304), and provides a welcome relief to the almost claustrophobic obsession with poetics.

For while one is constantly impressed by the rigour of the formalistic approach and feels that interpretations are well-grounded in theory, that terms are carefully defined, and that composition is not confused with representation, there are decided problems with such a study. First, a rigorous, formalistic study must tend towards hermeticism, must develop its own often awkward and impenetrable language. The potential audience for such a book is small and the function of the critic as mediator between the text and the potential reader is limited. And though it might be irrelevant to the hierarchy of academic values, it is worth stating here that if you did not know or love Amichai's poetry before studying Arpaly's book—however indispensible it might be to the literary scholar—you will not know or love Amichai's poetry after reading it. Second, while it is difficult to tell whether Arpaly was hampered by his method or by the declared scope of the book, he leaves us off precisely on the threshold of one of the most interesting critical questions. For while he does describe the transition from Alterman–Shlonsky to Amichai–Zach at the beginning of the period under consideration, that is, early Amichai, he does not mention the transition from the poetics of Amichai to that of Wieseltier, Horovitz, and Wallach, for instance, whose impact was most forcefully felt in the late sixties and early seventies, precisely at the juncture between what we would call early and later Amichai. This transition parallels the shift in the reception of Amichai's poetry mentioned above. If poetics-oriented criticism has some cardinal advantages, one should be in the rigorous, motivated delineation of periods. One anticipates such a move from Arpaly.

We move from Arpaly to Abramson, not only because of the historical sequence in the publication of their books (Arpaly, 1986; Abramson, 1989), but because the differences between them are so illuminating. While the Arpaly book is blatantly "academic", the Abramson book, written in English, aims to present a total view of Amichai as a creative writer to a wider audience, some of whom might have little or no Hebrew and know Amichai in his many English translations. Abramson undertakes to present Amichai in his totality: as poet, prose-writer, and playwright, and in the two major periods of his creative life: the early Amichai, through 1968, and the later, until the time of the writing of her study in the late 1980s. At the same time, the putative audience is clearly a literate one familiar with critical terminology, references to English writers such as Joyce, Eliot, and Donne, and with more than a little knowledge of the Bible and Jewish liturgy.

Rather than begin with first principles of poetics as does Arpaly, Abramson initiates her book with a presentation of Amichai as a representative of Israeli poetry of his times. She asserts, for instance:

> ... the growth of individualism and the loss of the cultural past, which so exercised the critics of the 1950s, form the conceptual basis of Amichai's thematic material. The widespread sense of disillusionment similarly characterizes his verse, as it does that of his contemporaries . . . . (p. 8)

After anchoring him in history, she proceeds to use a primarily New Critical method of close textual analysis of individual poems—without definition of terms or discussion of the general problems of poetics. This is New Criticism in its updated phase, disabused of some of the naive purism, its fear of contamination by history, but informed by a variety of Continental theorists.[2] These explications are organized around six topics, each getting a chapter: biography and autobiography; allusion and irony; the father and God; alienation and fragmentation; the love poetry; Jerusalem. Though the subtitle of the book indicates that this is a thematic approach, and one might think that this is so from the chapter headings of the last four chapters dealing with poetry, this is by no means true. The first two chapters which form the basis for the others are not thematic studies in the ordinary sense.

The first is a shrewd analysis of the "biographical" element in Amichai's poetry, conceived more as figuration than as representation:

> He has therefore not written an autobiography but a poetic myth of himself, a journey or progress of the self during which certain obstacles are encountered and challenged with varying degrees of success or failure . . . . Despite the autobiographical truths and despite Amichai's contemporary settings and language, much of his poetry exists within a world that is closer to legend than to the realities of modern Israel. (p. 17)

Once one establishes the lyric "I" in these terms, subsequent discussions of "themes" are never merely exercises in thematology, since these "themes" are never purely representational, and are, in fact, generated by complexes of words or images generated by words. This is clear throughout the book and the author feels no need to explain or justify this point. It is abundantly evident in her study of "Masot Binyamin haaharon mitudela", which she treats as the model poem of the study, analyzing it and referring to it repeatedly. The declared "thematology" is undercut not only by this formulation of the lyric "I": the entire second chapter is devoted to a study of "allusion and irony"—standard items in the critical vocabulary of New

Critical formalism; the "conceit" is treated several times, notably in the chapter dealing with the love poetry.

Precisely because Abramson is writing a book that comprehends the totality of Amichai's literary production, she can trace the poet's development from period to period, notably in his love poetry which she divides into two periods: 1948–68; 1968–84. She also notices shifts over even shorter periods. She notes: "In the poetry from 1962–68 the attitude of Amichai's lyric 'I' has altered, as has his notion of God" (p. 59). The reference is of course to the difference between *Shirim* and *Akhshav baraash*. The differences to which she calls attention are in attitudes, in self-projection, but not in poetics, which is what Nili Gold does in her study. The lyric "I" may speak with one voice in *Shirim*, another in *Akhshav baraash*; the "lover" embodies one set of attitudes before 1949, another after 1968.

Similarly, in her desire to present a total picture of Amichai, Abramson includes other genres: the novel, short stories, drama. Here, too, her focus is not on the comparative poetic aspects of the various genres, but rather on the generation of the figure of an author who, though primarily a poet, has worked in other genres, at least in his early period. The very existence of the author in considerations of literary or artistic production has been a major issue in both structuralist and post-structuralist critical theory over the past generation, and though none of these critics are post-structuralists, it is interesting to note how they would relate to one of the burning issues of contemporary criticism. For Abramson, the author is paramount; for Arpaly and Gold, he is almost absent—he is present, at best, in texts which manifest common defining features. Surely, before approaching a comprehensive study of any poet this question should be addressed.

Nili Gold's dissertation, soon to be a book, aims to argue a point which deals with a crux in Amichai criticism: in opposition to much of her predecessors, Gold strives to redeem the significance of the poetry of the later Amichai. Her project is forcefully stated in a recent *Prooftexts* article:[3]

> By analyzing the transformations in figurative language and structure, I wish to demonstrate that the poetry of the late 1970s and 1980s shows great command of poetic language and technique and should therefore be considered an integral part of his literary canon. To be sure, figurative and ready-made linguistic materials explicit in the earlier work also appear in the later poems, but here they create a unique, multifaceted texture. Most important, Amichai's voice becomes more suggestive and individual . . . .Tensions between sociolect and idiolect, between existing literary or spoken language and the poet's personal diction, combine to create the distinctive diction of the later poetry. (p. 50)

Just as Arpaly's discourse betrays his affiliation with Tel Aviv poetics, Gold's discourse reveals a heavy debt to the *Semiotics of Poetry* of Michael Riffaterre of Columbia University, that is, New York rather than Tel Aviv.[4] Aside from the distinctively linguistic terms—which are so useful for Gold—such as sociolect and idiolect, we find the notion of "ready-made linguistic materials" (explicitly mentioned here) and suggestions of the intertext which is not mentioned by name in this passage. In the second chapter of her study, Gold presents in brief Riffaterre's theory of the semiotics of poetry, a theory based on French linguistics and semiotics deriving from de Saussure. She takes from Riffaterre those aspects of his theory that she finds useful (she hardly makes use of the hypogram, for instance, since it adds little to her purpose), particularly his notions of how texts are made out of preceding texts, how idiolects are made out of sociolects. This was a wise choice, for in his description of the intertext Riffaterre produced a more adequate description of this poetic phenomenon than the vague notion of "allusion" used by generations of critics through the New Criticism and beyond it. Relying on intertextual investigation, Gold builds her argument that the use of intertexts in the later Amichai is more subtle and focused than in the early Amichai. Rather than attempting to achieve a comprehensive descriptive poetics of Amichai, she focuses upon one figure, the image, and within that ubiquitous figure she focuses primarily on botanical imagery to make her point.

The argument, though focused and thus limited, is crucial since, if convincing—and I find it convincing—it forces us to revisit and revalue all of Amichai's poetry after 1968, something Abramson actually does, though with less theoretical attention and precision. It therefore forms the basis for a more balanced study of all of Amichai's poetry and perhaps provides the tools for answering what I have already alluded to as a cardinal area to be investigated: the interaction between the poetics of Amichai and that of Horovitz, Wieseltier, and Wallach which emerges in the late 1960s and early 1970s. Until this new poetics is factored in, our understanding of the periods in Amichai's long, productive career will remain inadequate.

Each of these three works, by Arpaly, Abramson, and Gold, has contributed toward advancing Amichai criticism and preparing the way for future research. Arpaly has provided us with a methodologically solid base for understanding the poetics of the early Amichai in most of its manifestations. Abramson has paved the way for an overall understanding of Amichai, his periods, his genres, and his situation. Gold has argued convincingly for a revision of the evaluation of Amichai's later poems. Each has pursued the study of Amichai's poetry from a definable critical position: Arpaly from his Tel Aviv Formalism and semiotics; Abramson from a refined New Critical stance; Gold from a Riffaterrean semiotics of poetry.

Though an analysis of the problems of reading poetry manifest in these three critics is the subject of a different paper, it will be useful to conclude this study with one observation. When one reads the analyses of individual poems, one notices an interesting tension between the demands of a specific theory of critical interpretation and the impulse to include in the interpretation items which do not necessarily add to the argument presented. This tension is strong in Arpaly, moderate in Gold, and mild in Abramson, as one would expect, given the rigour of the critical stances they have adopted. It is very possible that further study in this direction might well arrive at the conclusion suggested by Paul de Man in the Preface to *Blindness and Insight*:

> . . . a paradoxical discrepancy appears between the general statements they make about the nature of literature (statements on which they base their critical methods) and the actual results of their interpretations. Their findings about the structure of texts contradict the general conception that they use as their model. Not only do they remain unaware of this discrepancy, but they seem to thrive on it and owe their best insights to the assumptions these insights disprove. (p. ix)

Notes

1. All Amichai's poetry has been published by Schocken (Tel Aviv and Jerusalem).
2. The variety of positions can be found in the excellent anthology, *Lyric Poetry*, edited by Chaviva Hosek and Patricia Parker (Ithaca and London: Cornell University Press, 1985).
3. January 1994, 14/1, pp. 49–69.
4. Michael Riffaterre, *Semiotics of Poetry* (Bloomington and London: Indiana University Press, 1978).

3

The Conceit as a Cardinal Style-Marker in Yehuda Amichai's Poetry

Ziva Shamir

The topic of my paper is the result of many years of close reading in these exceptionally versatile and heterogeneous poems. Despite the many generic and stylistic changes that Amichai's poetry has undergone since its early stages in the 1950s, the conceit[1] was and remained the most typical and widespread style-mark of these poems. To the best of my knowledge, it constitutes the core of Amichai's figurative language, and as a most cardinal marker, it can be traced in all textual levels—from microtext to macrotext. The abundant use of this style-marker in Amichai's works also emphasizes their innovative nature as precursors of a new poetic trend (especially when confronted with the total abstinence of Amichai's predecessors from this "artificial" poetic figure).

I shall allow myself a slight digression from this thesis, to mention a trial which was held in open court some thirty-five years ago. The accused sat with bent shoulders, listening carefully to the speeches of both his prosecutor and his defence counsel. Finally, he rose from his bench, uttered a few words on his own behalf and read two or three short lyrics, still in manuscript.

In Israeli high schools, pupils were still studying Zalman Schneur's "The Middle Ages draw near" under the title of "Contemporary Poetry". "Massada" by Isaac Lamdan and "Bluz" by Yaakov Cahan were also taught as avant-garde poetic works. In literary circles, the poems of Abraham Shlonsky, Nathan Alterman, and Leah Goldberg were recited. They, however, were considered by the overly conscientious members of the Board of Education as too "modern" to enter the curriculum. Amichai's poems, in contrast to the traditional modes of poetic expression, sounded so simple, so direct and prosaic, that they could hardly fall into any of the known and accepted poetic categories. However, there was something in the tone and atmosphere of these poems that captured immediate attention. There was an intuitive feeling in the air that modern Hebrew poetry was on the threshold of a new era. Today, in retrospect, it is evident that in the 1950s a new poetics was established and that Yehuda Amichai was one of its stimulators, together with Natan Zach, Daliah Rabikovitz, and others.

Indeed, when Amichai is confronted with his contemporaries, there is no real stylistic common denominator between them as may normally be expected from members of the same literary group. Nevertheless, a new generation of poets emerged in the 1950s, if not for the sake of poetic resemblance, then, at least, due to collective abstinence from certain poetic features: the withdrawal from national sentiment and ethos; the dismissal of all prosodic style-markers characteristic of the early modernists (mechanical rhythm, dissonant rhyming, regular rhyme schemes); the avoidance of a rare and ornamental lexicon, together with the readiness to forsake the verbal pyrotechnics of Shlonsky and his imitators; the renunciation of complicated syntactic structures, of phraseology, of high-flown epithets and of the rich vividness of the Shlonsky–Alterman School.

All these manifestations of conscious abstinence from over-elaboration eventually resulted in a sense of meagreness and asceticism. The young generation of poets replaced the polyphonic, high-mimetic mode of their predecessors with an anti-heroic, ironic mode, far from the magical impact of Alterman's poetry which was still prevalent at the time.

The critics of the new poetic mode were seemingly right in correct accusations against the "poverty" of Amichai and Zach, as they still bore in mind the poetic norms prominent in the 1930s and 1940s. These discriminating critics, however, refused to understand that this apparent meagreness is a voluntary renunciation of opulence on the part of young poets who detested the superfluous "Russian" sentimentality of Shlonsky and his many imitators. Amichai himself testified in one of his early poems, the bitterly ironic "Bemerhak shtei tikvot" (Two hopes apart): "I who resort to a small portion / of the words in the dictionary". He, who studied in a religious elementary and secondary school and could have exhausted the possibilities of intertextual language at will, demanded in one of his poems, "O Lord, why have you not forsaken me?" His aim was to discharge the ostentatious wealth of Old Hebrew and be able to move around with minimal load.

Almost two generations have passed since Amichai's poems have gained world-wide recognition, and it would not be an easy task to trace his innovations today. His personal style, with its typical irony and understatement, has been imitated by many young poets since the early 1950s, and has almost turned into a literary convention. I shall therefore review some of the vicissitudes of his literary career with the aid of one cardinal style-marker, namely the conceit. This scrutiny of Amichai's poetry may reveal that the few "cells" selected here are genetically identical to the whole corpus.

It is well known that the emergence of Amichai's poetry was induced by the antagonism of the young post-war generation towards the impersonal style of the Hebrew modernists of the Shlonsky–Alterman school and towards the collective standpoint of most *Palmah* generation writers who took part in the War of Independence in 1948. Amichai's sonnet "Ahavnu kan" (We loved here), for instance, the title of which served as a general title of a 23-poem-cycle, depicts the post-war atmosphere in a style that was yet unknown in Hebrew literature:

Sonnet no. 20

Elbow people pushed their way to a seat
while people of love dreamt a dream . . .
Troops waited behind the mountain
not discharged from their wars.
They won't go home again.

The unjust and anti-heroic end of a conflict that has hitherto been clothed with high-flown visionary words continues to harass the speaker in these poems—the "impractical" poet who meditates about the survivors and the dead. The sonnet "David hatzair" is a pertinent expression of the disillusionment of a modern anti-hero who faces the realization of the dream of statehood, discovering that the dream surpasses the reality in beauty:

Young David

After the outburst of the first few hails
Young David went back to the waiting boys.
Already those who clattered their hard mails
Were so disarmingly mature and poised.

They formed the usual shoulder-slapping queue.
Some swore, some spat, laughed hoarsely, even cheered.
But David stood alone. Henceforth he knew
There could not be another David here.
And suddenly he wondered where to put
Goliath's head that his numb hands were yet,
Through sheer inertia, holding by the curls.

> *Now it was heavy and superfluous. Birds*
> *Who flew into the bloodshot distance heard*
> *No longer, as he did, the shouts and snarls.*
>
> *(Tr. Abraham Birman)*

It is not by mere chance that David's comrades in this poem act and sound like veteran *Palmah* fighters. It is not by mere chance that David is presented simultaneously both as a hero and as an anti-hero whose victorious deeds are far from causing joy and whose only wish is to seclude himself from the meddling crowd. Amichai, who confessed in one of his poems "I want to die in my own bed", repeatedly presented in his poetry a weak and tired speaker, unsure of himself, questioning the solid truisms of the *Palmah* generation. Amichai, who could easily conform to the generation against which he rebelled, prefers to portray dim twilight pictures, states of "interregnum" and disorientation, reflecting constant dissatisfaction and instability. His refusal to belong within any frame of affiliation is expressed in the poem "My parents' immigration", where he describes himself as "too young to die, too old for games". In an early poem from the cycle "Pine cones on the tree", he describes himself and his beloved as two electric bulbs "too dark for reading, too bright for sleeping". States of disbelief, immaturity, insecurity, and instability characterize Amichai's poetry—poetry that is constantly illuminated by the vague colours of sunset, never by the bright colours of broad daylight.

The protest against all the solid truisms and confident slogans of the passing generation is accompanied by the many expressions of uncertainty and doubt scattered in Amichai's poems: "maybe", "sometimes", "if", "despite", "although", and so on. These words contribute to the argumentative nature of his poetry which reflects an eternal inner struggle. The speaker in the poems (as opposed to the "I" in the poetry of Abraham Shlonsky and Alexander Pen, who adopted the exaggerated egotism of Mayakovsky) presents himself as a fool and an *eiron*. Instead of the pathos of the 1930s and 1940s, the reader is confronted with expressions reflecting understatement and bathos typical of modern Anglo-American and German poetry. Amichai's figures too reveal an inclination towards the Anglo-American poetic style (as opposed to the French-Russian hyperbolic style) as they are closely related to the Metaphysical conceit which saw a renaissance in twentieth-century modernism. With this figure "the most heterogeneous ideas are yoked together by violence", or, in more modern phrasing, incongruous semantic fields are arbitrarily attached to each other, resulting in a cognitive dissonance. Usually one of these semantic fields is human, the other mechanical or inhuman; one is serious and one is playful.

These surprising innovations in the the formulae of figurative language, together with Amichai's unexpected typological innovations (the paradoxical figure of the anti-heroic fighter who is willingly "incriminating" himself as a coward with many human weaknesses), established the original nature of Amichai's poetry when it first emerged in the 1950s. Comparing people to small change (in "Misheloshah o arbaah baheder") is a conspicuous conceit; so is the comparison between the lovers and the electric bulbs or the multiplicative numbers in the cycle "Lemaalah baetz itztrubalim" (Pine cones in the tree). Similarly "artificial" and manneristic is the comparison between the human meditations and the unkempt hair in "Haishah halkhah" (The woman has gone). These Metaphysical conceits are often intermingled with Surrealistic features and pseudo-Romantic autobiographical themes.

Amichai may be defined as the Romantic mannerist of modern Hebrew poetry, and this definition contains an inherent oxymoron. His poems are Romantic in the sense that they obsessively deal with individual, personal memories as an everlasting thematic thesaurus (his parents' home, his paternal worries, his dead comrades, and so on). His poems are manneristic because of the over-sophisticated nature of their similes and metaphors, which manifest an inclination to wit. Conversely, Amichai sometimes tends to envelope his poems in a visionary veil which obliterates the manneristic and witty mode. Among his contemporaries who have used autobiography as an important thematic component (Arieh Sivan, Aharon Almog, and, to a certain extent, Natan Zach, Moshe Dor, and Dalia Rabikovitz), Amichai is probably closest to the poetic version initiated by Dylan Thomas—a poetic version which comprises memories, dreams, and visions, together with curious and rare conceits. This poetic version imposes upon the reader certain obligations: to read the text closely and slowly, and to treat it as a sophisticated enigma which requires intellectual engagement.

Similar poetic modes in the history of world literature are often the result of similar sociocultural conditions: the ecstasy typical of poems by Hopkins and Yeats bears a genuine resemblance to parallel phenomena in the poetry of Uri Zvi Greenberg, as they originated in similar sociocultural conditions. The intellectual and inherently paradoxical nature of the poems by T. S. Eliot and Ezra Pound was created simultaneously with the rediscovery of the treasures of seventeenth-century English Metaphysical poetry. Both historical periods—the seventeenth century and the beginning of the twentieth century—are characterized by a total crisis of values, by sweeping secularization, and by the collapse of most ideologies and faiths. A period of disorientation breeds a paradoxical art, as in John Donne's "A valediction forbidding mourning", where the lovers' souls are compared to the arms of compasses. The unorganic and surprising nature of this simile, which aggressively binds together playful wit and existential seriousness is typical of poets who have undergone a traumatic crisis of disorientation and disbelief.

Amichai's conceits may appear to be less elaborate than the typical Metaphysical conceit, but it must be undersood that they manifest the voluntary asceticism and leanness of an artist who has undertaken the risky task of uttering the most fundamental and substantial truths. Despite its anti-pathetic, light, and witty nature, the cry of the newborn and the cry of death echo through Amichai's poetry. Despite the Romantic style of some of these poems, death is portrayed in a disillusioned, transparent manner.

My Mother Died on Shavuot *(Imi meta bashavuot)*

My mother died on Shavuot when they finished counting the Omer,
her oldest brother died in 1916, fallen in the war,
I almost fell in 1948,
and my mother died in 1983.
Everyone dies at some counting,
long or short,
everyone falls in a war,
they all deserve a wreath and a ceremony and an official letter.
When I stand by my mother's grave
it's like saluting
and the hard words of the Kaddish a salvo
into the clear summer skies.

We buried her in Sanhedria next to my father's grave,
we kept the place for her
as in a bus or a cinema:
Leaving flowers and stones so no one would take her place.

(Tr. Barbara and Benjamin Harshav[2]*)*

In "My mother died on Shavuot", the speaker recounts his life story, making a witty remark about his survival in the 1948 war. The count of the Omer (49 days between the second day of Passover and Pentecost) is customarily associated with the interruption of the mourning observed during the Omer to celebrate marriages (*Lag Ba'omer*). The white bridal veil is associated with the whiteness of the old mother's shroud. These kinds of association are commonly found in poetry, and consequently they arouse little surprise or amazement. However, the association of reserving a burial place and reserving a seat in the cinema is incongruous and dissonant. A careful reflection upon this seemingly impossible comparison will reveal its congruity: the final target of the reservation of place in both incompatible situations is to spend the time—whether temporarily or eternally—near loved ones. Amichai's poetry often exploits the childish delight in going to the theatre, to the park or to the circus in order to evoke a harsh existential truth about the ephemeral nature of life and the scarcity of earthly pleasures awaiting mankind in this world.

The conceit (from the Italian *concetto*) bears a close relation to the riddle and the enigma. It immediately draws the reader's attention due to its unintegral features which force the reader to discover *post factum* its strange inner logic. This is the mechanism of "Hagibbor haamiti shel haakedah" (The real hero of the *Akedah*, *Sheat hahesed*, 1982):

The real hero of the **Akedah**

The real hero of the Akedah was the ram,
Unaware of the collusion of the others.
It apparently volunteered to die in Isaac's place.
I want to sing a tribute to its memory,
Its curly wool and its human eyes
And its horns, so quiet on its living head,
Which were made into trumpets after its slaughter
For them to sound their peals of war
And to blare their uncouth joy.

I want to remember the last picture
Like a nice photo in a refined fashion magazine:
The spoilt tanned youth in his fancy clothes
And beside him the angel in a long silk robe
For a festive reception.
And the two of them with vacant eyes
Staring at two empty places.

And behind them, like a colourful background, the ram
Caught in the thicket before the slaughter.
And the thicket his very last friend.

The angel went home.
Isaac went home.
Abraham and God had long since gone.

But the real hero of the Akedah
Is the ram.

(Tr. Glenda Abramson)

The ram caught in the thicket by its horns (Gen. 22:13), not the father and son, draws Amichai's attention. Through an indirect periphrasis Amichai argues that the real hero of the *Akedah* (binding of Isaac) was the anonymous ram who died far from the well-communicated post-war drama. Even his corpse was cynically used for making *shofarot* (rams' horns) for triumphal calls. Death is being commercialized in wartime, the poem says here with wry irony. This poem is an indirect pacifist manifesto bitterly proclaiming the injustice of war: slogans are being spread, vulgar albums of triumph are being published, only the innocent victim is being relegated or forgotten. Amichai, who wrote the unforgettable line, "I want to die in my own bed", directs the spotlight at the exploited victim who is bearing the iniquity of others in order to expose the aimlessness of war. As a pacifist who has always given preference to the anti-heroic, Amichai has often manifested iconoclastic inclinations. His poems tend to demythicize all slogans and to expose conventional lies. The human gaze of the ram's eyes is a reprimand and a memorandum. It is meant to recall those anonymous war victims who paid so dearly for the creation of all the well-known slogans that Amichai would readily have rejected.

It has already been claimed here that the conceit is etymologically connected with wit. Despite the tragic nature of some of Amichai's figurative language, it can often be associated with the cognitive mechanisms of the joke and the comic anecdote. In some of his inherently tragic poems, based on his autobiography, Amichai takes advantage of the same mechanisms exploited in joke-telling, and the reader is delighted by the uncovering of the pseudo-logical and pseudo-naive nature of the contents. A second reading will reveal that Amichai's conceits are not far-fetched and are far from being ludicrous or absurd. His witticisms are the output of a meditative writer and not of a *homo ludens* or a verbal acrobat.

In her introduction to a collection of seventeenth-century English Metaphysical poets, Helen Gardner describes the conceit as one of the cardinal characteristics, or style-markers, of Metaphysical poetry. According to Gardner, it attracts immediate attention due to its sharpwittedness and sophistication which overshadow its inner truth. The unorganic nature of Amichai's conceits compels readers to set in motion all their analytical abilities. They may discover, to their great surprise, that seemingly informative lines are to be interpreted as an emotional outcry; that "rational" statements are to be understood as emotive and sensual; that the seemingly logical is, in fact, pseudo-logical. The biblical allusions which apparently cloak the poems in a mantle of traditional respectability are, in fact, personal, undisciplined, idiosyncratic statements, free of any classical rules. At a later stage, readers may discover, again to their great surprise, that what appears pseudo-logical, even nonsensical, has in fact its own logic—not accepted logic, but a personal, associative kind of logic, the hidden rules of which must be carefully traced. Hence, the typical conceit in Amichai's poems requires three stages of comprehension: at first, the readers encounter a surprising and dazzling figure of speech; then, they discover that the apparently informative and rational charge of this figure is misleading; later on, they rediscover the rational side of the figure. For instance, in Amichai's well-known poem "Oh God, full of compassion", the opening statement sounds like a logical, even scientific, argument. Then the reader may discover that this is, in fact, an emotional complaint about God withholding his pity and letting the loved ones die (*El male rahamim* is, of course, the Jewish prayer for the dead). Now God does not appear to be overflowing with pity, but refraining from grace and love. Finally, the personal logic of the statement can be grasped: the opening words of this poem do not contain any blasphemous expression against heaven. They are the words of a soldier who has dragged his comrades' corpses from the hills, knowing that heaven is empty and godless—devoid of compassion. This logical exercise with its conditional mode is directed towards this delayed understanding: this is the expression of an unbeliever, of a godless atheist, not the naive words of the pious or the conformist.

This is the mechanism in many poems, including the poem "Matan Torah" (The revelation on Mt. Sinai) from the 1975 collection *Akhshav baraash* (Now, in the noise).

> *When Moses sat*
> *with God on Sinai, and wrote*
> *on a tablet, I was sitting*
> *in the classroom*
> *and dreamily drawing*
> *flowers and faces,*
> *aircraft and decorated names.*
> *Now I show it all to you:*
> *don't do, don't obey.*

Here, the well-known biblical story is inverted by an apparently childish pun (*luah* is both a school blackboard and one of the holy tablets of the Decalogue). Instead of evoking the revelation on Mt. Sinai and the tablets of the Law, the poem portrays a childhood picture of a daydreaming pupil who is scribbling flowers and airplanes instead of listening to the teacher.

Instead of the biblical phrase "all that the Lord has spoken will we do and obey" (Ex. 24:7), the child playfully teases: "Don't do, don't obey". The latent subtext beneath this playful facade juxtaposes the restrictions of the religious way of life and the freedom of secular individualism. This contrast underlies most of Amichai's quatrains, the best-known of which depicts the father harnessed to his phylacteries and the son to his dreams.

One can conclude and argue that the conceit is the cardinal microtext of Amichai's figurative language. Its impact is felt not only in the figurative language, but also in the allusive language, in the rhetoric, and on many other texual levels. Eventually, it constitutes the nature of the macrotext, or even Amichai's poetics, in general. The key to the understanding of Bialik's style is "ambivalence", and one can find its marks on every level. The key to the understanding of Alterman's style is "oxymoron", and it can be found everywhere—from texture to structure. The same applies to Amichai: the key to the understanding of his poetics is "conceit", and conceits can be found on every possible level of his poetry. It can be compared to a genetic code that may be found in every single cell, and eventually characterizes the poetic corpus as a whole. This rule applies only to some of the great poetic pioneers who break through poetic restraints and establish new codes. The minor imitators, the disciples and followers, usually change their style-markers from time to time, and consequently rarely have a personal, individualistic "fingerprinting". In the Shlonsky–Alterman generation they would have been admirers of the oxymoron and the hyperbole; in the 1950s they would have preferred ironic understatement, interwoven with manneristic conceits; in the 1960s they would have changed their style to the aggressiveness of Meir Wiseltier and Yonah Wallach. Conversely, Amichai's poetry, in all its stages and manifestations, is primarily based on one unchanging *ethymon*, namely the manneristic conceit. Amichai's imitators usually draw one component out of the entire complex and therefore their use of the conceit is frequently artificial and fanciful, whereas Amichai's use is genuine and full of natural grace.

Notes

1. A poetic figure, or image, which displays an over-elaborated analogy, often highly calculated, never totally spontaneous. In certain poetic periods, such as the Romantic age, this term gained derogatory connotations, was condemned as a fanciful manifestation of preciosity, and was often satirized. In other poetic periods (in the seventeenth century, the prime period of Metaphysical poetry, and in the twentieth century, with the emergence of early modernism), this figure was highly estimated and widely used.
2. *Meadam ata veel adam tashuv* (Schocken Books, 1985), pp. 15–16.

4

On the Political Significance of Amichai's Poetry

Boaz Arpaly

A

The major argument I wish to present in this paper is that, of all the poetry written in Israel since its establishment, there is probably no other corpus that can be likened to Amichai's poetry insofar as its potential political significance and influence are concerned. At first this significance and influence operated in a subversive and anti-establishment way against what were perceived as the accepted national ideologies. They also greatly helped to undermine these ideologies, becoming more and more an integral part of a new ideological and political consensus. Nevertheless, one cannot overlook the fact that claims of this kind are necessarily and always hypothetical premises (my use of terms like "perhaps", "probably", and "potential" is obviously not by chance).

In the first part of this paper, I shall make several remarks about the general theoretical topic (the political significance of poetry) and its specific application here (the political significance of Amichai's poetry). In the second part, which is the main body of the article, I will present several general aspects of Amichai's poetry that can be viewed as the factors responsible, to one degree or another, for the possible political influence attributable to this poetry. In the third part, I will briefly describe the general direction and subject matter which this political influence attempted to affect.

I have no means, nor apparently does anyone else, by which to determine, in a general, theoretical manner or in relation to a given period, what came first: a change in the social, cultural, political climate, the maturation of a new political consciousness in society, or their explicit expression in literature and poetry. To what extent does new poetry stem from a new social and cultural climate; to what extent does it influence the emergence of such a climate or spur such a consciousness? Does poetry, and of course literature in general, explicitly and knowingly reflect existing but unconscious moods, which are not expressly manifested but which take shape in the "silent majority" of society in response to changes in the political and social reality; or do its writers belong to the minority (or even constitute that minority themselves) which is the first to sense these changes and the responses they ought to elicit? Everyone assumes there are various kinds of links between literature and reality, but a well-founded and proven description of these links remains in the realm of an ideal. In accordance with these observations, I will cautiously reword the statements I made at the beginning of this paper: my major argument here is that if poetry can make a real contribution to a change in political mood and, in the final analysis, to a change in the political scene, I believe that Amichai's poetry has indeed done so.

At this point, in order to clarify the topic of my paper as it is worded in the title, I should like to draw a distinction (on the basis of E. D. Hirsch's writings) between the terms *meaning* and *significance*. By *meaning*, I refer, in the present context, to the message, information, and sense one can extract from a work of literature, or in our case, from a corpus of literary work, by one interpretive means or another. Both in regard to the definition of the term and the ways in which it is derived, there is no difference between a political meaning and other meanings extracted in this manner—be they ideological, metaphysical, psychological, or aesthetic—other than the thematic realm to which each relates. On the other hand, *significance* refers to the relationship between the poem or the poetic corpus, and more specifically between their meanings, and the personal or historical situation in which they are read. Significance denotes the role, influence, weight, and effect of a literary work or corpus in relation to its audience, in the specific cultural, social, and/or political context of that audience. Of the two domains which these terms signify, I am primarily interested here in the second—in the significance of Amichai's poetry—even though I may have to relate to its meaning as well.

It is obviously not difficult to assert that the connection between significance and meaning in a literary work or corpus is neither inevitable nor self-evident. Even when poetry on the face of it contains nothing political, or it is difficult to pinpoint any political stance, it may have a political effect and political importance in the specific circumstances in which it appears. In the right context, all poetry, no matter what its surface contents may be, can be accorded a political status and political significance. In certain conditions, poetry with a personal or metaphysical content will actually be perceived as embodying a consummately political stance, or even, in the eyes of the regime, as presenting a danger. A clear example of such a situation is the attack by the Communist establishment (Zhdanov) at the time, on Anna Akhmatova's poetry. In the Bolshevik context, her personal and universal themes were perceived as a subversive expression against the regime. Despite all the vast differences between contexts, there is a fundamental similarity between the charges hurled at Akhmatova and the criticism by certain conservative critics in Israel of Natan Zach's and Yehuda Amichai's early poems for their lack of values and nihilism.

In contrast to these examples that illustrate how political significance is attributed to texts that are seemingly apolitical, one can cite examples of blatantly political poetry which lacks any real political weight precisely because of the explicitness and extremism of its messages. Poetry of this kind often receives only minimal attention and does not arouse real opposition. Cultural and political establishments prefer to ignore it and often succeed in pushing it out to the margins of the public arena. Alexander Penn and Yonatan Ratosh are outstanding examples in Hebrew literature of writers who tried to convey clear-cut, blatant, political messages, but whose political influence was minimal (each poet, for reasons peculiar to himself).

As I stated, the political significance that can be attributed to the work of a poet is a function of the relationships between the meanings—political and other messages which can be extracted from the poetry through intratextual interpretation—and general contexts "external" to the poetry. If, as I will argue later, Amichai's poetry does indeed have political significance, then it is not only a direct outcome of the thematics and poetics embodied in this poetry itself; it is also, to a crucial degree, a function of the national, cultural, and political climate in which it was written. A different climate would have neutralized the political potential of those themes, or shifted their direction. Different thematics and poetics, on the other hand, are apt to operate differently in the very same climate. I do not intend to describe in any detail the cultural-political climate in which and under whose influence Amichai's poetry was written. However, I will present the political significance of his poetry as a fruit of the encounter between the poetry itself and that climate.

Amichai's poetry is not, on the basis of any reasonable definition of the term, political poetry. It cannot be described as serving a certain sector or a defined interest in the struggle over the distribution of national resources or the control of the sources of power. It is also difficult to find any of his poems that are distinctly and expressly political poems, namely poems representing specific political positions, which relate in a political sense to topical situations; protest poems; or poems representing clear oppositional stances against hegemonic ideologies, accepted social, political, or economic customs, and the like.[1] It is also not difficult to point to central issues in the internal and external politics of Israel which Amichai's poetry never really addressed, or did not relate to at all (even his direct references to the Arab–Jewish conflict, for example, are few in number). The political significance of Amichai's poetry—which I will argue is great and powerful—does not derive, therefore, directly from the "contents" or "messages" that can be extracted from the texts themselves, but from what is implied by those contents and messages in the historical situation in which the poems were written, from the time of the establishment of the State. This factor, which is symptomatic of the singularity of this significance, also makes it difficult properly to describe it.

An additional factor that may make it difficult correctly to evaluate Amichai's poetry in general, and its possible political effect in particular, relates to the paradoxical nature of its reception by the Israeli literary community. From several viewpoints, the key status of Amichai's work in the history of Hebrew poetry has been obscured because central trends in its poetics, central aspects of the fundamental world map it depicts, and the poetic, moral, and ideological values underpinning it have been assimilated into this history to such an extent that all those elements—first perceived as unique and innovative—have become what seems to be a common base immanent in all the poetry of that entire generation. This is all the more true in relation to the public of discriminating or less discriminating readers. While to this very day they regard the poetry of poets like Natan Zach and David Avidan as difficult, unclear, and "modernistic", Amichai's poetry has become self-evident to them, a kind of literary "daily bread".

It also seems that while several of the aspects, elements, and trends in the Hebrew poetry of the last thirty years are perceived as opposed, sometimes sharply or extremely, to the thematic and poetic centres of Amichai's poetry, they perhaps could not have taken shape or developed without it. Amichai's poetry (no less than, and in certain senses, perhaps even more than the poetry of others like Zach and Avidan) was one of the major factors in "clearing the area" and "preparing the ground" for the poetic growth of the poets who came later. It relieved them of the need to wage unnecessary battles and created a conducive climate for their development. The tremendous innovations that Amichai's work contributed to Hebrew poetry are not concrete and evident to his readers because these things have subsequently been flowing in the veins of Hebrew poetry and are embedded in the consciousness of its readers. Hence, it seems that a special effort of deliberate observation and "defamiliarization" is called for in order to extricate this innovation and this singularity from the flow, and to restore them to their rightful place.

These observations are particularly apt in regard to the political significance of this poetry. Those who have certain poetic and critical interests to advance try to represent this poetry as poetry which is supposedly restricted to feelings, emotions, and musings of the little man within his four walls, who takes no interest in anything beyond his private life and his circumscribed world. They depict it as a kind of everyday *petit bourgeois* verse which shies away from the ideological and political battlefield and refrains from taking a clear stand for or against views and actions, institutions and leaders that shape the public life of Israel. The comparison between the work of Amichai and poets like Wieseltier or Yitzhak Laor, as well as with later developments in the writing of poets like Nathan Zach and Dalia Rabikovitz, putatively confirms this impression. In my view, this is a totally erroneous impression.

The weight, influence, and political significance of Amichai's poetry do not rest on any explicitly political poems or from any directly political statements that an assiduous reader might cull from his work. Rather they are a product of its overall existence as a poetic system and of a combination of its global meanings as such. It does seem, however, that those very same characteristics that might serve as a basis for presenting Amichai's work as poetry that tries to eschew the political and ostensibly focuses on the personal emotions of the poet reveal themselves as some of the principal factors that imbue it with consummately political significance. This putative paradox will be understood much better, however, when these characteristics are considered in the poetry's overall contexts: as a system and the product of the historical situation in which it was written and received (as well as the link between the two).

The political significance of Amichai's poetry is a general aspect, among others, of its influence as poetry; it is not a result of an aggressive struggle or of direct confrontation, but of a vital and multifaceted penetration of the psychological and social fabric of the community of readers: a penetration that can appropriately be described according to the model Amichai himself proposed in his poem "Not as a Cypress" (*Shirim 1948–1962*, p. 76). Everything stated above about the all-embracing link between Amichai's poetry and that of later poets, even those who represented themselves as its opponents, is also true of its political influence. It is possible that in the absence of this seemingly modest influence, the sharp outspokenness of younger poets might not have resonated so strongly in the political realm some years later.

B

If—as I suggested in the previous section—the political significance of Amichai's poetry relies on its overall existence as a poetic system and on a combination of its general meanings in its own contexts, then it is impossible to describe its political significance unless one first systematically and thoroughly delineates it as a cognitive and poetic system.[2] I shall limit myself to a brief presentation of five of the general aspects of this system, not necessarily in order of importance, which can be viewed as the major factors or combinations of factors underpinning its possible political influence. (1) Amichai's poetry has an intimate connection to the material and spiritual world of its generation and its time or, at any rate, to the material and spiritual world of many members of that generation. (2) It portrays in detail a world picture and world view (ideology), new and different from those previously accepted by writers and readers of Hebrew literature. (3) The introduction of familiar elements from the material and spiritual world of the generation and the time into this unique world view and world picture, and the modes of their compositional, rhetorical, and poetic structuring in Amichai's poetry, led to a change or inversion of their meaning, "releasing" them from the emotional and value-laden charge attached to them, and stimulated readers to think about them and everything they represented in a new, more sceptical and rebellious way. (4) Although he displayed quite radical critical attitudes towards the conventions of culture and ideology, Amichai showed restraint, moderation, and caution in presenting these positions. In this way, instead of arousing strong objection, he encouraged thought and agreement. (5) The last aspect is the popularity of Amichai's work, perhaps the only canonical poetry since Alterman which has been and still is being read by many.

These elements work in combination; hence the strength of each one and of all of them together is enhanced. I shall now describe each one separately, without trying to determine their relative weight. The reader will bear in mind, however, that their possible political significance is a function of the interaction between them, and that it is nearly impossible to describe the influence of any one of them on its own.

(1) The connection of Amichai's poetry to the "here and now" of Israeli life, both in the limited, literal sense as well as in the broader, metaphorical sense, are close and intimate. There has probably been no other Hebrew po-

etry like it in this regard since 1948. It contains a variety and a profusion, which grows from book to book, of topical, historical, cultural, traditional, ideological, and mythological basic materials that serve as reference points and key components in the political existence of Israel, and signify, through metonymy and metaphor, the broad contexts of the personal and collective existence within it, which are also its parts. The Israeli reader of Amichai has encountered these elements and contexts again and again; they are not only aspects of a present reality or of historical memories but also motifs and chapters of written and oral texts, which are a living part of his or her cultural heritage. These are texts Israelis have studied and come to know in childhood and adolescence as texts that helped shape their perception of themselves as people and as the children of a nation. From the mouths of spiritual and political leaders, they again and again heard those texts and others like them. I can neither discuss here these elements and topics, nor relate to the variety of ways—ranging from hints and echoes to explicit statements—in which they are revealed in Amichai's poetry. I can, however, allude to several of the more striking and symptomatic among them: in the direct political domain (the wars) and the geopolitical (Jerusalem), in the general conceptual domain (history, archeology, eternity), in the domain of personal existence (body and soul), and in the domain of culture (the attitude to the traditional thematic and linguistic sources).

(2) It may be vital for components and aspects of the type alluded to here to be present in a literary corpus before it can have any political significance and influence on its audience. However, the nature and depth of such an influence are a corollary of the ways in which they are presented and structured in the contexts of the literary corpus. And indeed, Hebrew readers have encountered materials with a political potential in Amichai's poetry from the standpoint of its composition as well as (primarily) from its conceptual point of view, within contexts that are generally different from those to which they were accustomed prior to its appearance. Such materials are not present in Amichai's poems on the surface, and they usually do not appear in poems in their own right.

Amichai's poetry is primarily and principally poetry of the individual which narrates, in a rather intimate manner, details of his private life, his family and its past, his lover or wife, his friends, and the events in his life, and particularly tells about his love and the difficulty of sustaining it. Within this poetry which, from many standpoints, can easily be likened to a personal autobiographical diary reporting on the life of the protagonist-poet from day to day and from year to year, elements from geographical, social, and national contexts are interwoven, as if of their own volition, within the most private and personal contexts and according to the needs of the specific personal situation. One can learn something about this interweaving from the words of the poet about his life:

> Since I happen to be a Jew, and happen to live in Israel, and have participated here in everything I was commanded to do and in everything I wanted to do—I am living in my natural surroundings, and everything I went through and everything that passed before me, has been stored up in me and is expressed in my poems . . . every personal experience, when the individual is sensitive to the outside world, obviously becomes an historical experience. Since I belong very much to my time and my place, every personal experience of mine belongs to my time and my place. (Interview in 1978)

The composition of Amichai's poetry which shows the link between the collective and the historical, between the life of the individual as "fortuitous" from the outset and "inevitable" in retrospect, and intersperses the former into personal situations, making them subject to "autobiographical" contexts, is only a symptom of a fundamental world picture and world view, embedded in the entire corpus of Amichai's poetry from its inception. These were and still are revealed in diverse ways, direct and indirect, in the bodies of his various poems. Into that conceptual frame, into that philosophy perhaps, many of the materials were interwoven, changing their status and value, sometimes even their significance. To put it differently, within this conceptual frame they acquired a status and a meaning that undermines their conventional content and their accepted status in sanctioned hierarchies and prevalent cultural and ideological contexts.

From the cognitive standpoint, Amichai's poetry does not recognize the metaphysical and the mystical, and this is consistent with the world view that shapes or informs it. It only acknowledges the existence of "this world", as it is perceived through our senses and our common sense in the "here and now" of existence, or, insofar as the past is concerned (history, archeology, the history of culture), those things that can be verified on the basis of facts. From the standpoint of values and morals, the life and happiness of the individual in this world are the decisive yardsticks with which Amichai's poetry measures everything.

The view that there is no reality except that which is perceived by our senses and common sense (this world is the only one that exists) is tantamount to denying the validity of all those principles that provide guidance and significance, which originate in "other worlds" (religious, metaphysical, or poetic-visionary). On the other hand, the adherence to personal subjective experience as the decisive criterion for observing the world and judging its values and events also leads one to perceive those principles which ostensibly originate in rational thought—the natural and social sciences, social and political systems—as baseless, ridiculous, and even, at times, harmful. The orders of nature (death, the irreversible direction of time) as well as the orders of society are perceived as indifferent to the existence and happiness of the individual, which from their vantage point are accidental and transient. This existence, fragile and ephemeral, whose value is nil in the world as it is, is the most precious and valued reality in the poetic world of Amichai.

The scale of values articulated in Amichai's poetry is thus an inversion of the one that directed Israeli culture in the years preceding the establishment of the State, continued to direct it either openly or covertly afterwards as well, and whose dominance may not have been totally undermined until the present day. According to this inverted scale of values which guides Amichai's poetry, the concrete is preferable to the abstract, the specific (the individual) to the general (the collective). And in particular, whatever is close to the world of ordinary people, whatever benefits their happiness and their existence, is preferable to whatever is distant and likely to impair them. The "here" is preferable to the "there" and "everywhere". "Present" is more important than "past" (history) or "future" (collective aims and social-national planning). One is more important than many; an individual, a family, more than the state; a chair, bed, table, more than the three religions, than churches and temples, than archeological remains, no matter how glorious they may be. A soldier is more important than the "regiment"; a father, child, more than the "nation", its leaders and heroes. A "flower", a "tired man", more than the law of nature, than "God". The experienced reality is more important than understanding, remembering, or recounting it; the very fact of existence, more important than purposes attributed to it or the "designs" it is supposed to realize. The more things fall into the category of "I" or "mine" (in relation to each and every individual) and are included in "my" existence, as they become less general, comprehensive, or "objective", they come closer to the centre of the values, in relation to which they are judged and evaluated in this poetry. In total accord with these principles, Amichai's poet- protagonist is not a man of action, a man of vision, or a poet-prophet possessed of extraordinary imagination, and certainly not a heroic figure. He is akin to the man in the street, an individual among individuals, passive (the passive stance is the only rebellious attitude he recognizes), a man who is "competent only for love, disabled for any other craft"; lacking in initiative, who makes no pretence of knowing even himself, a man swept up by his destiny, one who rather than being in control of his life is controlled by it.[3]

Within this system several phenomena that shape the Israeli collective consciousness assume new values. One of the most striking of these, and the most relevant to our discussion, is the war. Throughout all of his work, Amichai comes back to the wars of Israel, but in general he does not "eulogize" these wars, he does not laud the victories or lament defeats from the national or Zionist standpoint which could have given these wars justification and meaning. He looks at the war, the soldiers going forth to battle, the army camp, the call to reserve duty, from the vantage point of the separation from loved ones, of the kindergarten, of the wounded and the fallen (who are always ordinary people, not heroes), of the individuals whose world is damaged and devastated by wars. The individual's fate is the criterion for judging wars and the individual's life is the perspective from which they are observed. In this sense, Amichai's poems could have been written anywhere in the world and incorporated into any poetry protesting against the subjugation of the individual to national destiny and the state's interest.

The attitude towards wars is the extreme expression in Amichai's poetry of his general attitude to central aspects of Israeli existence. This is summarized in his great poem "Journeys of the last Benjamin of Tudela" (*Akhshav baraash* [Now in the noise], pp. 95–139), which, on the basis of one of its contextual frameworks, is an interpretation of Zionism from the viewpoint of one who has succeeded in realizing it. Also in this rich poem, which can be regarded as a sort of recapitulation of Amichai's earlier poetry, the Israeli situation is rendered in a wide diversity of aspects but from the viewpoint of an individual life. Despite its distinctly autobiographical nature this poem depicts the fate of an Everyman caught up in circumstances he is forced to endure. The poet-protagonist of the poem does not come to the country as a conqueror, or as a settler, or as a Zionist poet. He is brought as a child to the land of his parents' dreams, without being consulted about his own wishes. The flags he hoists are not flags of the nation or pennants of battle, but "a woman's little, triangular panties hanging on a line / on a Jerusalem roof signalling to the old tired / sailor from Tudela". The "last Benjamin of Tudela" has come to the end of his Zionist journey only to learn that no ideal can serve as a substitute for life. Only against his will and having no choice does he reconcile himself to the tragic historical trap ("the trap of the homeland") in which he is caught.

In a society controlled by militaristic leaders and in the ideological context of "statism", the attitude in Amichai's poetry towards every kind of apparatus of government has revolutionary significance. Governments that are supposed to lead their people in fulfilling national goals are depicted in this poetry as alienated apparatuses, and their decrees, which determine the fate of individuals without their knowledge or consent, are described as arbitrary and likened to "machine guns shooting direct fire". The people whose fate they determine are represented as soldiers or civilians injured or killed when they mistakenly cross those machine guns' line of fire ("The clouds are the first to die", *Shirim 1948–1962*, 88/104[4]). This condensed metaphor, which portrays the apparatus of government in terms of war, is not accidental in poetry which views war as the extreme outcome of the indifference of the rulers to the individual's life and concerns.

The way history and the historical are shaped in Amichai's poetry is no less symptomatic of a political subtext. In the cultural and ideological context of a nation that regards itself as a "historical" people, in a country in which every inch of ground has a rich past and in which historical events serve as a justification for political decisions, and even for the society's very existence, the sceptical attitude towards history (in both the general and the Israeli sense) in Amichai's poetry is striking. He up-ends history and its related descriptions, divesting them of their accepted value. This is a distinctly subversive attitude, which seems to encourage critical judgment relating to the way in which this history is usually perceived.

In Amichai's poetry, "history" is the opposite of life and the experience of living. One can re-think history, but one cannot live it. The time described by history is "time emasculated of humans", an impotent time. In the final analysis, history is nothing more than an arbitrary list of names and dates, a catalogue signifying things that are already dead (*Shirim*, p. 271/307). The information that history provides, the connection between past events and the buildings and ruins around us, are perceived as lacking in any importance, as "the gossip of generations", the "decoration of passing hours", "entertainment", "adornments of time", surrounding what is paramount—the existence of the individual (*Shirim*, p. 165/200). Written history is akin to a dirge, an expression of a hopeless and futile struggle against the ironclad rules of time and death, which inevitably ends in submission. By virtue of its systematic nature, history is in opposition to the spontaneous, chaotic flow of life, an ineffective attempt to introduce linear retrospective order into something which by its nature is fortuitous and multi-directional (*Akhshav baraash*, p. 114). Perhaps one ought to note at this point that, in Amichai's poetry in general, "order" is the absurd or dangerous opposite of "life" which is manifested more as "chance" or luck. All writing, including that of the poet, is perceived as a pitiable substitute for life whose disappearance it reports. No wonder then that the attitude expressed in Amichai's poetry toward collective acts of memory and commemoration is also quite cynical.

History and the "historical" are negatively assessed in Amichai's poetry particularly because of their alienation from everything it regards as the supreme criterion for judging both values and realities: the life of the individual. Within the broad lines of world history, the concrete, discrete life of the individual is swallowed up and disappears. From this standpoint, history is likened to an "eating binge" or, to be more exact, to "digestion"; in "digestion" all of the individual differences between things and people vanish, "everything descends into the awful resemblance". Written history is compared with the "fruit of intestines", a result of this digesting. Just as all the differences between the various types of food swallowed by their eaters disappear in the digestive juices, thus written history effaces the individual uniqueness of people, events and experiences, turning them all into a thick mush ("Journeys of Benjamin", *Akhshav baraash*, p. 114).

Amichai's poetry imputes no importance or purpose to the historical process. The hidden, but true, story of history is that which has not been recorded, but is concealed under the oft-repeated theme of the theft of life and happiness, destroyed in the "circus arena of world history" according to the will of generals and ideologues for the sake of aims and ideals instilled in people by others, for the sake of a future in which they will have no part and a past which no longer exists ("Elegy", ibid., p. 92). The story of history is based on archeological excavations and filed away in museums. In neither of these is there any trace of the love and pain of the individual. One need only recall the status of archeology and of the preservation of Israel's heritage in its culture and ideology to understand the revolutionary significance of this approach.

Another symptomatic example of the change which central elements of the Israeli collective consciousness undergo in Amichai's poetic system is the way Jerusalem is represented in his work. In the Israeli collective consciousness, Jerusalem is not merely a geographical reality. It is perhaps primarily perceived as a condensed symbol of all facets of Israeli existence that both the secular and the religious regard as sanctified, but also as a political touchstone of contradictory ideological positions. Jerusalem serves in all these contexts as a metonymy for the entire Land of Israel, as a mirror reflecting the "external" struggle between peoples and religions, and the internal political controversies, as well as a metaphor for the Jewish-Israeli entity as a whole. Jerusalem, within these contexts and their reverberations, is a theme that recurs throughout all Amichai's poetry. Jerusalem in Amichai's poetry incorporates negative, grotesque, painful, ugly, and inhuman aspects, which one cannot help but associate with the touristic, religious, and political exploitation of the city. The city's spiritual and historical traditions are underscored, with growing intensity, along with the love the poet feels for it, and the pain he shares with its inhabitants. Even in Amichai's poetry, which strives to restore Jerusalem to human and Jewish reality, to strip it of the mystification and distortion which seem to have become part of its essence, Jerusalem is more than a literal entity, for whatever is true about Jerusalem is also true to one degree or another of the social, cultural, and political existence of Israel as a whole.

(3) The statements I made about Amichai's world picture and its cognitive structure and values ought to be supplemented, in the context of this discussion, by a review of the rhetorical structure of his poetry, a structure which is their analogy and parallel. Three major factors are involved: (a) the fact that Amichai's poetry refrains from fashioning other, mythical or metaphysical, worlds; (b) the structure of the phrases, the images, and the poem as a whole in Amichai's poetry; and (c) the way this poetry treats the Jewish sources (biblical and others).

(a) Within the contexts of the "here and now", words that usually refer to "other worlds" lose their customary meaning in "standard" language, in the language of Amichai's poetry. These words and idioms can only be understood in his poetry according to the sense attributable to them in "this world", in relation to common sense and the evidence of our senses. Moreover, their customary meaning is dismissed or apprehended as ridiculous. (b) The catalogue-like structure of an Amichai poem creates an equivalence between words and concepts from heterogeneous spheres of the dictionary and of life. The structure of his images also brings together linguistic materials from different domains. The reader is encouraged to grasp these materials in a new way, and—since their traditional capability to make things meaningful is undermined—to reexamine them, using the realistic concepts of his or her life and world.

In this context, materials from the vocabulary and concepts of religious faith, in addition to others, assume special importance. Thus, for example, "eternity" in Amichai's poetry is not, as is usually the case, a term carrying a positive implication of the valuable and the everlasting. Rather, according to meanings that can be attributed to it in "this world", it is a term with ironic or negative implications for things that have no life, or are outside life, a term denoting the non-life that "exists" after our death ("Everything that lives and exists, from the moment of our death and thereafter is eternity", *Akhshav baraash*, p. 168); in a different context, after the death of our love, or our separation, we move to "a land without me and a land without you . . . an eternal land", *Shirim*, p. 216/250). Something of the traditional meaning of "eternity" is preserved in a parodic sense as a hyperbolic quantitative term within the existence of the individual ("My eyes are full of eternity like the pocket of a boy's trousers" [*Shirim*, p. 68]; "There is no greater eternity than a door on which the words 'Closed Today' are written" [*Shirim*, p. 264/300]).

In Amichai's poetry, "prophecy" has a meaning which is the reverse of its traditional one. It appears as a term for self-evident knowledge, knowledge of things that will take place by the force of natural or social laws (the change of seasons, the waging of wars, separation, pregnancy, and birth). Amichai's "prophet" is the newspaper that comes out in the morning, is sold at noon and read in the evening. If his "prophet" is a man with moral sensitivity and the ability to identify with suffering, pain, and distress, he is not a superior being, possessed of supernatural wisdom, but a man like all men. More than expressing the suffering of a people, he expresses the suffering of individuals. Reproach is alien to him; he brings no momentous message. There is no room in our world for the traditional roles of the prophet. "Prophet" can, at the very most, serve as a derogatory term for someone bringing destruction upon his followers through his unwanted fanaticism.

In these and other ways, Amichai's poetry divests of their customary meaning many words and concepts which refer to religious and metaphysical worlds, such as "resurrection of the dead", "angels", "miracles", and so on. Amichai also examines the meaning of terms or concepts that are not necessarily associated with the world of religious faith. I will take the word "soul" as an example. Amichai, who defines himself as "belonging to the last generation of those who know body and soul separately", would not give "soul" a spiritual-metaphysical definition, as is usually done. Rather, based on the fundamental assumptions of his world picture, he would pose the question about the nature of the soul according to its possible concrete manifestations: "Where do you sense your soul inside you?", and the corresponding reply would be: "Between my mouth and my anus stretches / a white cord, not transparent breath. / It is cramped in a corner between two bones, / with pain. / when it is satisfied, it disappears, like a cat." ("Journeys of Benjamin", *Akhshav baraash*, p. 113). "Soul", if it appears in Amichai's poetry, is not a term denoting any spiritual or metaphysical entity, but rather bodily functions, feelings of sorrow and pain manifesting themselves physically, even if their source is, on the face of it, emotional, psychological, or spiritual; when the poet is satisfied and happy, the soul "disappears". Spiritual, cognitive, and emotional events occur in Amichai's poetry "inside" the body, in a space separated from the world surrounding the speaker only by the physical shell that sets up a barrier between the stones beating from the inside and those beating from the outside. In the end, only by means of the things and words absorbed from the outside into this inner space can he "externalize" his feelings and thoughts and endow them with a singular lyric expression which finds its way again into the external space, into the world.

I have presented only a few of a long list of items from the religious-metaphysical sphere. I will end with the concept from which all of these are derived: the concept of the Divinity. Here, just as anyone wishing to define, or impart meaning to, a term such as "soul" must indicate the conditions and feelings that call up the concept and define it, so anyone wishing to point to the presence of God in this world or to define his essence must indicate those phenomena in this world that attest to that presence or enable one to define the concept denoting it. The word and the concept "God" are strikingly present in Amichai's poetry, but there is no divine presence in his world. The life experience of the poet, who brought "corpses from the hills", who searched for God where he is worshipped and in other places, in the poet's own life and in the lives of "weary people", has taught him that there is no God in this world. There is no point in searching for him, or for any other entity that may possess the qualities attributed to God in the religious tradition.

Therefore, in Amichai's poetry, "God" serves as a term for world orders, in particular the orders of nature, indifferent to the life of the individual, which allot him a short and fleeting life and condemn him to a fate of separation and death. In other contexts, "God" signifies human aspirations for pity, justice, love, and happiness, aspirations directed towards phenomena that do not exist in the reality of this world, and values that *do not* guide it; or "God" embodies the incapacity of man to understand his world (Amichai's poetry does not ask theological questions nor does it take any interest in the possibility that "God" exists in "other worlds"). It is therefore no wonder that religion and its institutions are described in his poetry as empty shells whose contents have shrivelled up and faded away, but which through their illusory sanctity protect narrow and earthly interests.

The consummate secularity of Amichai's poetry is also revealed in the use it makes of sources from the Hebrew literary tradition, which is, in the main, religious. In Amichai's poetry, verses and phrases from the sources are endowed with a secular meaning, frequently through parody or parodic inversion. The jet aircraft "makes peace in His heavens" (*Shirim*, p. 21), the "writing on the wall" is written and read by human beings suffering pain and destruction, but also causing others to suffer (*Shirim*, p. 219/253), the man "beneath his vine" telephones to the man "beneath his fig tree" (*Shirim*, p. 71), and the poet "wants to wager with Job on how God and Satan will behave / who will curse man first." Job wins the wager: "Damn it, Job, accursed is the day you were created in my image, your mother's cunt,

Job"—"God cursed, God blessed" (*Akhshav baraash*, p. 116). In the recurrent battle between God and Satan, the vanquished is really always Job (Everyman). These are only a few examples from a possible list of hundreds.

The importance of Amichai's "treatment" of words and concepts from the religious sphere—prophecy and miracle, the resurrection of the dead, God and his entourage, the biblical heroes, verses and phrases from the Bible, the midrash and the prayers—is not self-evident in our context, because the reading public that Amichai is addressing is not particularly religious. Nonetheless, it seems that this "treatment" is significant, particularly for readers who can be described as "free-thinking" or secular. Among these readers, there is a tendency to blur the lines separating a simple fondness for Jewish tradition from the conferring of serious significance on its religious elements. Pseudo-religiosity of this type, no matter how abstract and sentimental it may be, obscures unpleasant truths, creates conscious and unconscious hypocrisy, and directly and indirectly helps provide ideological reasons for actions that are driven by militaristic political interests. These reasons are totally unrelated to the feelings they exploit in order to realize themselves. Amichai's poetry obviously helped, perhaps indirectly, to expose sentimentality, to disclose hypocrisies, and encourage a more sober view of the "metaphysical" world.

A combination of linguistic and existential elements which, by their nature, have a political potential in the structural and thematic system of Amichai's poetry, as well as the way the elements are rhetorically and poetically fashioned, activate processes that can be described as those of *deconstruction*. Words and ideas which carry a political or ideological significance in the Israeli, Jewish, and Zionist context, overturn their accepted status. Amichai's poetry strips these words and ideas of every aura of esteem, it demystifies them and encourages a probing, ironic, and sceptical attitude towards them. The lack of seriousness towards more-or-less sacred cows that Amichai's wordplay, usually parodic, sometimes ironic, reflects in words, phrases, and concepts, has an extremely serious significance in guiding readers to new insights into their own reality, and in perceiving their political reality in particular. It also directs their attention to existential values from which this poetic "playfulness"—amusing as it may be—stems, and to which it points.

(4) The reference to the tension between the ironic playfulness and the existential seriousness, in relation to accepted and unaccepted values, which is so pervasive in Amichai's poetry, leads us to an additional factor also responsible, paradoxically, for the possible subversive political weight of this poetry. I refer to the moderation, the caution, the restraint and balance that characterize the way in which Amichai presents his position in

relation to every topic. To put it differently: the political positions that characterize Amichai's poetry are implied by it in indirect ways, and only rarely are they extreme in their content or formulation. The poetry is frequently aware of the limitations of these positions, on the one hand, and of the relative merit of opposing positions, on the other. Sometimes it even grants these opposing positions a sort of right of speech. My argument is that it is these among others that have made this poetry important from a political standpoint, and enhanced its power of exerting influence.

Probably the main reason that Amichai's poetry does not usually arouse any opposition, certainly not political opposition, is because it does not directly attack positions it dislikes: it does not contain a "passionate protest" against anything. On the other hand, it does not inflate or exaggerate the worth of values precious to its hero-protagonist, even if they serve as the underpinning of his "I do not believe" and play a central role in his worldview. The "anarchistic" stance of Amichai's poetry is balanced by an awareness of the human and national limitations that make it imperative to maintain collective mechanisms of various kinds. More than Amichai wishes to destroy the bureaucratic ruling establishments, he wants to restrict as far as possible the damage caused by their existence, an existence which ultimately he perceives as unavoidable, even necessary. He wishes mainly to reinforce the human as opposed to the establishment. Although his poetry always prefers the individual in the here and now to the historical past, and family life to the values of tradition and nation, his poetry is filled with historical concepts, traditional values, and "national problems".

The Amichaic man knows himself to be a cultural and social creature, a mortal who has no existence other than in the brief space between birth and death. Although he views himself first of all as an individual who refuses to be perceived as one of many that are counted and "summed up" according to "common denominators", which he often regards as alien to the very principle of his life, he is aware of the existence and power of national and social frameworks that pigeonhole him into various categories, determine his place within the national and social order, and grant him identity. He unwillingly takes part in the national endeavour and senses the workings of the historical and cultural consciousness based on values of the past as it determines his fate. However, he often perceives these values and norms to be artificial and coercive.

The poet-protagonist of Amichai's poetry is deeply rooted in his country and its cultural world and symbols. He lives in the present, but is also a captive of memories and of nostalgia. The fact that Amichai places the individual, his life and happiness, in the centre of the life experience in his poetry does not cause him to forget mankind's weaknesses, the brevity of human life or its limitations. The secular stance through which Amichai mocks the religious establishment and abjures illusions and divine consolations does not prevent him from relating with affection and a certain amount of respect, albeit mixed with ironic sobriety, to the linguistic and cultural values that originate in religious faith. All of them, even if their meaning is inverted or if they serve as material for his "games", find their place in Amichai's poetic world. His poetry, despite all its realism, is filled with love, albeit painful and sad, for the land and its geographical and human landscape. And within this love, that same Jerusalem from which the poet does not withhold his mockery and anger plays a leading role. The slogan "make love not war", popular among American youth in the 1960s, is relevant for many of Amichai's poems. However, it does not become a radical flag of protest, partly because of his sober awareness of the uniqueness of Israel's situation, of the dangers threatening its existence, and of those which endanger the existence of each individual in the country. Readers of Amichai who cannot grasp his irony may feel that the absence in his poetry of any extremism, or aggressiveness towards adversaries and those with opposing views, is a flaw; in my opinion, this absence is one of the secrets of its strength and influence.

The moderation with which Amichai employs irony and humour has not dulled the sting of the criticism embodied in his poetry, but it has made its apprehension easier, like the sweet coating on a bitter pill. Despite the fact that Amichai presents material with a fundamentally subversive political potential, from a perspective opposed to conventional social and national ideas, it has not aroused anger. Readers have reacted with restraint. They do not feel it necessary to defend themselves against provocation or to launch a counter-attack of the kind they might have contemplated had they felt themselves or their ideas being assailed. Only on reflection do Amichai's readers notice that, in diverse indirect ways, he undermines their accepted beliefs or formulates issues they have already recognized in some unarticulated layer of their consciousness. Like many phenomena I have mentioned in this paper, one can also view this effect as one aspect of a general quality of Amichai's poetry: the misleading, sometimes unbearable lightness of the poems, which penetrate the mind with great ease, while their often weighty influence is recognized only later, like the intoxicating effect of champagne, experienced only after the drinker has imbibed many glasses.

(5) An additional factor which may explain the possible political status of Amichai's poetry is its popularity. Of his contemporaries or successors none since Alterman has been his equal from this point of view. Amichai is prob-

ably the only canonical poet read by so many, even by those who do not really belong to what is known as the literary community. In this regard he certainly has no peers. From this standpoint at least, even today, he can be regarded as a "national poet", an appellation which does not suit his poetry in any other sense. Amichai achieved this status with great ease. A short time after he began to write, the stature he enjoyed among critics and scholars, as well as among the public at large, became an incontrovertible fact. Poets who are no less important have not earned this special status. Gershon Shaked wrote in 1970: "One cannot describe the poetic idiom of the poetry of this generation, its rhythm, its relationship to the world, without Amichai; in his generation Amichai is like Shlonsky in his." I am tempted to add the words of Shlomo Grodensky, who said on a radio programme in response to a letter from a listener ("We have had our fill of Bialik and Tchernichowsky, we want Yehuda Amichai"): "Apropos of Yehuda Amichai, it is strange that he is so universally admired in Israel. We are divided on everything except on Yehuda Amichai. That worries me, particularly because I am one of his first admirers" (published in writing in 1975).

In an issue of the *Haaretz* supplement devoted to the crisis in poetry (19 August 1994), Amichai was one of the few to assert that he himself did not sense any crisis. In response to claims voiced against him ("When Amichai says there is no crisis, what he means to say is: I continue to receive stipends"), he wrote in the following issue (26 August):

> I never received (and thank God, never needed) any public stipends, etc. I was awarded literary prizes for my books—the Shlonsky, Brenner, Bialik prizes, the Prime Minister's Prize, and the Israel Prize in 1982. When I said I wasn't complaining, I meant to say that my books are selling well to this very day. The royalties I receive from their sale and royalties from the Composers and Authors Society (for the publication and readings of my poems in various places) provide me with a good livelihood. That's why I said I had no complaints about my reading public of all ages.

This is not the place to discuss the reasons for this popularity, some of which can be found in the "internal" factors of his poetry, others in external, social, and cultural factors that stimulated its reception. However, one can offer two generalizations as hypotheses worth examining. According to the first, Amichai's poetry became popular because readers, even those unaccustomed to reading poetry, found in it direct and indirect echoes of their own world and of the topics preoccupying them, more than in the poetry of other poets of their own or earlier generations. I refer to the affinity of Amichai's poetry to the Israeli social, cultural, and political world as well as its affinity to the world of the "private citizen" and to his private life. I also refer to the fact that his poetry has taken as its protagonist an individual who is Jewish, Israeli but also Everyman, who is not a "personality", or "above the people" in any sense.

Other factors that made it easy for the Israeli Everyman to absorb Amichai's poetry and identify with its world belong to its poetics. Of these, its language, which on the one hand alludes to broad cultural systems, and on the other, sounds conversational, even "folksy" and very simple, seems to be of special importance. In its unique modernism, characteristics of more conservative poetics are incorporated and this combination of the new and the familiar, on various levels of language, is similarly one of the factors that has made Amichai's poetry accessible to a broad and heterogeneous reading public. In any case, there can be no doubt that popularity of this kind, even if not a sufficient condition for a politically significant influence, is surely a prerequisite for such an influence.

C

What is that influence and in what sense does it have any political significance? First, it is the influence of the experiential perspective to which the reader is directly and indirectly exposed by means of a rich diversity of contexts and details. This influence is apt to encourage readers to re-examine the ideological and political values to which they adhere. They must sense that the examination of these values and the reality guided by them which they absorb from Amichai's poetry has not stemmed from a clear political credo, or from some ultimate truth, but from within his real life, which the poetry has re-illuminated in its own way. Although this putative influence has not made Amichai's poetry political in the conventional sense nor has it enabled one to draw specific political messages from it, it enables one to attribute to it political implications. From the first appearance of this poetry and in the contexts in which it continues to develop, "simple words on eternal themes of death and love, or hope and despair" (Amichai, 1968), in the spirit of "make love, not war", express political implications, and reflect a new set of references, constantly expanding toward the political and helping to crystallize it. The point of departure Amichai has chosen, from which he challenges the significance of the political and the public in the consciousness of his generation, has exerted a greater influence, with political implications, than Zach's abstinence from place and time, his focus on ultimate truths of existence, on ethics and the aesthetics of the poetic medium; than Avidan's virtuosity and egocentricity; than Dalia Rabikovitz's musical magic and imaginative worlds.

If indeed Amichai's poetry has not directed its readers towards defined political activity, it has demarcated an ideological domain of political thought by means of which such activity can be explained and justified. For the sake of brevity, I will chart this domain according to several well-known, perhaps over-used, keywords.

The first is *humanism*. Amichai's poetry is humanistic in the literal sense of the term, not because it is associated with a lofty grouping of values but because at the centre of its values stand "people" and their experience. This signifies a refusal to subjugate their lives in the "here and now" to the historical past, or to mortgage them for the sake of an unknown future. If we add another word we could say that Amichai's humanism is *democratic*. In Amichai's poetry, there is not the slightest trace of élitism of any kind.

Then there is the word *scepticism*. Amichai's poetry casts doubt on every collective, class or national, ideology, on every religious or secular theology, and on every social or political solution that presumes to solve man's fundamental problems. Political, national, and social apparatuses are depicted in Amichai's poetry as absurd, alienated, and inept, not only because, according to his poetry, they lack the ability to provide answers to the authentic problems of existence, or because in one way or another it regards them as its destructive enemies, but also because they do not even possess the ability to resolve the problems for which they were established. Amichai's is not scepticism for its own sake, not total and certainly not nihilistic. This is scepticism which is driven, on the one hand, by the system of values I previously called humanism, and on the other hand—our fourth and fifth keywords—by *sobriety* and *realism*.

Amichai's poetry is a sober poetry in several senses: despite the fact that it assigns priority to the reality of the individual's life on earth, it is all too aware of the limitations of this life. It never ignores the political and social contexts that invade the private world of lovers and it often recalls the inevitable interaction between them. Although his poetry suspects and teaches others to suspect the platitudes of any social or religious establishment, its protagonist-hero belongs, and knows that others also cannot escape belonging, to the national and social frameworks that determine his and their identity. He also knows that dismantling or undermining these frameworks may have serious consequences for the security of his life and others' lives.

This realistic sobriety may also be the reason why the scepticism in Amichai's poetry regarding political values and institutions does not take extreme forms. His poetry does not incite any violence towards the ruling order, any refusal to fulfil civilian duties, or any real acts of protest. Amichai knows that the damage caused by aggressive acts, even when they are based on good intentions, is greater than any benefit they may bring. In particular, his poetry's consciousness of the unique national situation in which Israel and Israelis find themselves, its sense of belonging to the life of Israel, is, for better or worse, too powerful to allow it to adopt any other stance. For example, even if Amichai finds the continued occupation of the Territories repugnant, he will not support Israelis who refuse to serve in the army.

One cannot overlook the possibility that the poet's wariness of extremism and activism, which in his view have very slim chances of achieving their aims and are certainly damaging to the lives of individuals, his very fear of impairing what he perceives as the foundations of the state's existence, his advocacy of caution, as well as his eschewal of positions that seem to involve some danger to Israel, may be some of the reasons why a large public of readers identify with his poems.

Amichai's poetry demands of its readers that they adopt from the outset a suspicious attitude towards political establishments, misgivings about their motives and unrelenting scepticism about their theological and ideological justifications. This demand is manifested, as I have already noted, in Amichai's attitude towards war—the counter-experience, or the conclusively negative experience, in his poetry. Implicit in the poetry, which does not directly address the establishment, is the demand it makes of every regime to prevent the ultimate consequences of ideology and politics. To the people, or as Amichai puts it "the weary people", it implies the demand to reject the justifications that governments attempt to peddle in order to lead them to destruction and death. From its inception to the present day, Amichai's poetry has demanded peace. This demand, however, is usually implied in indirect ways, with humour and understatement.

After the Yom Kippur War, the call, expressed in Hebrew poetry, for direct political involvement and a clearer delineation of the characteristics of the political situation, in particular those relating to the occupation and the attitude towards the Palestinians, reappeared and intensified. The demand for a direct political struggle (through poetry) against all these phenomena increased. The "civil", humanistic, and anarchistic aspects of Amichai's poetry became the object of disparagement. His poetry was perceived as conciliatory and non-political. It seems to me that even in this context, Amichai's poetry—whose positions also became more extreme to a certain extent—continued to fulfil its role in the way I have described above. In the wake of these changes in Israel's political climate and in the political character of Hebrew poetry, there were those who argued that the political implications of Amichai's poetry are rather general and flimsy, insipid and non-committal. I do not find this argument persuasive. These implications have left their imprint on the Israeli mentality. Based on them, poets and other artists, holding more explicit views and advocating more defined goals, have gone much further in formulating them.

Amichai's poetry has indeed embodied its fundamental values primarily via the internal Israeli situation; its "Everyman" is usually the Israeli-Jewish individual. The distressing results of the social and political situation the poetry reflects—and in its way, also tries to subvert—are primarily those affecting this individual. However, this in itself does not refute the main arguments put forth in this paper. From the standpoint of political influence, calling the reader's attention to the suffering and demoralization that the collective brings upon itself and the individuals belonging to it may be preferable to "pure" moralizing that places a stress on catastrophe and the pain it causes to others.

In any case, the poet who, early in his writings, felt compelled to remind his readers, "with all the exactitude of pity", that members of his generation who "learned too soon to read the / awful writing on the wall" also knew how "to write [this writing] on others' walls" (*Shirim*, p. 219), felt at the same time the need to shift, or at least to allude to the possible shift, from the general world view he embodied in his poetry to more sharply defined political positions, as one of his early poems of Jerusalem, among others, already proves:

> *On a roof in the Old City*
> *Laundry lit up by the last light of day;*
> *A white sheet of an enemy,*
> *A towel of an enemy*
> *With which to wipe the sweat of his brow.*
>
> *And in the skies of the Old City*
> *A kite.*
> *And at the end of the string—a boy*
> *Whom I didn't see*
> *Because of the wall.*
>
> *We hoisted many flags,*
> *They hoisted many flags.*
> *So we would think they are happy,*
> *So they would think we are happy.*
>
> **(Shirim, p. 164/199)**

From the ability to express empathy towards the other with such great simplicity and such restrained emotion, from the feeling of shared fate and entrapment in the same terrible, absurd, and artificial situation, it is but a small step to the specific political conclusions that could be drawn by readers influenced by these values and the consistency with which they are expressed in Amichai's poetry. It is therefore not difficult to assume that Amichai's poetry played a meaningful role among those factors that prepared the ground for change in the Israeli political climate in recent years, a change that enabled the reversal of Israel's policy in the direction of the peace process.

Notes

1. For a thorough discussion and an extensive bibliography on political poetry in general and in Hebrew in particular, see Hanan Hever's book, *Paytanim uviryonim: tzmihat hashir hapoliti beEretz Yisrael* (Jerusalem: Mossad Bialik, 1993).

2. I tried to write such a systematic and detailed description of that cognitive and poetic system a few years ago in my book *The Flowers and the Urn: Structure and Meaning in Amichai's Poetry 1948–1968* (in Hebrew), in particular chapters 9–12, 14.

3. On the basis of Nili Gold's comments about the father figure in his poetry, quite a few traits of the Amichaic male can be depicted as "feminine", namely, as fitting female stereotypes, and can be viewed as Amichai's contribution to the struggle against the Israeli macho culture. See Nili Gold's "The 'Feminine' in Yehuda Amichai's Poetics" in this volume.

4. The first page number refers to the 1963 edition, the second to the enlarged edition of 1977.

5

Yehuda Halevi and Solomon Ibn Gabirol in the Early Poetry of Yehuda Amichai: Two Different Poems—Two Different Styles

Masha Itzhaki

In the first book of Yehuda Amichai's *Akhshav uvayamim haaherim*, there are two poems which are titled quite differently from all the others: the first one is called "Yehuda Halevi", and the following one "Ibn Gabirol". The purpose of this paper is to study some aspects of the early poetry of Amichai with reference to medieval poetry and poets in general, and to these two poems in particular.

Yehuda Halevi

The soft hairs on the back of his neck
are the roots of his eyes.

His curly hair is
the sequel to his dreams.

His forehead: a sail; his arms: oars
to carry the soul inside his body to Jerusalem.

But in the white fist of his brain
he holds the black seeds of his happy childhood.

When he reaches the beloved, bone-dry land—
he will sow.

(Tr. Stephen Mitchell)

This poem contains five stanzas. Four of them describe the well-known poet through the eyes of an unidentified speaker. The fifth is the only one referring to the future, pointing out the fact that he will reach the promised land, the "beloved and deserted" one, and on arriving there he will sow the seeds of youth and happiness, meaning that he will put an end to waste and ruin. One must pay attention to the fact that there is no question of "if" concerning the future, only a question of "when".

How should we understand this concluding phrase? How should we decipher the poem as a whole in the light of the final stanza? As happens quite often in the early poems of Amichai the closing sentence suggests two different modes of reading: either an optimistic one, signifying a hopeful future for a young generation to come, or an ironic one, full of question marks. This is an irony based on the simple historical fact that nobody knows for certain whether Halevi ever reached the land of Israel or not.[1] However, both readings are based on a conventional metaphor typical of the secular Hebrew poetry of Spain, a metaphor used more than once in the poems of Yehuda Halevi himself. I am referring to the contrast between white and black as signifying not good and evil, as expected, but old age and youth. In fact, it is quite logical; the basis of this metaphorical comparison is the hair: white hair (usually curls) for an old man while black hair for a youngster. Sure enough, following this metaphorical structure, black means something positive and hopeful, while white signifies the approach of death. Realizing this, one might understand several phenomena concerning this poem, for example: why hair and beard are the main components of the physical description of Yehuda Halevi; why from the start there is an impression of an old man although there is not a word concerning the question of age; how black seeds could possibly have a positive meaning; and so on.

This confrontation of white and black, signifying old age and youth, is the basis of a certain analogy between the third and fourth stanzas: the third contains an image of an ocean (oars and sails), reminding us of the real journey of Halevi to Egypt, and creating in the reader's mind the picture of the froth of waves, which is connected to the curls in the second stanza. The second line evokes the body, which contains the soul inside itself. Neither colours nor age are mentioned, a typical medieval motif concerning the concept of the body as a vessel of the soul.[2] One thing inside another is the basic picture in the fourth stanza as well: in the hands of his white—therefore old—mind he is holding the black seeds of happy youth. The analogy is evident: the old body (with its white hair, white beard, and a forehead like a white sail) is holding inside itself the soul, full of dreams and hopes, young, and therefore—black.

So far, the medieval method of comprehension leads to an optimistic reading of the poem. But is one allowed to disregard the universal signification of black and white? Is it really possible in the twentieth century to absorb black seeds or a black soul as positive elements meaning hope and optimism? It is here, at this point, where the other reading, the ironic one, is required. This reading, by its nature, leads to a certain doubt: will he really reach his goal? And if so, what sort of seeds are black seeds? In addition to the universal interpretation of white and black as good and evil, the ironic reading takes into consideration the great question mark in the unfinished biography of Yehuda Halevi, as well as the famous legend connecting his arrival in Jerusalem with his own murder. The absolute tone of optimism regarding Halevi as a messenger of renewal, of renaissance, somehow becomes weaker when confronting the poetic text with the external historical and traditional contexts. On a more general level I am suggesting that Amichai, by using the historical model of Halevi, is referring to the questions of immigration and the generation gap in general, a problem he treated more than once in his early poetry, always with ambiguity although usually from a very personal point of view.[3]

Nevertheless, medieval poetics is quite essential for the process of reading this poem, and not only on the level of simple interpretation. The fact that the figure of Yehuda Halevi functions historically as well as poetically creates a rigid external model which organizes the various components of the text and enables the reader to reach its different readings. In other words it could be regarded as a sort of puzzle, and in order to solve it the reader requires certain hints that refer to the external context, historical as well as poetical. It is as if the unknown speaker were drawing some kind of a picture, leaving some parts blank, and it was up to the reader to turn to the external model in order to fill them in.

This technique is characteristic of medieval secular poetry. In the process of reading the reader is expected to use a method of rational thinking, a shrewd analysis based on intellectual activity and knowledge of external cultural models (*adab* in Arabic), while the emotional impact based on personal experiences is considered secondary, if considered at all. What is needed in order to decipher a secular medieval text is an aesthetic distinction of stylistic improvisation based on rigid poetic structures. I believe that Amichai, in his early poetry, turns often, in the medieval manner, to rigid external models. This is obviously the case in poems such as "Rei anahnu shneinu misparim" (See, we are two numbers) or "Sonnet habinyanim" (The sonnet of buildings). In "Yehuda Halevi" the model in the text's background is of a historical nature; in the two other poems it is either mathematical terminology or grammatical observations. These two models function in the process of reading in a very similar way: in order to reach the core of the poem one has to think, puzzle-like, from the text to the outer context, and vice-versa, rather than following an emotional interaction based on personal sensations, images or allusions. In this regard the only difference between those two examples and "Yehuda Halevi" is in the nature of the external models. Certainly a national medieval context, charged with religious ideas, is accepted more easily than a mathematical or grammatical context, referring to the experience of love. The two poems referred to earlier were considered as unlikely to be compatible and therefore a linguistic amusement rather than lyrical expressions. What I am claiming here is that although "Yehuda Halevi", because of the nature of its historical context, seems more "poetical" in the conventional meaning of the term, it is as much an intellectual amusement as are the two other examples. Therefore not only does the text claim an outside model, but all its components are comprehensible only with regard to this model. Is it possible to understand in any other way metaphors such as "his forehead is a sail and his arms, oars"? Is there a way to avoid mathematical terminology in order to reach the ambiguity of the last verse of "Rei anahnu shneinu misparim"?

Terms like "amusement" or "game" are deliberately invoked in cases such as these. Certainly they could have negative significance concerning modern poetry, but not at all in the case of medieval verse. On the contrary, as mentioned before, the intellectual interaction between words and sounds, the shrewdness of an image, the linguistic ornaments, and even the absence of a personal narrator are characteristic of Hebrew secular poetry. I believe that in this sense the poem "Yehuda Halevi" represents a medieval stylistic tendency, typical of a number of Amichai's early poems. Its title not only signifies a code which defines the external cultural model as referring to the poetic message, but is, as well, a sort of declaration of a very particular stylistic tendency.

Ibn Gabirol

Sometimes pus,
sometimes poetry—

always something is excreted,
always pain.

*My father was a tree in a grove of fathers,
covered with green moss.*

*Oh widows of the flesh, orphans of the blood,
I've got to escape.*

*Eyes sharp as can-openers
pried open heavy secrets.*

*But through the wound in my chest
God peers into the universe.*

*I am the door
to his apartment.*

(Tr. Stephen Mitchell)

The second poem, "Ibn Gabirol", should be considered from the start as a completely modern personal poem, *in spite of* its title. It is true that one must have some knowledge about Ibn Gabirol in order to reach the core of this poem: one must realize that he was a poet, that he was very ill, that he was an orphan. Otherwise, mentioning the pus, the wounds, the suffering, and so on, is redundant. However, contrary to "Yehuda Halevi", neither external pattern nor puzzle-like technique are required. In other words, there is no description of Ibn Gabirol in this poem, only of an identifiable suffering speaker who takes advantage of certain qualities of the medieval poet, qualities which emphasize the relationship between agony and poetry, between suffering and creativity. Ibn Gabirol himself is mentioned only once, in the title. The "I" or "me" of the speaker is the subject of four stanzas out of seven. The other three are generalizations.

In order to penetrate the inner layer of the text one must be confronted with almost contradictory components from different, if not opposite, semantic fields, such as, for instance, pus and moisture versus tree or wood; God and poetry versus an opener or a door. These components are, quite obviously, not made of one piece, they do not possess unified characteristics, and they do not correspond to any external model which could, if it existed, organize them as one meaningful unit. On the contrary: on the surface there is no sign of any order or logic, external or internal. It is up to the readers, using their sensations, their associations, their personal experiences, and their cultural background, to try to identify the connections among all details and to organize for themselves meaningful groups of components in order to reach a comprehensive reading. The poem, in spite of its very concrete title, is an open one, not only from the formal point of view, but from the figurative and thematic aspects as well. The only means of attempting to "close" this text, that is, to reach its deep message to which all components correspond, is by referring to motifs like the father, wounds, the allusion to death, the very particular sort of God so commonly personified, and so on. In other words: if one needs to seek help outside the poem itself, this will be found in Amichai's poetic work as a whole rather than in the life of Ibn Gabirol. The divine idea of poetic inspiration turning into a bleeding wound which functions as a window through which God looks at the universe—or, to put it differently, the concept of the tortured poet as an instrument through which God glances at his own cosmos—has nothing to do with the attitude of Ibn Gabirol towards his own poetry, he, the master of his art, the speaker for God on earth. On the other hand, it has everything to do with Amichai's anger with God, an agonized anger deeply expressed in a number of his early poems. In "Ibn Gabirol" there is nothing "amusing", either on the linguistic level, or on the thematic one. There is, on the contrary, much pain, which is obvious, needing neither sophistication nor any puzzle-like technique.

The sophisticated wall between the historical model and the poetic message, the wall which forces the reader to use his or her intellect rather than emotional sensibility, does not exist here. From the very beginning of the poem there is a total integration between the two protagonists—the speaker and Ibn Gabirol. Technically, one could ask who is speaking in this poem, but even then, the only thing that matters would be the question, since the answer is not at all important. The wounds of young Ibn Gabirol, dying of a certain illness, are melted into the loneliness and agony of the rebellious young speaker, discovering that there is no real poetry without suffering. This is the idea at the core of this poem, purely lyrical, purely modern.

Notes

1. On this matter, see H. Schirmann, "Hashlamot lehayei Yehuda Halevi", in *Letoldot hashirah vehadrama haivrit* (Jerusalem, 1979), pp. 319–342.

2. On this matter, see my book, *Hahai gefen vehamavet botzer* (Studies in the Spanish *Tohehot*) (Tel Aviv, 1987), third chapter.

3. It mainly concerns his poems about his parents, such as "Laem" or "Avi bepesach", and many others, in the book *Bemerhak shtei tikvot* (Two hopes apart).

6

Portrait of the Poet in a Landscape

Glenda Abramson

Yehuda Amichai is not a topographical poet in the conventional sense. Only two aspects of his use of landscape in his poetry are considered in this paper: the landscape as part of the act of memory, and the landscape as an unstable element in his poetry. The Jerusalem poetry is excluded from this discussion: the Jerusalem poems reveal a complex and somewhat paradoxical version of landscape poetry if they are landscape poetry at all. They certainly do not describe an urban landscape but a symbolic or even mythic Jerusalem compounded of texts, both sacred and literary, the speaker's own personal history, and the history of Israel. Other, equally symbolic urban landscapes in Amichai's works are that of Weinburg in *Lo meakhshav lo mikan* and Buenos Aires in *Velo al menat lizkor*.

Landscape and Memory

In the eighteenth century, literary history and the life of the individual had their analogy in the English landscape garden. Careful arrangement of natural growth, statuary, and other structures were typically used by gardeners to re-create the stages of history and human life, and the lyric or topographical poem corresponded in some detail to these features of landscape gardening. The stroller in the garden was aided by its artifices to view the area in a particular manner: the variety of scenes and structures in a landscape poem was designed to evoke a corresponding variety of aesthetic and moral values. In such classical gardens—and indeed in such poems—the spectator/reader could move from scene to scene and experience symbolically a broad range of situations, events, and moral conclusions.[1]

    The Israeli landscape as a whole can perhaps be "read" historically in the sense that an eighteenth-century garden was read, through the placement of monuments, war detritus, memorials, and ornaments which create recognizable emblems of a cultural or political "life" and which evoke a corresponding variety of emotional responses. This becomes a rhetorical rather than moral discourse through which the promenader strolls—or more relevantly, a motorist drives. Israeli poetry has no tradition or analogy of gardening, with the result that the poet has to create his or her landscape epic anew. Without previous gardens, all the poets have are previous *texts*, either shared cultural texts or more abstract personal ones. Tova Cohen has already demonstrated the way in which to generations of pious Jews the landscape of the Promised Land accorded solely with descriptions in the Bible, and even maskilic visions of Palestine ignored the reality of heat, dust, and swamps to see only a verdant pasture and clear rivers where the desert should have been.[2] For the contemporary writer this has, of course, changed. Apart from its having been described *as it is* from the time of the *yishuv*, the Israeli landscape as a whole has accreted a political component. Perhaps it is true to say that its historical and political dimensions correspond to the morally didactic dimension of the classical garden. The Israeli landscape is perceived at one and the same time as a topos and a text, the physical embodiment of biblical demands and pledges.

Yehuda Amichai's landscapes echo the broadest understanding of the Israeli landscape as a collective historical discourse. They most often enclose, and intensify, a private narrative. While landscape seldom prevails over the action in which his speaker is involved, at the heart of his work lies a spiritual truth of which the establishment of *place* is an essential component. Amichai is therefore not a landscape poet in the sense that he merely describes an external place, one intended as a backdrop or a "scene" for its own sake, for the purpose of straightforward description with no apparent ulterior motive. He does not "simply stand and stare". This accords with Jacques Ellul's formulation of visual images, which, devoid of meaningful continuity between past and future, provide nothing but external appearances, never inward meaning.[3]

Amichai's gaze, then, seldom lingers on the external view but seeks to infer truth in a recollected view rather than in a static and presented visual form. In his poetry the landscape is more likely to serve as a stimulus for his speaker's personal reflections or his philosophy of memory; that is, it becomes a construct of his own personality instigated by his gaze. This more complex method of landscape description ranges from description that infers some sphere of meaning beyond the landscapes themselves, such as, for example, Tchernichowski's famous "Ayit, ayit", to a description which may incorporate some form of pathetic fallacy. Or, in an even more abstract development, the poem transforms an external scene entirely into a region of the poet's mind. The external landscape is metamorphosed by the imagination in transmutations that lead inward, resulting in Rilke's *Weltinneraum*, "inner-world space", an interior space through which the poet can configure things so that they accord with his perceiving eye.[4] His stroller does not *see* as does the visitor to the eighteenth-century garden, but *constructs* the stages of history and human life. This is a landscape either manipulated by the imagination or entirely situated within the imagination in poems in which the poet and the place temperamentally unite.

Amichai's landscape is generally not an invented landscape in this sense but a reconstructed one according to the emotion accompanying an act of recollection stimulated by a real place. His walks take place within his memory, creating the topography of the *inner* eye. He indicates as much by placing the word "memory" (*zikkaron*) or many synonyms for it as frequent landmarks within his reimagined landscape. The primary function of the landscape for Amichai's speaker is, therefore, its signification of the emotion accompanying memory. His topoi are "areas of remembering", which involve individual experience and history, and the historical life of the country.

> But now I do what every dog of memory does,
> I howl quietly
> and urinate an area of remembering around me
> so no one will enter it.[5]

Amichai's vision of place is modified by previous knowledge, in other words he employs what John Noyes has characterized as a "visual hermeneutic".[6] He mythicizes space according to his previous personal experience of or in it, and also in accordance with the broader collective vision of his generation. Many of his poems are titled with place names; the opening statement of the poem briefly summarizes the place's character but it is then radically appropriated and transmogrified into *Weltinneraum*, to become an element of the speaker himself: his youth, his love, his nostalgia, and so on. The *name* of the place, such as Akhziv for example, evokes a mood or the incentive to contemplation far more than the geographical location of which it is the indicator. Significantly, places retain the characteristics apportioned to them by the poet even when they have objectively changed. Edward Said claims that the traveller's eye acquires, organizes and controls space according to knowledge imposed on it in a form of "primary narcissism"—his phrase. Amichai renders the space he encounters subservient to his desire, which, in most cases, is memory or memorialization. His landscapes are therefore not spatial but temporal elements.

Amichai's landscape elements are particularly significant in the context of war, or more precisely the War of Independence, and of love. His method of "writing" the landscape provides a topography of war in which the entire country is able to be "read" (precisely like the classical garden) as a verbal map of battle sites and war memorials, sites that have significance only as battlefields of 1948. Place names provide the geographical locations and specific signs within the poems indicate their memorial nature even when the poem itself is devoted to personal memory. The sites are immediately recognizable as belonging to a particular realm of the nation's consciousness. The place names in the poems' titles themselves constitute the memorials, much like Ypres, Normandy, Passchendaele, or Arromache, which have no identity in the collective memory other than their signification of battle. For one engaged in memorializing the war, few existing Israeli monuments appear in Amichai's poetry. The monuments are all created internally, consistent tropes of death and memorialization constituted by sites or at least the names of sites. As he writes: "Memorials are placed in everything like weights / so that the country's history shouldn't fly away in the wind / like paper does."[7]

The War of Independence reappears in *Gam haegrof hayah paam yad petuhah veetzbaot* within vastly altered contextual formations. The poems in the *Yovlot milhamah* (Jubilees of war) section of *Gam haegrof* emerged from Amichai's visit with his children to some of the battlefields of 1948. He describes this as a "nostalgic" visit, a paradoxical designation in view of the harshness of his war poetry composed in the 1950s shortly after the experiences it describes. However, Amichai interprets nostalgia as "remembering" (*hizakrut*). In an interview he said: "I explained to my children at Tel Gat, for example, that there was a position here, a machine gun here, we began a retreat from there and there my good friend was wounded and I dragged him to the field ambulance."[8] These factual details have been recapitulated in other poetry, notably in "Meaz",[9] and appear to be the accepted metonyms of the war as explored in retrospect by Amichai's poetic spokesman. The poems of *Yovlot milhamah* are suffused with quasi-mythical or even pastoral landscape elements which have more to do with collective memories of youth than explicit individual memories of the war: flowers, gardens, orchards, warm weather, trees, sea. They have no hint of the rain or cold which distinguished one of Amichai's most famous early war poems "Rain on the battlefield" and many others in which autumn, with mist, fog and rain, was the predominant season. In "Tel Gat" the topographical outlines and landmarks and their colours are clearly marked; there is no mist or fog in a war which has become sanitized, almost beautiful in memory, different from its stark incarnation in the poetry which was closer to the event. Yet the pathetic fallacy of the earlier war verse paradoxically intensified the romanticism of the poetry far more than the bright sunlight suffusing "Tel Gat", the poem and the place.

"Tel Gat" opens with the restatement of Amichai's comment in the interview: "I brought my children to the hill where once I had battles / so that they should understand the things I did / and forgive me for the things I didn't do" (p. 9) Since the appeal for forgiveness is immediately followed by the suggestion of forgetting this may be the fault for which forgiveness is required. The duty to remember is a national obligation. In the context of war, Amichai promotes the communalization of his own experiences by utilizing them (visiting and naming the battle sites, recalling dead comrades) to memorialize the communal effort. For example, Dickie, Amichai's own commanding officer, killed in 1948, is frequently memorialized in the poetry and the fiction. In one case he seems to constitute a feature of the external as well as internal landscape. He "remains standing in the landscape of my memory / like the water tower at Yad Mordechai".[10] Yad Mordechai becomes for all time an embodiment not only of the war but of one of its victims. Memorialization is subsumed into the landscape, creating an unbreakable psychological bond between the landscape and the people.

Because of the general indeterminacy of Amichai's memories of war and their non-specific character, they can be deemed to relate not only to him, but to the activities of his entire generation. The vistas and smells he invokes to recall the battles and their topographical locations remain vague and unspecific: various valleys, beaches, and orchards, smells of eucalyptus and yellow sand. Amichai's memories of war reside in the lexicon of tropes and words of the terrain that together define the topographical parameters of his war poetry: hills, trees, the wind, sand, and orchards, rather like the red poppies, barbed wire, and rows of white crosses which immediately summon up the First World War. For example, there are hills and orchards at the site of a *Palmah* reunion; the temporal "then" is defined by hills and sand in a poem entitled "Bagivot hanegev" which recalls a battlefield. Cypresses, orchards, and sand are the only topographical elements in the famous war poem "Meaz". A hill and the wind mourn a casualty on the battlefield in "Halal basadeh". The foot of the "hill of horrors" in "Abu Ghosh" is the wind's habitat. The only line in Amichai's famous "El male rahamim" relating to war reads: "I, who carried bodies down from the hills . . . ". These repeated elements provide the modules of Amichai's visual language of war.

In "Tel Gat", the hill upon which the speaker and his children sit is covered with chrysanthemums, with an allusion to Genesis 6:1 underscoring their power of multiplication. The hill ceases to be the hill "where I once had battles" but presents a flower-covered site concealing the historical connotations of the terrain and neutralizing it, with only the ex-soldier, unlike the casual stroller in the garden, aware of what is obscured under the carpet of flowers. One implication is that since the terrain forgets, it is the duty of the man to remember. "We were the resurrection of the hill / and even this is as temporary as this spring, and as eternal" (*Gam haegrof*, p. 9). The ex-solder's real memories, other than those he shares with his group or the nation as a whole, are irrelevant to his geography of war and remain enclosed within a secluded and protected area. The communal memories are evoked by the place name, the hill, and the wind. The word "memory", *zikkaron* (*z-kh-r* in many grammatical permutations occurs fourteen times in three pages of verse in *Gam haegrof*, pp. 11–14), therefore becomes no more than a framework or a poetic cloak, like the chrysanthemums themselves.

Amichai's loci in poems about memory of war often unite landscape and text so that the landscape is preconditioned by the text. For example, in "Tel Gat" specific memory is summoned by a *textual* wind which alludes to a *Palmah* song: "Haruah noshevet kerirah . . . " (The wind blows coolly)—Amichai: "Ruah tzohorayim noshevet kalah" (A noonday wind blows lightly). In "A memorial service for those who fell at Ramat Yohanan" the hills and valleys which mark war sites become monuments to the dead soldiers:

> *The trees planted in their childhood*
> *now almost conceal their graves on the hilltop.*
> *From afar the white tombstones*
> *are like the hives of the bees of the sweet honey*
> *of forgetting.*
> *In the valleys grow grain, barley and wheat, corn and alfalfa*
> *and on the hills fruit trees are in bloom,*
> *all the poetry of geography books*
> *that the dead learnt in their childhood.*[11]

The tombstones are, ironically, the signifiers of forgetting: they are not tombstones but something else, their memorial function deferred in an act of denial rather than forgetting. The natural landscape is the only true memorial, one unknown to the geography books. Yet another text imposes itself on the landscape in an ironic and neutralizing misrepresentation of it.

Sometimes the landscape derives its character not as much from its description in the poem as from its textual source which lends the events taking place within it a transcendental significance. For example, the elegiac "Pegishat anshei hapalmah" in the collection *Shalvah gedolah—sheelot uteshuvot* reads like a collection of motifs or signs most closely associated in Amichai's work with war in general and the *Palmah* in particular. Yet its geographical location evokes a more abstract entity than a single war: it takes place at the foot of the mountains of Gilboa, less a landscape than a historical association with tragedy and heroism. By placing his reunion in this location Amichai unites an archetypal heroism with his own generation of heroes and provides a historical continuity to Israel's valour. The name, Har Gilboa, sets the locus of this poem in the Bible in its interior and exterior landscapes. Together with this powerfully rhetorical setting are the emotional topoi of the War of Independence itself: orchards, cypresses, and the *ruah hanoshevet*, Amichai's contemporary points on his map of war.

There has to be some disjunction between the ex-soldiers' memories, which are not conventionally pleasant ones, and the pastoral metaphor of their setting, rendered by Amichai as a flock of sheep at pasture in which the memories can graze in peace, the pastorality which infuses all his later poetry of wartime memory. *Zekhirah*, "remembering", is a voluntary act, unlike "memory" (*zikkaron*). Like the pastoral memories of war, the remembering itself occurs on sunlit days and perfumed nights, among peaceful cypresses and orchards. Words of tranquillity, together with the idyllic landscape, belie the surface sadness of the poem with its remembrance not so much of dead comrades but of youth and the past. The speaker recalls a path among the orchards leading to memory and forgetting "but we didn't go down it". He remained halfway, in a limbo between the recollection and the possibility of forgetting. For once the speaker decides to remain safely outside the "area of remembering" and allow the landscape itself to constitute the ideological and historical monument. In fact, Amichai's lyric "I" is rarely "within" the objective landscape at all: it is from the outside that he does his transformative work.

In the context of love the landscape constitutes less of an aide-memoire for Amichai's speaker than a powerful *symbol* in his poetry. This is an important theme in itself. One short poem serves as an example for the relationship between love and landscape throughout all the verse:

> *I know a man*
> *who photographed the view he saw*
> *from the window of the room*
> *in which he had loved*
> *and not the face*
> *of the one he had loved*
> *in that room.*

Although the phrase "I know a man" indicates some amazement, the man's action is consistent with the relationship of the lyric "I" to the landscape, for throughout the poetry the sight of a landscape instantly recalls the act or event of having loved. Therefore a photograph of the landscape may mean more about the love than a photograph of the lover herself. Landscape appears to recall not only the love but a complex system of emotional responses relating to the memory of love rather than its object. The landscape therefore becomes a solipsistic symbol of love itself and loving. Its task is to stimulate the act of remembering rather than the memory itself. It is important that the poet be engaged in the *act* of remembering for, in addition to commemoration, remembering for him is a creative enterprise. In his earlier books, particularly in the Akhziv and Caesarea cycles, an event reported to have "happened" in the past was a poetic principle by which the remembering of the event was akin to creating it. "Remembering" had to do with the creative process itself, a form of wish-fulfilment rather than a recollection of an experienced event, particularly in the context of love. The equation of landscape and this procedure of "remembering" love is a constant throughout Amichai's verse.

In the metaphorical transformation of love and memory, spatial and temporal distance are related. The following poem is almost a continuation of the previous one:

> *A deep window allows one a distant view*
> *like a deep firearm.*
> *Distant things attract me.*
> *Even the woman standing beside me,*
> *her voice reaches me from time to time,*
> *like the sounds of celebration in a distant valley*
> *that come to my ears on gusts of wind.*
>
> **(Sheat hahesed, p. 80)**

"Distant things", being vague and undefined, are capable of manipulation, even creation. The woman's voice is something other when heard indistinctly from afar—her words are more pleasant ("the sounds of celebration") for not bearing clear meaning.

Movement and Instability of the Landscape

Amichai's speaker is a variation of the urban *flâneur*, he is a person who strolls through landscapes but instead of describing them he appropriates them subjectively. He is rarely, like Wordsworth, a static observer but moves from scene to scene. He moves and everything constantly moves past his gaze despite the beguiling stasis in a new "still-life" vision which promises security and quietude:

> *In an evening when olive trees breathed deeply*
> *and the hills again learned to dance like the sons of gods*
> *I saw my son's face when I was alone*
> *I was so alone until I saw it.*
> *Rest in me, said this landscape, rest, rest.*
>
> *I saw birds flying up and down*
> *like when people leave you*
> *and others return in their place.*
> *I saw people sitting in their house*
> *shouting "home!" and their faces*
> *were peaceful like those people*
> *sitting in their house.*
>
> *Rest in me, said this landscape, rest, rest.*
>
> **(Hazman, p. 60)**

As his wanderer is always on the move so is his poetry, little of which is what it appears to be. Through his idiosyncratic reliance on metaphor and conceit his object is continuously being displaced. This is a stratagem of linguistic disguise which is extended from the simple mask, such as the chrysanthemums cloaking the battlefield, or the illusion of the beehives in place of tombstones, to actual transmutations of language and the displacement and deferment of meaning rendered by his densely concentrated tropes, and particularly by the recurring image of darkness which appears in many of his poems and which draws the reader's attention to the obscuring of the referential outlines. For example, in "Pegishat anshei ha-palmah" there was a path among the orchards leading to the "perfumed darkness" of memory, a pleasant darkness in which memory and desire could be conflated. Elsewhere, love assumes the guise of an old toolshed whose interior darkness deflects clarity of memory.

His poetry therefore conceals rather than reveals: not only are the obsessive metaphors a strategy for disguising meaning but the landscape as well is one of the poetry's most unstable and deceptive factors. First, as we have seen, in the context of war, it is reduced to a few repeated metonymic elements which disguise its authenticity: sand, sun, sea, hills, and valleys. These features obscure or replace the ugly particulars and facts of battle. Second, the contents of the poem confound our anticipated sense of the landscape elicited either by the place names or by the classification of the place. For example, the poems set in Akhziv are rarely seascapes but agonized contemplations of love. The most cognitively unstable topos is the public park in Amichai's expressionistic *Baginah hatziburit* which, for all its grass and trees, is a beautifully ironic metaphor for the urban jungle, the modern technological city. The grass is green but the "end" (*ketz*) sits on it; the trees are lushly in leaf, but from one of them hangs a suicide who "deleted the inapplicable" and the homeless sleep on benches beneath them. The "garden" or "park" encloses modern technology, poverty, depression, isolation, and thwarted love.

Third, many poems refer to the *alteration* of the natural topography. In one of the poems in *Hazman* (p. 80) human activity rearranges and controls a landscape by reclaiming the seashore to suit people's view; nature is domesticated and enrolled in their purposes:

> *People's actions bring the seashore closer*
> *other actions push it away.*
> *How does the sea know what they want? Which jetty*
> *clings like love*
> *and which disdains and rejects.*

In an article written soon after the Six-Day War, Ehud ben Ezer analyzes the changes in the portrayal of the Israeli landscape from the *yishuv* to 1967 and the landscape's loss of innocence in the face of war and expulsion. He cites Amichai's "Mayor of Jerusalem" as an example of a nightmare in which the Arabs, the border and the view become a "demonic and threatening entity":[12]

> *It's sad to be*
> *the mayor of Jerusalem,*
> *it's terrible.*
> *How can a person be the mayor of such a city?*
> *What will he do there?*
> *He'll build and build and build.*
> *At night the mountain stones will draw nearer*
> *and surround the houses*
> *like wolves coming to howl at the dogs*
> *that became men's slaves.*[13]

Ben Ezer interprets this poem as representing the sense of menace from primitive elements existing outside people's houses, elements which encroach upon their enclosed, civilized lives and threaten to destroy them. In fact the poem is another representation of the transformation of the landscape from its primitive and natural wildness, represented by the stones, into subservience as the structured and configured walls of human dwellings. The mountain stones which are still free elements of nature skulk near the houses and lament or mock the servility of the stones appropriated by the mayor of Jerusalem in order to "build, build, build". Humans compel the landscape to surrender its liberty. Just as wolves lost their freedom when they became dogs, mountain stones are domesticated into buildings and reconstituted into a new, man-made landscape.

At the same time nature of its *own* volition shifts and obscures its forms: sand, salt, and wind reshape the landscape. Human creations, which add contour to natural topoi, are also constantly transformed: for example, a Roman column becomes a museum artefact and then finally a constituent of the soil.[14] Even the landscape in Amichai's poetry is therefore not to be trusted. It shifts and dissolves, it masks and reinvents itself as the speaker gazes, and in his memory. Ultimately his consciousness reconstructs it, with nature's power of change assisting him in his imaginative formulations.

In "Abu Ghosh" nature asserts its transformative control:

> *We were silent up to Abu Ghosh*
> *I'll love you up to old age*
> *at the feet the hill of horrors,*
> *in the wind's habitat. At Shaar Hagay*[15]
> *the angels of the three faiths came down to the road.*
> *Faith in one God was still heavy. In words of pain*
> *I must describe the fig trees*
> *and what happened to me which was not my fault. Sand*
> *blew into my eyes and became tears. Little airplanes*
> *and the great dead without names*
> *parked in Ramallah. The scent of orchards*
> *touched my blood. My blood looked over its shoulder*
> *to see who had touched. Winds, like actors,*
> *began to disguise themselves anew*
> *in order to act in front of us*
> *and to don masks of a house, a mountain or a forest,*
> *the mascara of sunset and night.*[16]

The wind is the great dissembler here, first blinding the speaker with sand so that he can no longer discern the real landscape and then creating a new form in front of his eyes. The ancient landscape is refabricated to displace the war, the "hill of horrors" in which things happened "which were not my fault". When the pain of remembering becomes unbearable the speaker relieves it by reconstituting the landscape: in Abu Ghosh the transforming wind obligingly screens the usual synechdoches of battle, hills, valley, orchard, by mimicking more peaceful, domestic elements: a house, a mountain, a forest, sunset, and finally the darkness. All this constitutes both an imaginative enhancement and concealment, like the chrysanthemums, of the truth of the battlefield.

In addition to constituting a general map of *events* rather than places—for Amichai says more about things that happen in the places than about the places themselves—and serving as a memorial narrative, the landscape in Amichai's poetry structurally resembles his putative poetic autobiography. His verse presupposes autobiography through its almost constant first person singular speaker, its recourse to personal experience and its chronological and narrative continuity, an effect reinforced by Amichai's declaration, "I have always written my life."[17] While the composite effect of his work is that of a coherent life history, it consists more accurately of a selection of events from a life which become the basic propositions upon which his entire literary output is based. These elements and certain *dramatis personae* are consistently present in the poetry, all contributing to Tzvi Atzmon's assertion: "Amichai deals with the 'great', the 'classical' things: love, the passage of time and of a man, youth, death, war, memory . . . ".[18] The *real* life is obscured by these repeated tags. This is the case as well with the poetry in which landscape occurs. When one recollects Amichai's poetry in tranquillity one is aware of its general ambience: the middle eastern sunshine, dust, the sea, tall trees, sand, and wind. While there is ambience there is only a generalized and repeated topography. The landscape too has been transformed into a sustained poetic myth which through certain repeated elements provides both introspective references and the landmarks of a generation's history.

Amichai uses few adjectives in his poetry about landscape. This lack precludes any evidence of the speaker's real feelings about any individual landscape, any evaluative response other than a blending of the landscape and significant human experiences such as love and war. The dearth of adjectives places the speaker at some emotional distance from his subject. There are few individual moments of recognition during which he responds to the landscape as it is rather than as a trope of memory or nostalgia, or as an extended personal and historical narrative, like the eighteenth-century garden.

Notes

1. See Brigitte Peucker, "The Poem as Place: Three Modes of Scenic Rendering in the Lyric", *PMLA* Part 96 (October, 1981), pp. 904–912.

2. *Mehalom lemetziut: Eretz Yisrael basifrut hahaskalah* (From dream to reality: *Eretz Yisrael* in the literature of the *Haskalah*) (Bar Ilan University, 1982).

3. Martin Jay, "The Rise of Hermeneutics and the Crisis of Ocularcentrism", *Poetics Today*, vol. 9, no. 2, p. 311.

4. Peucker, p. 912.

5. *Gam haegrof hayah paam yah petuhah veetzbaot*, p. 11.

6. John Noyes, *Colonial Space: Spatiality, Subjectivity and Society in the Colonial Discourse of German South West Africa 1884–1916* (Reading: Harwood Academic Publishers, 1991), p. 217.

7. *Meadam ata veel adam tashuv*, p. 73.

8. Dalia Karpel, "Mekaveh lanobel" (Hoping for the Nobel Prize), *Ha'ir*, 3 November 1989.

9. *Shalvah gedolah—sheelot uteshuvot* (Schocken Books, 1990), pp. 9–11.

10. *Meahorei kol zeh mistater osher gadol*, p. 89.

11. *Meadam atah veel adam tashuv*, p. 70.

12. "Portzim unetzurim" in *Keshet*, Summer 1968, no. 4, pp. 133–134.

13. *Shirim 1948–1962*, p. 185.

14. This is the reverse of the process described by Ilan Sheinfeld: "Poem after poem . . . presents everything in the world as a reflection or an incarnation of something else which also was an incarnation of something more ancient which was an incarnation of a primeval source." "Vehakol masekhot", *Al hamishmar*, 9 July 1990.

15. Lit. "the valley's mouth".

16. *Shirim 1948–1962*, p. 168.

17. Dalia Karpel, "Mekaveh lanobel", *Hair*, 3 November 1989.

18. Tzvi Atzmon, "Yad Amichai baolam", *Iton* 77 (January 1990), p. 23.

7

The Metaphor of the Persona

Ziva Feldman

Yehuda Amichai was born in 1924, in Würzburg, southern Germany. Würzburg was at that time the cultural centre of Jews throughout south Germany. Amichai was raised in a traditional Jewish manner. His father was a travelling salesman, selling haberdashery. In 1936 the family emigrated to Israel, settling first in Petach Tikvah and then moving to Jerusalem. In 1942 Amichai graduated from school and immediately joined the Jewish Brigade in the British Army. He became involved in smuggling arms and illegal Jewish refugees into Palestine. After leaving the army in 1946, he began teaching education at the Bet Hakerem Seminary and in high schools. He enlisted in the *Palmah*, serving in the Negev Brigade. During the 1960s Amichai taught education at the Greenberg Diaspora Teachers' College in Jerusalem. In 1957 he won the Shlonsky Prize for his first book of poems, followed by the Brenner Prize (1969) for his second book, the Bialik Prize (1976), Israel Prize (1982), and Agnon Prize (1986).

Amichai has brought about a change in Hebrew poetry, within the transformation from the sublime to the mocking.[1] His works, like Shlonsky's, illustrate a prevailing lack of direction and orientation.[2] In this regard, Amichai is a follower of Shlonsky, although he lacks the motif of the heroic death that becomes the horror of the single individual. His poetry does not reach metaphysical heights, but remains within the physical and down-to-earth. Amichai creates poetry expressing modern humanity which accepts the burden of an existence without God. These new norms are part of the change overtaking the modern community, creating a new Israeli society with all its complexity and lack of homogeneity. These factors have led, from the 1950s to the 1990s, to the creation of literature which becomes more personalized, without separating the poetic persona from the speaking persona. It is literature which is less communicative, based on a very powerful persona at its centre. This is not ideological or political work, but the sole esoteric persona expressing his feelings. This is illustrated in poems such as "I want to die in my bed" and "I'm a poor prophet", among others. The viewpoint created does not allow perspective, and transforms the persona poetry into "poetry within its own reflection".[3] Amichai is considered to be one of the creators of this change. Another expression of this era is the moulding of the persona as an untrustworthy, anti-heroic figure, constantly failing and self-reflexive within the Hebrew literature of the "self-image".

Hebrew literature is engaged constantly in the process of overcoming the Hebrew language. Hebrew confronts the changed conceptions of humanity and the arts in the modern era, in addition to its struggle to become a language transformed from biblical into colloquial. This process is laid bare in contemporary Hebrew literature which, apart from its creation of a colloquial language, undergoes a transformation from a high register into a lower type of language. Amichai goes further and demonstrates manipulation of the language through the use of linguistic dislocation and manneristic structures. Diaspora writers would speak the local language but write in Hebrew. This meant a transformation of language from daily down-to-earth into sacred. The Israeli writer uses sacred language as a colloquial one, creating a reduction of the biblical language. Amichai does so by manipulating parts of the Bible and other sacred sources. Dualism and oxymoron, characteristics of Alterman's poetry, also characterize Amichai's, although they are used differently. Amichai utilizes the same tools, introducing them into the most modern poetry, unbound by any of the restraints to which Alterman adheres in his poetry.

Amichai's work expresses "metaphors of self"[4] as its contemporary spirit. The poet attempts to focus on the struggle of forces between conservative and modern, by using words. His poetry does not exist in a vacuum, but generates a dialogue with another modern medium, such as the visual (Magritte, Buccioni, Marinetti, among others); it is nourished by the Imagists, Futurists, and Surrealists. It derives also from Rilke's works by silencing the soul or animating the still and abstract. It derives from Proust through the activation of memories and objects, the object manipulating its operator.

Amichai functions through the object which has undergone a transformation as a means of conducting a dialogue with the absolute, rather than rejecting it or renouncing its existence. He attempts to understand his own existential situation between blasphemy and the values of his parents' home. Hebrew literature itself has attempted to deal with this situation since the nineteenth century, but Amichai is able to express it with fresh clarity. His work is located between things, not within the things themselves. His struggle is not that of a person who has to decide between worlds, but of someone who cannot find his place in any world. His metaphorical space is *shetah shel hefker*, no-man's-land.

No-man's-land: place is the central focus of his poetry, rather than time, although the motif of time is also essential. The place is not a defined one, because it is anywhere. Amichai's Jerusalem is a city in which he and his children live. Its stones belong not only to him, but to many other peoples. He finds its stones in the ruins of Würzburg, the city in which he was born, and in the Rhine which is also the Jordan. The concept of a place as non-defined creates a reality by means of a dynamic space figurative system.

Physical dynamics deals with elements that create motion, and the influence of forces on the movements of objects. Kinetics deals with the phenomena resulting from these influences. "Kinetic" indicates existence in motion through space and time, as opposed to stasis. Amichai's work is expressed by constant kinetic movement, the result of a biographical process which has created that movement. This is analogous to physical dynamics, all on the assumption that kinetic self-expression is open to many interpretations.

With the annulment of the unilateral representation of artistic expression, the work assumes movement with the aid of a figure which is essentially metonymic and fragmented. This creates a form that aspires to overcome unity and symmetry, as a means of expressing an era of uncertainty. The figure in Amichai's work is, first, a means of expressing the feelings of the lyric persona; second, memories of the persona in constant movement; third, dynamic expression, creating kinetic transformations. Therefore, the images in Amichai's work are thematically and compositionally kinetic transformations.

In Amichai's poetry the images move between two temporal axes: synchronic and diachronic. It is possible to find in his work a place known as "the golden intersection" in a work of art,[5] situated between excitation and reaction, between conveying an experience and drawing an existential conclusion. At this specific meeting point, experience receives a meaning while being transformed from presented picture into subjective expression. Aesthetically a symmetrical dynamics is created, resulting from the relationship between all the parts of the work.

The image of the lyric persona lies between situations of "activating" and "activated". First, an object as an involuntary element activates the memories of the lyric persona; second, the persona activates the object by means of memory. Movement is created through these forces between an unconscious object, being an activated object, and a conscious object which is the operator. This movement moves on the axis of time which is between memory and immediate experience. The movement of the lyric persona is between his parents' home and the absolute, and progress and change, that is, an aspiration towards the kinetic focus at the "golden intersection":

My God, The Soul[6]

```
       a    My God, the soul
            you gave me
            is smoke—
            from never-ending burnings

 c—         of memories of love.

            The minute we are born
       b    we start burning them ——> Kinetic focus
            and so on
            until the smoke
            dies, like smoke.
```

From elements creating the "smoke" the lyric persona moves to describe the existential phenomenon of fear of death and the approach to it from the moment of birth. Two fragments create a unity between unbalance and balance at the point of kinetic focus or "golden intersection":[7]

$$\frac{a}{b} = \frac{b}{c}$$

This structure exists also in Amichai's fiction which is defined as "lyrical fictions". It is expressed in the short story in the same manner in which it appears in poetry. The figures describe the persona and are reflected within his image. The persona is in the "no-man's land" and in a fragmented world of uncertainty and disappointment. The stories are autobiographical, creating a plot without development. *Not of This Time, Not of This Place* is a lyrical novel describing an attempt at vengeance which has never been realized. Between the internal and external narratives the figures are no more than reflections of the persona.

Amichai's works cannot be divided into periods, as there is no fundamental difference between them. It is possible, though, to divide them according to the changes within the creative persona as he grows older, from meeting death as a soldier to the fear of death as an adult facing the end. From the 1960s, a time in which the persona already bids farewell to his parents and his children are growing mature, his address is not to existing time, but to fear in the face of the loss of time and its rapid disappearance.

Amichai's works have been translated into many languages and have reached a broad spectrum of readers, since they are not identifiably local. This proves the power of literature which is not lost even in translation, assuming that translation implies an entirely new work but preserves the same kinetic structure at the meeting point which creates a balance within the fragmented system.

Notes

1. See Hillel Barzel, *Hashir hehadash: misagav lehitul* (The new poetry: from the sublime to the mocking) (Tel Aviv: Eked, 1979).

2. Baruch Kurzweill, *Beyn hazon leveyn haabsurdi: Perakim laderekh sifrutenu bameah haesrum* (Between vision and the Absurd: Chapters on the progress of our literature in the twentieth century) (Jerusalem and Tel Aviv: Schocken, 1966), p. 173.

3. See Ruth Karton-Blum, *Shirah barei atzmah* (Poetry within its own reflection) (Hakibbutz Hameuchad, 1986).

4. James Olny, *Metaphors of Self: The Meaning of Autobiography* (Princeton University Press, 1972).

5. Gila Blass, "Hatakh hazahav baomanut" (The golden intersection in art), *Mahshavot*, no. 59 (1990), pp. 37–40.

6. Yehuda, Amichai, *Shirei ahavah* (Love Poems) (Tel Aviv: Schocken, 1986), p. 63, pp. 103–104.

7. Blass, pp. 103–104.

8

The "Feminine" in Yehuda Amichai's Poetics

Nili Scharf Gold

A few years ago, in a class on Israeli women's literature, a student, angry and curious, asked me: "How is it that you, a woman who teaches women's literature and argues that not enough is written about it, devote so much time and energy to the work of a man?" The man, of course, is Yehuda Amichai. Silent for a moment, I blurted an answer I had not thought of before that student's challenge: "I think I connected to his feminine side." She was not satisfied, but that's another story. A week later, I met Amichai and, with some trepidation, recounted to him the incident in my classroom. "I hope the word 'feminine' doesn't bother you", I said. "Bother!" he exclaimed. "That is the greatest compliment you could have paid me." Emboldened by that reply, I shall here try to reveal those feminine strands in his poetry.

I use the term "feminine" in its most conventional sense, the one accepted in culture, in literature, and in the sociolect.[1] By that I mean the reservoir of stereotypes whose sources and reflections spread over a very wide range: classical texts, sometimes called patriarchal; Freud and his followers; even feminist writing, essentialist and other.

I do not consider in this paper the whole colourful menu of stereotypical views of women. I refer only to those views of femininity relevant to poems by Amichai discussed here. Two central concepts in this reading are femininity defined through binary oppositions, and the idea of the maternal.

The attempt to define femininity through binary oppositions takes many forms. On the one hand, in his lecture on femininity, for example, Freud acknowledges the difficulty of defining the term, and turns to stereotypes. He says that when we use the term masculine, we mean active, while by feminine we mean passive; aggression is the quintessential attribute of the male, whereas we clearly see the female as the caregiver and nurturer of the young.[2] On the other hand, in their attack on patriarchal culture, contemporary French feminists, notably Hélène Cixous, enumerate traditional feminine and masculine pairings: active/passive, culture/nature, logos/pathos, intelligent/sensitive, head/emotions.[3] Her efforts to cancel these pairings are not the purview of this paper.

The dominant quality of femininity, in both recent theory and the general culture, remains nurturing. Protecting and caring for a child, and the image of the womb as exemplary container, sustain many conventional metaphors. A central concept in the work of an English psychoanalyst, D. W. Winnicott, is the "good enough mother" who provides the child with a "holding environment".[4] A worthy mother is a kind of vessel for her child's emotions and desires. Following Winnicott, W. Bion says that the psychoanalyst has a maternal function, indeed calls him or her a "container".[5] The enclosure is a central archetype in women's literature, says Annis Pratt. Here, I believe, is the container transformed, this time from a feminist angle, which paints marriage, the closed container, in prison colors. In other words, the woman as container is trapped in another one, the institution of marriage.[6] The mother, says Melanie Klein, is a flowing breast who gives her love with infinite generosity;[7] and Cixous, generally light years separated from Klein's thought, also speaks of woman's capacity for selfless giving. According to her, the woman is a boundless body like water, also associated with the feminine, offering the comfort and security of the womb.[8] Woman, then, or at least the stereotypical mother, cares, worries, loves, nurtures, feeds, and gives like the earth.

Identifying woman with nature's cycle—roundness, birth, death, and rebirth—is an archetype found in texts as foreign to each other as Pratt's book, Homeric hymns, and Jewish law (*Halakhah*). Jewish women, for example, are exempt from time-bound commandments, as if they function in a different circular time, rather than the historical linear time of men.[9] While man's power bursts forth in one stroke, like a spear point, woman is a wide plain, the earth, the cushioning of the nest. Even observations of child psychology contribute to this view: boys build vertically, girls horizontally.

The tensions between Amichai's ideolect[10] and cultural conventions (prayer, God, and so on) have been examined from many points of view, but not from the one in this paper. Critics from Barukh Kurzweil and Hillel Barzel to Tovah Rosen and me have, in one way or another, discussed the intertextual tensions between Amichai's language and the materials of the sociolect, classical or colloquial.[11] How this poetry treats ideological and perceptual conventions and Amichai's unique world view has been looked into by Natan Zach and Shimon Sandbank, Dan Miron and Boaz Arpaly, for example.[12]

Now what does Amichai do with what we call feminine? How does he manipulate and sculpt this stereotype? Does he, as he did in the early poems, turn the convention upside-down, changing a "God full of mercy" (*Y.A.: A Life*, p. 31)[13] into a God who empties the world of mercy? Does he digress from convention to ambiguity and nuance as he does in many late poems? Reading the poems about women, love, parting, courtship, and love-making reveals that shaping the love object in these texts usually obeys the familiar "patriarchal" mould. But this is not my concern in this paper.

Amichai always assimilates anything that comes to hand. However, the integration of the "feminine" is not a coincidence. Let us begin with a poem that struggles not only with conventions I have already mentioned, but with others that will become clear later.[14] The poem's complexity calls for more than one translation. Here, first, is a recently published translation, to be followed by my own literal translation. The discussion will draw on both versions.

A rosebush hangs over the wall

A rosebush hangs over the wall, witness to bliss
of others, in closed gardens that break your heart
With so much yearning,
Plenty and loss, like the last bread
Tossed over the wall of a besieged city,
A sweet seized moment in red ardor
On the faces of prophets of the End of Days
Death and lust, sleep of the waking, talk
In a dream, and time in vain. A rosebush covers
A letterbox holding the letter of pain:

Between the event at the window
And the event at the door
Sometimes a whole life passes.
A rosebush over the wall.
I know a scholar of hard history
Who sired three soft daughters,
Beauties who grew up and left home.
But a rosebush hangs over the wall.

(*Y.A.: A Life*, p. 390)

A rosebush over the wall

A rosebush over the wall, testimony to happiness
of others in closed gardens that break the heart
out of much yearning,
abundance and destruction, like last bread
cast over the wall of the besieged city,
sweet life of the moment flaming red
over the faces of prophets of the end of days, death and orgasm
sleep of those awake, speech from a dream
and time in vain. A rosebush covers
a letter box, in it the letter of pain:
between the event near the window
and the event near the door
a whole life sometimes passes.
A rosebush over the wall.
I know a scholar of hard history
who begat three daughters, tender
and beautiful, who grew and left the house.
But a rosebush over the wall.

(Meadam ata veel adam tashuv
[From man you are and to man you will return],
p. 64, my translation)

In addition to the title, the full image "A rosebush over the wall" appears in four strategic places; but exactly in the middle of the poem, it turns into a mere rosebush. The rose's sociolectic load is used: it is the king of flowers (the Hebrew word *vered*, rose, is masculine) symbolizing love, passion, and their object—woman.[15] The convention of rose poems draws from such ancient texts as the *Song of Songs*, if we think that *shoshanah* equals rose,[16] or *The Romance of the Rose*, the medieval allegory that ends with red petals opening to the man.[17] In ancient Rome, the rose symbolized the sexuality of Venus, but in Christianity the pagan symbol became a symbol of purity, the Virgin Mary whose garden is the womb.[18] The sociolectic associations are dialectical—sexuality and virginity, but also beauty and thorns. The opening sentence of the poem, throughout its almost nine lines, interprets the central image in statements or marginal images. The rosebush is "testimony to happiness", but "happiness of others". It awakens the imagination of the person standing outside, who thinks that if there are roses, there is bliss, but it is beyond his reach, behind a closed garden wall, recalling the *Song of Songs'* "my beloved is a closed garden". The bush breaks the observer's heart, but it is also a thorned fence that, along with the stone wall, protects a sleeping beauty.

The bush is characterized in a series of contrasts: "abundance and destruction". The original *shefa vaavadon* is a loaded phrase. *Shefa* means "plenty" or "abundance", *avadon* derives from the verb root *abd*, meaning "loss" or "perish". The noun *avadon* is stronger, for it contains "ruin", "hell", "abyss" . . . *abaddon*. The beauty is abundant, but the blossoms will wilt quickly, hence the reference to death. "Last bread cast over the besieged city's wall" says that beauty is like bread, the last gift of grace to the outsider; but the "besieged city" is a marker for prison, not for happiness and security. Moreover, if the last bread is thrown from the besieged city, it is a kind of waste, perhaps self-destruction, *avadon* in the language of the poem. The "last bread" connects to Jesus and the Last Supper in Jerusalem, the model for a besieged city: "And the daughter of Zion is left as a cottage in a vineyard, as a lodge in a garden of cucumbers, as a besieged city" (Isaiah 1:8). On the mimetic level, Jerusalem is a city with a wall at its heart, and in the city there are gardens surrounded by stone walls and rosebushes. Perhaps all of Jerusalem oscillates between happiness and heartbreak, abundant beauty and flirtation with danger: "Sweet life of the moment flaming red over the faces of prophets of the end of days." The city's prophets passionately, with flaming faces, give themselves to pleasure, despite the destruction they prophesy, or perhaps because of it. And maybe the prophets of the end of days are the city's people who say "eat, drink and be merry, for tomorrow we die", and prefer a short-lived flower to eternal redemption. The red flower is a kind of orgasm, burning, impassioned, and short-lived; its elixir disconnects its addicts from reality and forces them into lethargy, a twilight state: "speech from a dream", "sleep of those awakened".

The first half of the poem gradually transforms the rosebush from an object of longing (as expected from the sociolect) into something on the edge between life and death. The contrast is in the image itself, "a rosebush over the wall": the rose is the moment, the wall is eternity. The complete image is introduced as a preference for ephemeral enjoyment (orgasm, sweet seized moment, red flame, last bread) over eternal spiritual life (wall, besieged city, prophets). Textual remnants of the conventional rose (redness, sweetness, happiness, heart, yearning) are scattered through the first lines, but the digression from convention is crystallizing. The dialectic between yearned-for happiness and despair, between life of the moment and eternity, is enriched by the parallel dialectic between the rose as a locked garden, symbol of purity and virginity, and its description as bursting sexuality.

There is a sharp turn exactly in the middle of the poem: the wall disappears and one can glimpse that the rosebush covers pain. The person outside was deceived. The bush does not attest to happiness, but camouflages sorrow. The letter was mailed, perhaps; it lies in the "letter box" but it is also the handwriting on the wall. The source of pain is in awareness that life and love are ephemeral. "A whole life sometimes passes between the event near the window", falling in love, "and the event near the door", perhaps parting. The image's content and the way it is expressed have changed. Complex syntax becomes simple, sentences are shorter, and dramatic enjambments disappear. It is as though ambiguity has vanished with submission to pain; it is no longer necessary to hide the truth with figures of speech.

The speaker identifies himself in the second stanza, which illuminates the first: "I know a scholar of hard history / who begat three daughters, tender / and beautiful, who grew and left the house." The connection between the two stanzas demands that the reader fill in the gaps. Did the scholar study the city's history, its prophets and destruction? Did he and his daughters dwell behind the rosebush? In any event, he begat beauties who left him. The event near the door is indeed parting. Isaiah's voice echoes again: "I have nourished and brought up children, and they have rebelled against me . . . children that are corrupters: they have forsaken the Lord . . . " (Isaiah 1:2, 4). The daughters grew up and left; the children in the prophecy were raised and forsook God. (In the original Hebrew, the roots for growing / being raised (*gdl*) and leaving / forsaking (*'zv*) are the same.) This is how the prophecy is laced into the poem. A typographic wall is erected by repeating the first and last lines in the second stanza; the typography participates in transmitting the message. But the rosebush is now superfluous, the tender daughters have left, the father who built a fence around them is like a rosebush over a wall with nothing behind it. This is a kind of emptied container-womb. The richness of this image is in its being a cover for happiness and a cover for pain; it is both the protecting wall, the father, and the protected treasure, a beautiful woman who is likened to a rose. The image is the poem's matrix, the simultaneous existence of pain and bliss, impermanence and eternity, closeness and parting, purity and sin, perhaps man and woman.

In the use of feminine stereotypes—enclosure, locked garden, container, protecting womb—in a text about a man; in the preference for the flame, the emotional, impulsive, stereotypically feminine over the intellectual, spiritual male option; in the ambiguity of the rosebush's identity—grammatically male but in literature female, and in the poem perhaps both: in these three choices we see fingerprints of a male who appropriates female stereotypes and describes himself through them.[19]

Conventional feminine materials are clearly evident in the poetic rendering of the "I" and of the father who is his "metaphoric hero". Miron claims that the fundamental cognitive principle in *Akhshav uvayamim haaherim* (Now and in other days), Amichai's first book, is the perception of the body as a box, a container whose content is protected between its walls, or seeps outward or inward, moving in space or time.[20] Miron points to the connection between this pattern and a view of reality of a soldier who is anxious lest his body/container be struck and spill its life fluids. Making the father a vessel is one realization of this principle, Miron says. For our purpose, the point is the sexual, not the historical implication of the box pattern. The oft-quoted lines from the poem "My father" sketch, in a few strokes, a maternal portrait: "Like a magician who pulls rabbits and towers out of his hat / he pulled from his small body—love" (*Shirim*, p. 27, my translation). The magic container is nothing but an overflowing, fatherly womb. It is, according to another poem, a small body that, during the First World War, formed the son, even before he was born "out of / his calms so few and scattered" (from "Ahavnu kan" [We loved here], *Selected Poetry*, p. 8). The same magic container nurtures the son throughout his life. The womb not only protects its contents, but also keeps worrying about it up to the edge of "the territorial waters of fear", in the language of the late poem, "Travel by train" (*Y.A.: A Life*, p. 396).

Miron speaks of the danger of self-destruction to a container/father with such a fragile exterior, a father whose generosity and love flow towards the other, as the poem says: "The rivers of his hands spilled into his good deeds" ("My father", *Shirim*, p. 27, my translation). And behold, the quality of giving without limit, without thought of self, at the risk of shaking the foundation of self-protection is a feminine quality par excellence. Both "giving" and "container" create the feminine father in this poem.

The paternal womb and its ties to the foetus, and later the child, appear again and again throughout Amichai's poetry. In the opening scene of "Autobiography 1952": "My father built over me a worry big as a shipyard / and I left it once, before I was finished, / and he remained there with his big, empty worry" (*Selected Poetry*, p. 2), these lines can be read to mean a depiction of birth. Even if afterwards the womb—or shipyard, or worry, or garden—remains empty, the bond between father and his issue is eternal. Even when the father does not contain the child, he is the only one who hears him. "In the mountain of the wind" reads: "No one heard / that in your swollen belly is a foetus screaming"—no one, of course, except the father-speaker (*Shalvah,* p. 81, my translation).

". . . the way one was worried about . . . will to some extent be reflected in the way one worries", says Adam Phillips, a Winnicott disciple.[21] It comes as no surprise, then, that the father's qualities turn up in the son who then becomes a father, as well as in other father figures in the work. This is a man with a womb, with a history of military battle, with memories of "nameless dead" of trenches and bunkers ("We loved here" I, *Selected Poetry*, p. 8).

"Seven laments for the war dead", which opens with "Mr. Beringer, whose son / fell at the Canal . . . ", says that he "has grown very thin, has lost / the weight of his son" (*Selected Poetry*, p. 92). Mr. Beringer exists in an upside-down birth: a woman, after she gives birth, loses the weight of her baby, and this father, after his son's death, not birth, has grown very thin, having lost the weight of his fallen child. But in a strange kind of logic, the father will carry in him the aborted life forever. "A man whose son died in the war / walks up the street / like a woman with a dead fetus in her womb. / Behind all this, 'some great happiness is hiding'."

The man who has studied war is a maternal father who worries about his children, and his wish is to replace God the Father in "the worry business" ("Eyes", *Great Tranquillity*, p. 65). "Worries are imaginative creations . . . anticipated catastrophe", says Phillips (p. 50), and so the father who knows the land's history and God's works tries to protect his children from them. "The eyes of the Lord run to and fro around the earth / and my eyes are always looking around my house." And the children? They are "all sweet in my worry". Like the shipyard, worry is a container, but here the children marinate in it as in a sweet syrup. "Eyes", which calls the children's eyes figs, grapes, and orange sections, is not alone in connecting father, food, and sweetness. Needless to say, at least conventionally, responsibility for food belongs to the feminine realm, beginning with suckling and ending with grocery bags and cooking. The Amichai father "cooks jam stirring . . . white, sweet foam for future generations" (*Y.A.: A Life,* p. 274) and is always there for his son, even after death: ". . . Happy are those / who have a patisserie next door to a coffee house, / you can call inside: 'Another cake, more / Sweetness, let's have more' // Happy is he whose dead father is next door to him / and he can call him always" ("A second meeting with my father", *Shalvah,* p. 88). The equation father=cake and sweetness, father=womb or box, is perhaps another aspect of man=woman.

However, the container, the enclosed garden, nurture, giving are not the only feminine elements. The perception of space reflected in a poem like "Not like a cypress" (*Selected Poetry*, p. 12) has clear, conventional feminine features. The cypress, like a spear point, shoots upward in one stroke, while blades of grass and spring blossoms are scattered on the plain. The poem continues explicitly: "And not like the single man / . . . but like the rain in many places . . . to be drunk / by many mouths, to be breathed in / . . . ." It is difficult not to see here a potential suckling, or at least a wish to spread over the earth a desire conventionally associated with a feminine perception of space. Moreover, all the verbs that state the desired form of being are in the passive voice: "to be absorbed", "to be drunk", "to be breathed in", "to be scattered".

The perception of time is the flip side of space perception. It is cyclical and circular, connecting in the sociolect with the feminine, in contrast to linear male perception. Redemption will come from the cycle of life and nature, based on caring for the young and cushioning the nest, even if it is a "lion's maw" ("I want to die in my bed", Y.A.: A Life, p. 37). The speaker in "Tourists" ruminates in prose: "I said to myself: Redemption will come only when they are told: 'You see over there the arch from the Roman period? Never mind: but next to it, a bit to the left and lower, sits a man who bought fruit and vegetables for his home'" (Y.A.: A Life, p. 333).

In effect, the perception of time and space, like the metaphorical description of the man through feminine convention, has political, ideological implications associated with Amichai's "demonstration against death" ("Since then", Y.A.: A Life, p. 310) and against the worship of heroism and victory monuments darting upwards ("A dangerous land", Meadam ata, p. 73). Juxtaposed to the male forceful eruption forward and upward stands the typical female option of survival and adjustment: staircase to a home ("From man", Meadam ata, p. 45), a flowerbed ("I work . . . ", Sheat hahesed, p. 74), and a kindergarten where a tower of blocks collapses and spreads over the floor ("Shnei shirim . . . ", Shirim, p. 20). A gently caressing palm is better than a fist ("Even the fist", Gam haegrof, p. 12), a sleeping baby's room lit by a small light-bulb is better than the "terrible / three-sided race between consolation and building and death" ("Seven laments" VI, Selected Poetry, p. 95).

It is no coincidence that "To my land" by the poet Rahel finds an echo in Amichai's Meadam ata veel adam tashuv (From man thou art and to man thou shalt return). The meeting of plants and walking as a means of creating a bond with the land devoid of "heroic deeds and spoils of battles" is a feminine, Rahel-like connection.[22]

However, it seems to me that the feminine description of a father carrying grocery bags and containing his child has a central function in Amichai's poetics beyond its political and perhaps autobiographical meaning. The male womb is the source of words. Just as the maternal womb protects and nourishes the foetus until it emerges into the world, so the food the paternal womb provides the infant, the poet to be, is words. Just like the womb, the father, too, will protect his son with all his might. In "Travel by train", the speaker, that is, the father, adopts a metaphorical feminine anatomy, a womb, perhaps even amniotic fluid.

> *Do I think of the children of my children, yet unborn?*
> *What is the length of my arms into their future,*
> *What is the area of womb protection,*
> *The span of body heat,*
> *The range of feelings, the private domain of hope?*
> *What are the courtyards of love,*
> *The defended preserve of worry,*
> *The territorial waters of fear?*
>
> **(Y.A.: A Life, p. 396)**

The paternal womb's uniqueness is that it continues to nurture and protect with words even after death. The father owned a small notions store, sold women's merchandise "in tired travels. But his words he kept in his heart: Therefore I am now rich with them", says Amichai ("Therefore I am rich", *Meahorei,* p. 118, my translation). Poem 10 in the *Time* collection is one of the fullest, richest expressions of the maternal father's poetic function: "This child, sleeping, like a compass needle / trembling slightly at night: / But his head doesn't / move, secure in the holy ark / of his father's worry." The child's head is secure because the worry container is like the holy ark, the most protected place in the synagogue. Reading the modern word *mazpen* (compass), according to the ancient root *zpn*, reveals that the child, like the Torah, is *muzpan* (hidden) in the father's worry, the holy ark. Moreover, the rarity of the root *zpn* in the Hebrew paradigm for "hiding" directs the reader to the intertext, the story of Moses, whose mother hid him (*hizpina*) in an ark of bulrushes (Exodus 2:3). Like the child in the poem, Moses is hidden (*muzpan*) from danger in a container of love. Again like Moses, the child has an intimate relationship with the words of the Torah; his head lies, after all, in a holy ark. "The child sleeping like a compass needle" pointing to its destiny. His fate is determined very early by the unique word-food he absorbs from the womb of worry. Another line in this poem, "No dream ever dreamt this child", connects him to Joseph, the quintessential dreamer whose father, Jacob, has become *the* exemplar of love. As Yael Feldman has shown, Jacob is a very feminine patriarch,[23] perhaps like the Amichaian father. In its second half, the poem sets forth an anatomy of love:

> *In ancient times they used to say:*
> *"Loved, like the apple of his eye." What, what*
> *like the apple of his eye? This child.*
> *What is the apple of an eye? A ball made*
> *from tears and paint.*
> *Oh, all my words, sad*
> *and happy nails of my life.*

The apple, or more precisely the pupil of the eye (*bavat haayin*), is the source of tears, according to the poem's definition, and the homonym *yevava* (weep) resonates from the word *bava* (pupil of an eye). The father's tears, the expression of his love, together with the words of his Torah, nourish the son's soul. They are the building materials, the hardware, "nails", of his life and poetry. Or, in a different version that mixes tears and prayers: "the tears that my father cried over me on Yom Kippur do not yield me. / In the laboratory of my heart I stand and work / to turn them into other things" ("Shnei shirei Yom Kippur", *Akhshav baraash*, p. 161, my translation). But the heart's laboratory performs additional miracles; casting the father in the image of a mother and adopting his words has deeper origins.

What Spitz calls "the bath of language" was in Amichai's case, "the bath of the German language". He was immersed in it when he was born. Well-known historical and biographical circumstances are not the only reasons why he chose Hebrew, *not German,* as the language of his poetry. There were inner processes at work. The mother-tongue surrounding the baby in the pre-verbal stage is the only language in which the "I" and the world merge. There is a symbiotic connection between child and mother, then there is rupture; later the child learns to separate "I" and "other".

R. R. Greenson's study offers the hypothesis that the sound "mm" that many people murmur in moments of happiness "expresses the fantasy of union with the mother and of holding her nipple in the mouth". In fact, this is the only sound that can be produced with the mouth shut. "So it is not purely by chance . . . that in so many languages the word for mother contains the sound: *meter, mater, mère, Mutter, madre, mamma, ama, umm* and *em*".

The authors of *The Babel of the Unconscious,* psychoanalysts Jacqueline Amati-Mehler, M.D. and Simona Argentieri, argue that Greenson's work shows "how closely the origins of a language are linked to the first sensory experiences . . . ". "Mm" is not yet a word, but the first word will be produced from it in "the only magical, true and universal conjunction between 'word' and 'thing'". Such idioms as mother tongue, *madre lingua, alma mater* are verbal images suggesting that the function of language is internalized and learned with the mother's milk; the baby recognizes the mother's voice at the dawn of development. Jean Piaget, Noam Chomsky, and others have shown that a four-day-old baby identifies not just the mother's voice, but her language.[24] Studies reported in June 1994 confirm that babies acquire a vocabulary in the mother's language as early as the first four months.[25] It is possible, then, to connect between the mother's language and merging with her in primal and complete bliss. Jacques Lacan presents the appearance of the father, of his language, and of the "symbolic order" he imposes on the child's life as the moment of rupture. By saying to the baby, so to speak, that the mother's place is with him and not with the child, he causes a tear in the child's psyche. This tear is the eternal source of longing and, on the other hand, allows the emergence of an independent self. Lacan's "language of the father" or "law of the father" imposes on the child what is permitted and what forbidden, especially by prohibiting incest. These terms are partially parallel to the Freudian patriarchal order and Oedipal crisis.[26]

What about Amichai? Although his father spoke German, one may perceive Hebrew, especially synagogue Hebrew, as the language that bonds them. Hebrew, not only when spoken by a biological father, is the divine word, the language of the law of God the Father—of "thou shalt nots", of commandments, of prayers, and of Torah.

I argue that in a very original, perhaps paradoxical process, Amichai transforms the father's language into a mother tongue or, rather, into language before separation of inside and outside. He softens hard law-language into one that answers his needs, one that "symbolizes the beginning", in Julia Kristeva's words.[27] With this language he can return to infancy, to the happy land where borders between "I" and world are blurred, the place where the moon can be a jug, or perhaps suckle a baby ("Beheyoti yeled", *Shirim*, p. 11). Rigid classical Hebrew is bent, relaxed, made pliable, to serve maternal purposes. It is the food, so to speak, the paternal womb bestowed on his foetus: words.

Such a reading explains the liberty and facility with which Amichai plays with language, breaking down specie into small change, dissolving frozen idioms, playing with it like a baby who does not recognize the borders of reality. In the poem "Forever and ever, sweet distortions", for example, Amichai plays on the different ways to say "God" in Hebrew, including deliberate distortions designed to conform to the commandment "Thou shalt not take the name of the Lord in vain" (Exodus 20:17). Thus, one of God's names, Elohim, becomes Elokim when used in a secular context.

> *What is the Jewish people? The quota that can be killed*
> *in training,*
> *that is the Jewish people.*
> *Which has not yet grown up, like a child that still uses distortions,*
> *the baby talk of its first years*
> *and still can't say*
> *God's real name but says*
> *Elokim, Hashem, Adonai*
> *dada, gaga, yaya, forever and ever, sweet distortions.*
> **(Shalvah gedolah, p. 57)**

The father tongue that becomes a mother-tongue allows the baby to soil himself and return to the courtyards of love, to the protected regions of worry. This reading offers grounds for shaping the father like a mother and describing his love and worry as womb-like containers. It explains both the father's tolerance when his son throws off the yoke of commandments, and the myriad allusions to prayer and the Bible in the poetry of a non- or perhaps anti-religious artist.

I conclude with an interpretation, based on the position I have taken here, of the magical poem "A letter of recommendation" (*Selected Poetry*, p. 101):

A letter of recommendation

On summer nights I sleep naked
in Jerusalem. My bed
stands on the brink of a deep valley
without rolling down into it.
In the daytime I walk around with the Ten
Commandments on my lips
like an old tune someone hums to himself.
Oh touch me, touch me, good woman!
That's not a scar you feel under my shirt, that's
a letter of recommendation, folded up tight,
from my father:
"All the same, he's a good boy, and full of love."

I remember my father waking me for early prayers.
He would do it by gently stroking my forehead, not
by tearing away the blanket.

Since then I love him even more.
And as his reward, may he be wakened
gently and with love
on the Day of the Resurrection.

The Ten Commandments are an old tune (*pizmon*) the speaker is humming (*mefazem*) to himself. The Commandments—the Lacanian language of the father par excellence, the language of laws and borders—ignore their purpose and become a hummed tune, a kind of happy, domestic, familiar, non-threatening mother tongue in which even the "mm" sound (*pizmon, mefazem*) appears. "Oh, touch me, touch me, good woman! / That's not a scar . . . ." Although the scar is under the shirt, one may see in it a remembrance of circumcision or "the law of the father". But no, this is a letter of love. Instead of imprinting a scar of commands on his baby's flesh, the father gives him a letter, and what is a letter if not written words, poetry? It testifies that the son is still a child, and even if he does not obey the Ten Commandments, he is a good child "all the same". The father who contained his child created a son in his own image, and the son, too, is a container "full of love". This father, even when he awakened his son to fulfil commandments, did not tear him from a blissful sleep, but gently and tenderly caressed his forehead with an open palm and with his fingers. "And because of this / let him be woken up gently and with love / on the Day of Resurrection."

Notes

1. See Michael Riffaterre, *Semiotics of Poetry* (Bloomington, 1978). Sociolect, following Riffaterre, is the pool of linguistic habits, hidden myths, descriptive systems, clichés, and familiar classical texts that are known by readers and speakers of a common language (p. 5).

2. See particularly S. Freud, *New Introductory Lectures on Psycho-Analysis* (1933a [1932]), chapter 33 "On femininity", GW XV; SE XXII, pp. 112–135.

3. As quoted in Toril Moi, *Sexual/Textual Politics: Feminist Literary Theory* (London, New York: Methuen, 1985), p. 104.

4. D. W. Winnicott, "Ego Distortion Terms of True and False Self"; "The Theory of the Parent–Infant Relationship", *The Maturational Processes and the Facilitating Environment* (New York: International Unversities Press, 1965).

5. Concerning the use of maternal metaphors to describe therapists, I was helped by a not yet published article: Susan B. Kraemer, "Betwixt the Dark and the Daylight: Some Meditations on Material Subjectivity". Also see W. Bion, *Learning from Experience* (London: W. Heinemann, 1962).

6. Annis Pratt, *Archetypal Patterns in Women's Fiction,* Part 2 (Indiana University Press, 1981).

7. As quoted in Moi, p. 115.

8. See Moi, p. 117, and Hélène Cixous, *Three Steps on the Ladder of Writing,* trans. Sarah Cornell and Susan Seller (Columbia University Press, 1993), pp. 104, 118.

9. Timebound commandments are called in Hebrew: *mitzvot shehazman graman.* A classical depiction of mother earth can be found for example in the hymn "To Demeter". See *The Homeric Hymns,* trans. and introduction Apostolos N. Athanassakis (Baltimore and London: The Johns Hopkins University Press, 1976), p. 1.

10. *Ideolect* is a concept Riffaterre borrowed from semiology and redefined. According to him (p. 146), the idiolect is the language unique to the poet or his poetry—a pool of names, words, word combinations, and personal images that define and separate a specific writer from others who use the language. For the relationship between text and idiolect, see the introduction to Joshua V. Harari, *Textual Strategies: Perspectives in Post-Structuralist Criticism* (Ithaca: Cornell University Press, 1979), pp. 17–72: "textual idiolect . . . the style of a text . . . a prescriptive and limitative subcode, and it is this subcode that imposes itself on the reader's attention" (p. 67).

11. Barukh Kurzweil, "Autobiographical Poetry in the Vast Desert", *Haaretz*, 12 July 1963; Hillel Barzel, "Yehuda Amichai, Assaulting Holiness", *Shira umorashah* II (Tel Aviv,

1971), pp. 153–159; Tovah Rosen Moked, "Samuel Ibn Nagrila and Yehuda Amichai", *Mehkerei Yerushalayim* 15 (1994); Nili Scharf Gold, *Lo kabrosh: gilgulei imagim vetavniyot beshirat Amichai* ("Not Like a Cypress: transformations of images and structures in Amichai's poetry") (Tel Aviv and Jerusalem: Schocken, 1994), pp. 69–116. All in Hebrew.

12. Natan Zach, "On the Single Stanza and the Poet's Handwriting", *Yocheni* 5 (1967), pp. 40–44; Shimon Sandbank, "Amichai: The Game and the Plenitude", *Lamerhav*, 28 November 1969; Dan Miron, "The Present Reflecting into Other Days", *Zemanim*, 17 June 1954, p. 4; Boaz Arpaly, *Haprahim vehaagartel* ("The flowers and the vase: Amichai's poetry", 1948—1968) (Tel Aviv, Hakibbutz Hameuhad, 1987), pp. 173–242. All in Hebrew.

13. Citations of poems here are principally from two general collections: *Yehuda Amichai: A Life of Poetry, 1948–1994*, trans. Benjamin and Barbara Harshav (Harper Collins, New York 1994) (henceforth *Y.A.: A Life*), and *Selected Poetry of Yehuda Amichai*, trans. Chana Bloch and Steven Mitchell (Harper & Row, New York, 1986) (henceforth *Selected Poetry*). A few poems are quoted from *Time,* trans. Yehuda Amichai (Harper & Row, New York, 1979) (henceforth *Time*), and *Great Tranquillity: Questions and Answers*, trans. Glenda Abramson and Tudor Parfitt (New York, 1983) (henceforth *Great Tranquillity*). My own translations, marked as such, will be identified by their transliterated Hebrew book titles.

14. For a more detailed discussion of the poem, see Gold, *Not Like a Cypress*, pp. 33–42.

15. For example, see entry "Rose": Kate Greenway, *The Illuminated Language of Flowers* (New York: Holt, 1978).

16. For the controversial identification of *shoshana* with "rose" see, for example, entry "Flowers of the Bible" in *Encyclopedia Judaica,* as well as Asaf Goor, *The History of the Rose in the Holy Land Throughout the Ages* trans. Max Nurock (Tel Aviv: Massada, 1981).

17. Guillaume de Lorris, *Romance of the Rose* (Hanover, New Hampshire: University Press of New England Edition, 1983).

18. Barbara Walker, *The Woman's Encyclopedia of Myths and Secrets* (Harper & Row), p. 323 and pp. 866–869.

19. A possible reading of the poem is to interpret the rosebush as a description of poetry itself. The Hebrew *siah* means bush, but also discourse. Such a reading would perceive, for example, the cast-out bread as the poet's desperate attempt to communicate with the outside world. This interpretation is part of a work of my own in progress, but even an alternative reading cannot ignore the fact that the poet conceives his own creation in feminine terms.

20. Dan Miron, *Mul haah hashotek* ("Facing the silent brother: Reading the poetry of the War of Independence") (Jerusalem: Open University and Keter publishers, 1992), pp. 273–313.

21. Adam Phillips, "Worrying and its Discontents", in *On Kissing, Tickling and Being Bored: Psychoanalytical Essays on the Unexamined Life* (Cambridge, Mass.: Harvard University Press, 1993), pp. 47–58.

22. See, for example, the poems "Sage, jasmine, vine and oleander" and "Elizabeth Swados" in this collection (pp. 40, 90, translated in *Y.A.: A Life,* pp. 381, 400), and also the discussion in Gold, *Not Like A Cypress*, pp. 189–190.

23. Yael Feldman, "And Rebecca Loved Jacob, But Freud Did Not", in Peter Rudnytsky and Ellen Handler Spitz (eds.), *Freud and Forbidden Knowledge* (New York University Press, 1994), pp. 7–25.

24. Spitz, Greenson, Piaget, and Chomsky are quoted in the discussions on bilingualism and multilingualism: Jacqueline Amati-Mehler, MD, Simona Argentieri, MD, and Jorge Canestr, MD, *The Babel of the Unconscious: Mother Tongue and Foreign Languages in the Psycho-*

analytic Dimension, trans. Jill Whitelaw-Cucco (Madison, Connecticut: International Universities Press, 1993), pp. 67–71, 139–140.

25. Josck, as quoted in B. Bower, "Babies head toward budding vocabulary", in *Science News*, 18 June 1994, p. 389.

26. Freud's and Lacan's "Rupture", "Fear", or *Spaltung* are discussed in a similar context in *The Babel of the Unconscious*, pp. 260–261. Dr Raquel Zak de Goldstein's lectures at the Psychoanalytical Institute at Columbia University in Spring 1994 helped me to clarify Lacan's ideas, especially those he expressed at the Conference of Romance Languages in Rome, 1953.

27. Julia Kristeva, *Powers of Horror: An Essay on Abjection*, trans. Leon S. Roudiez (New York: Columbia University Press, 1982), pp. 56–68.

9

Amichai and the *Likrat* Group: The Early Amichai and His Literary Reference Group

Gershon Shaked

I

The codes of literary transitions are determined by genotypes. A genotype is the repertoire of possibilities which literary tradition places at the writer's disposal in the various realms of his or her creative work (genres, styles, themes, literary styles, and so on). Each literary work is the singular manifestation of the writer's ultimate decision made from the possibilities available to him or her, be it his or her choice of units or the rules of composition.[1] The shift to a new repertoire of possibilities breaks the readers' horizon of expectations (the customary structural and thematic norms) forcing them to modify their literary expectations. Yehuda Amichai and Natan Zach are two prominent poets who transported Hebrew poetry from one genotype to another. Even the most conservative of Amichai's contemporary critics admitted that he shattered the horizon of expectations; that his work was a severing of ties with an old tradition and the heralding of a new one.

Gideon Katznelson, a conservative critic who published annual vilifications on the nihilism of young writers in *Lean hem holkim* ("Where are they heading?"), gave vent to his amazement and surprise at Amichai's having broken the horizon of expectations, on the one hand, and at his success, on the other:

> We have received the first fruits of Amichai's poetry (*Now and in other days*) with mixed feelings. We witnessed how in his poems he broke the majority

of frameworks we accepted as poetry's only frameworks. And it seemed to us that this disruption was malicious. His frequent use of unrefined images seemed to us a desecration of poetry. Even the form of language was confounded and came astoundingly close to stark prose.

Nevertheless we noticed that Amichai's poetry yielded that same powerful spirit of concise and rich expression characteristic of poetry, and perhaps even great poetry. We were therefore puzzled by his poetry and found it difficult to define to ourselves what we were witnessing. These puzzles are unravelled in his second collection of poems, "Two hopes apart". Now it is beyond doubt that this is good poetry, although in our neck of the woods we are still unaccustomed to calling it poetry. The conventional frameworks of poetry have been disrupted in a way that thwarts any possibility of sealing the breach.[2]

In both Amichai's and Zach's work there was a shift from one genotype to another. To understand the nature and significance of this transition we turn to its initial stages and a group of young poets. These poets were younger than Amichai, although it was with them that he first appeared on the literary stage and in their literary journal, *Likrat*. Unlike most of Amichai's contemporaries, who were born in the 1920s, these were all born in the 1930s.

A late bloomer, Yehuda Amichai differed from the outset from both his biological and his literary peers. His first poem, *Bemotzaei hahofesh* (After the vacation), was probably published in 1944 in Kol Yisrael's magazine, *Hagalgal*, while he was still serving in the British Army. This sonnet is not necessarily a beginning, but rather a single swallow that was yet to herald a spring.[3]

Bordieu defined a literary system as a mode of production, a type of functional relationship in which a hierarchy of enclosures exists. The chief competition for domination amongst the "indigenous generation" *dor baaretz* (born in the 1920s) was between prose and poetry. Poetry had the central position amongst the third and fourth *Aliyah* generations (those who began their literary careers after the First World War and before the 1930s). In the 1930s the arena was dominated by such poets as Shlonsky, Alterman, Leah Goldberg, Raphael Eliaz, Eliyahu Tessler, Yocheved Bat Miriam, Avot Perlmutter-Yeshurun, and Alexander Penn. Some of them began their careers in *Ketuvim* and continued in *Turim*, until Shlonsky turned to the left and his loyalists remained affiliated with *Itim* and *Mishmar*. Another faction, headed by Alterman, Horowitz, and Zmora, set up *Manhbarot lesifrut* and were closer to *Davar* and *Haaretz*. Yonatan Ratosh, poised between the two factions, acquired a stand of his own.[4]

These poets led the revolt against Bialik's generation. They saw themselves, and were seen, as his successors. They formed a new poetic language based chiefly on the neologism created by a new Hebrew like a pit being filled with its own heap of sand: the measured ultimate accented (*milra*) rhythm, erudite and lyrical figurative language, and at times an overly dramatic and conative rhetoric. Their poetry expressed both the *weltschmertz* of the modern individual and the needs of the collective singing its own hymn of praise. The heritage of Symbolism (Alexander Blok) and Russian Futurism (Mayakovsky),[5] suited to the poetry of the Russian Revolution, was adapted to the Zionist Revolution. With them, Lamdan's and Uri Zvi Greenberg's Zionist Expressionism fought to make this a lasting revolution.

II

Avraham Shlonsky headed the group and set up various organizational tools that would provide him and his following with the seats of power from which to manipulate the strings of literature. Sifriat Hapoalim became the leading publishing house for young literati, and also translated several of Russian literature's most influential writers. Shlonsky and Leah Goldberg were the publishing house's chief translators.[6] The journals which Shlonsky edited—*Turim, Itim,* and *Orlogin*—published some of the first works of young writers and poets. Since poetry still held centre-stage, while prose and drama remained peripheral, most of the capable and gifted voices in the first two journals were poets. Even the most prominent of the few prose-writers in *Ktuvim, Turim,* and *Mahbarot lesifrut*—Ya'akov Horowitz and Menashe Levin—were not hailed with the same enthusiasm and appraisal as the poetry.[7]

The poets of the younger generation stood in the shadow of these poets. It was not until the mid-1950s that they began to break away from the influence of the previous generation. A closer look at the poems of those born in the 1920s reveals the extent to which they were shadowed by the dominant group and by several poets on the margins of this group (particularly Ratosh). The genotype created by these forefathers left its mark on the early attempts of Shlomo Tani, Haim Guri, Natan Klein (Yonatan), Binyamin Galai, Matty Megged, Natan Shaham, and Haim Feiner (Hefer),[8] whose poems were thematically naive and epigonic in their structure.

III

The initial poems of the *dor baaretz* were published in the mid-1940s, five years before Amichai's first poems were published (except for his poem in *Hagalgal*), and they remained loyal to the previous generation's rhyme-schemes, rhythms and diction. These poetic elements appear in extremely personal poems as well as in social and national poems. Many of those who continued to write poetry did not adhere to the poetics of their youth, and both the poetry and the poets changed in the fifty years of the development of their poetry in Israel.

They were also influenced, although not entirely, by the new trends in poetry (Amichai, Zach, Avidan, Rabikovitz, and others), and primarily by the social and cultural changes taking place in Israeli society.[9] In any case, poetry did not make a breakthrough in its initial stages and did not pave any new artistic courses. The prose writers held the reins of cultural leadership in the *dor baaretz*. Some of these writers later became playwrights as well. Poetry remained on the margins, and until it hit upon new paths in the poetry of Pinchas Sadeh, Yehuda Amichai, Natan Zach, David Avidan, and Dalia Rabikovitz, as well as Israel Pinchas and others, it failed to regain its seat of honour in the literary arena.

IV

The shift from one genotype to the other was not a smooth one. Many of those born in the 1930s continued in the same vein as those born in the 1920s and did not bring about any polar changes in conventions and themes. One might say that Zach and Amichai were alone in fighting for another repertoire of language and a different style.

A historic illustration of a literary development can concentrate on various focal points: the "entry time" of a new literary work; or the literary work's reception by the public; or the moment of influence, when the work begins to have an effect on other writers and on society. Ideally, literary history would investigate these focal points simultaneously.[10] I would like to examine Amichai's development from the point of view of "entry time".

At one point, Amichai and Zach were affiliated with the *Likrat* group when it was headed by Zach and Hrushovski.[11] It should be stressed, however, that there was a rift between the members of the group from the outset. In social terms, this split was between new immigrants and the faction of native-born writers. Yehuda Amichai (born Würtzburg, 1924; arrived 1936) was amongst the *olim* poets, as were Binyamin Hrushovski (born Vilna, 1928; arrived 1948), Natan Zach (born Berlin, 1930; arrived 1935), Israel Pinkas (born Sofia, 1935; arrived 1941), Gershon Shaked (born Vienna, 1929; arrived 1939),[12] Gabriel Moked (born Warsaw, 1933; arrived 1946), Maxim Gilan, and Yonah David. These *olim* writers were nourished mainly by German and English culture, more so than by the poetic forefathers of Shlonsky's generation who were closer to various schools of Russian and French Symbolist poetry.[13]

The leading figures in the native-born group were Moshe Ben-Shaul (born Jerusalem, 1930; seventh generation in Israel), Moshe Dor (born 1932, Tel Aviv), Arieh Sivan (born 1929, Tel Aviv), Pesach Meilin (born 1930, Vienna; arrived 1938. Meilin was not an "immigrant"; his poems are a continuation of Shlonsky's generation), and David Avidan (born 1934, Tel Aviv) who has carried the Shlonsky tradition to its extreme and thus carved out his own unique poetic style.

Subsequently, some of them admitted to the nativeness in their poetry, even though they began to drift further and further apart, each going on to create his or her own literary self-portrait. This faction, affiliated with the *Likrat* group, appeared in Agudat Hasofrim's *Pamalia* anthology edited by Israel Cohen. The poems by native-born poets featured in this anthology are more mature than those in the initial volumes of *Likrat*. I will thus venture an understanding of the early Amichai vis-à-vis his literary contemporaries by comparing the poems of the native-born generation featured in *Pamalia* and Amichai's and Zach's first poems.[14]

In its publication of the *Pamalia* anthology, Agudat Hasofrim had a clear and what it considered to be a positive aim: it wanted the "Young Turks" to remain under its wings, and, by providing a hearth, to yoke the wild colts. In the editor's own words:

> Every generation is obliged generously to nurture many talents and link them up with the fine tradition of the general creative body. Even if some of them do disappoint, the effort will not be wasted. Those who remain make this effort worthwhile, for they carry on the golden chain and remember the kindness of the helping hand.

It seems to me that it is no coincidence that Natan Zach and Yehuda Amichai are not part of this collection, although Amichai did publish (with no qualms whatsoever) in Agudat Hasofrim's literary journal, *Moznayim*, and I have before me the original correspondence between him and B.Y. Michali.[15]

Israel Cohen describes the social make-up of the participants and stresses their thematic and structural populism:

> Nothing human and national is alien to this entourage of young writers. The growing pains of youth and the struggles of puberty, love and disappointment, the concrete and imaginary worlds, individual and social misery, landscapes and settling the homeland, revolt and surrender, affliction and redemption, immigration and creative joy, bereavement and failure, despair and hope—images of these essentials of life are inscribed in this book, each writer according to his ability and talent.[16]

Almost all members of the *Likrat* group (barring Hrushovski, Zach, Amichai, and Rabikovitz) participated in this collection, along with other writers and poets who were not affiliated with this group of students, who gathered in the early 1950s in Jerusalem, and in 1952 brought out their first journal in stencilled copies.[17]

Members of the *Likrat* group who did appear in *Pamalia* were, in order of appearance: Moshe Ben-Shaul, Arieh Sivan, Yigal Efrati, Moshe Dor, Yosef Bar, Aharon Gefen, Israel Pinkas (a short story), Itzhak Livni, Pesach Meilin, Israel Pinkas, and Yonah David.

I will take a closer look at the poems of Moshe Ben-Shaul, Moshe Dor, and Arieh Sivan. All three began printing in the youth press (particularly in *Bamaaleh*) as well as in the same newspapers in which the previous generation printed (*Al Hamishmar, Ayin,* and *Mevo'ot*, amongst others). They all published in the first and second editions of *Likrat* that came out in July and August 1952.[18] In 1953, Dor and Sivan, along with Natan Zach, brought out a collection of poems, *Beshlosha*, printed by *Likrat*. This collection preceded Amichai's book of poems, *Now and in Other Days,* that came out in 1955. Amichai himself participated in the second edition of *Likrat* that came out in August 1952.

I begin with a poem by Moshe Ben-Shaul, a native Jerusalemite, whose first books were *Migdal Shemesh* (Sun tower, 1954) and *Mifreshei melah* (Sails of brine, 1960):

> ***Your faded roadways ("Darkayikh hadahot")***
>
> *How the city runs helter-skelter with us*
> *tiredness burdens us—*
> *you have a halo of drunkenness, mottled city:*
> *You go,*
> *round and round you go,*
> *like cogs in a machine.*
>
> *And how laughter is pushed to the rear:*
> *rancid smells from the edge of town, chimney smoke*
>   *towering to the sky,*
> *round and round*
> *and rising*
> *from towers of tin.*
>
> *Woe to you, city, sadness on your threshold,*
> *your childhood's body—your faded roadways.*
> *How has the blush of your cheeks vanished*

and shut down
like forgotten memories in dreams.
(Pamalia, ed. Israel Cohen,
Tel Aviv, 1953, p. 13)

Ben-Shaul's poems are written in the vein of the Shlonskian tradition:[19] the iambs (in Hebrew) organized in extending and shortening lines, the set meter, and the very euphonic rhyme are reminiscent of this tradition, yet all the metaphorical elements are literary: the town, the chimney smoke, the mottled city, the rancid smells—there is no connection whatsoever between them and any city in Israel of 1953.

If the city is European, Ben-Shaul did not give it any local landmarks, and if it is a local city it has been abstracted and given the metropolitan signs of a modern industrial town as far from the Tel Aviv of 1953 as Tel Aviv is from New York. The use of *segolate* words (*keret* instead of *kirya*) to allow for a trochaic "feminine" end-rhyme is a common Shlonskian invention; just as the idiom from Ecclesiastes, *holekh sovev* (round and round), is frequently repeated in the same source. There is not that much of a difference between Ben-Shaul's metropolitan poetry and the poetry of Amichai's biological contemporaries (Shlomo Tani, Natan Yonatan, Haim Guri, Natan Shaham, Binyamin Galai).[20]

Arieh Sivan was, along with Moshe Dor, one of the native-born founding fathers of the *Likrat* group, and one of the three poets who brought out *Beshlosha*. Not unlike most of his generation he is particularly versed, so to speak, in Alterman's poetry. Born 1929, he served in the *Palmah*, and his first "independent" book of poems, *Shirei shiryon* (Poems of armour), came out in 1963.

Arieh Sivan: Our Room ("Hadrenu")

Our room is innocent and cryptic. In it nothing
but your body and mine, and the wick of love apart:
and the cypress's top—the ancient partner,
from its breath in the window to the flame's heart.

The room is closed. No one goes in or out.
Seventy wolves with tangled fur—
for winter outside is grudging and cruel—
lurk with alien shadows at the door.

You'll go out, girl, to be mercilessly stoned
they'll hang you on the scaffold of fable and scorn.

> *As if deaf the grey one will stand*
> *when for mercy you reach out, to beg, importune.*
>
> *You'll go out, girl, and the innocent room*
> *will shiver with cold with its bareness revealed.*
> *The throats of its four walls will stifle*
> *the sigh of the flame that dishonour had killed.*
>
> *Don't go out, don't go out. Our room will be seen*
> *and will warm and burn seventyfold.*
> *Together we'll quiet the burning need*
> *on spring nights of wheat and dew.*
> *See, the treetop bends, surprised,*
> *to spring's breeze which dares to blow.*
>
> **(Pamalia, ed. Israel Cohen,**
> **Tel Aviv, 1953, pp. 54–55)**

Alterman's influence is evident on various levels of the text: the anapaestic meter and the abundance of anaphoric rhetorical effects (for you'll go out) and repetitions (don't go out), elements of archaic language that exist in both Alterman and Ratosh's poetry (none goes out and none returns), *yiskelukha* (you shall be stoned), *yokiukha* (you shall be hanged), *ergat kadim* (burning desire) as well as literary-linguistic elements (seventy wolves)—these are typical of the influences on Sivan.

In its structure, its rhetoric, and its linguistic and thematic elements, the poem remains close to Alterman's *Simhat aniyim:* "The houses are destined to sink, / they are not destined to stand. The eyes are destined to wither, / they are not destined to desire. / The sleeper is destined never to awaken, / and the waking man is destined never to sleep" (*Simhat aniyim*, p. 168); "Do not wear your festive dress / Do not ever laugh" (p. 159). Sivan's poem is more concrete and easier to place than Ben-Shaul's—he at least has a local pine tree for a backdrop: "At the edge of the lonely skies stands a pine tree" (Alterman, "Zimra", in *Kokhavim bahutz* [Stars outside]). Yet even in this poem, there is no great innovation when compared to the poetic forefathers of the 1920s, 1930s, and 1940s.

Moshe Dor, the third in our study of this generation, was born in Tel Aviv in 1932. Although one of the first poets to join the *Likrat* group, he did publish prior to *Likrat* in various journals and newspapers (primarily in the youth press). Hrushovski devoted the only essay in the first edition of *Likrat* to Moshe Dor.[21] He was also one of the three, along with Sivan and Zach, who brought out *Beshlosha* (1953), published by *Likrat*. His first independent book of poems, *Broshim levanim* (White cypresses), was published in 1954, about a year before Amichai's first collection of poems. Dor's second book of poetry, *Im nagia veim lo nagia* (If we do and if we don't), came out in 1957.

"Tav" (Note)

Night encloses until senses are lost
streaming, silently clasping your throat.
No path swoops freely
to grasp your legs while fire rises
to anoint their good light like wine from the vessel.

All around, rustles of strange shadows,
a plot lurking in the thornbush,
the hatred of looming mountains pierces your back
and the fear that they'll descend
to stifle your cry with cold hands,
with a sudden cruel lunge.

You cowered low, your hand filled with grass.
Darkness held your heart as warm as a wound.
The scent of the field bends unnoticed
over the tears of the solitary man. A note burns on the brow.

(Pamalia, ed. Israel Cohen, Tel Aviv, 1953, p. 110)

This poem also has several evident features typical of the poetry of Shlonsky's generation (and Shlonsky himself in particular): the iambic hexameter (at times replaced by an iambic pentameter); alternating male and female end-rhymes; euphonic rhyming (*metzah* and *petza*); particularly the widespread use of invented *segolate* words to "enrich" the language and rhythm with various neologisms and upper-accented (*milel*) phrases (*demem* [bleeding], *sheli* [quietness], *keli* [vessel, annihilation], *zemem* [plot or scheme], *mayit* [downfall]); and *kamatz* end-rhymes instead of the regular *segolate* end-rhyme (*dokra, hofna*)—all these are distinct stylistic trademarks of Shlonsky's poetry. The realization of "missing pictures" (*hashekha* [darkness] *demama* [silence]) is also typical of the poets of the previous generation: "The silence in the heart, midnight hush looming in the piazza" (Alterman); "silence lies and wallows in the clefts of the road" (Shlonsky). The shaping of anxiety through its manifestations in nature also has its roots in the same literary source: *mishol* (lane), *shayit* (thorn-bush), like shapeless mountains (*kegolmei*), dust (*efer*), grass (*deshaim*).[22]

V

We can safely assume from what we have seen so far that the beginnings of some of the members of Zach's and Amichai's literary generation were no different from those of their older siblings, Amichai's biological peers, and that the breakthrough initiated by these two poets touches on both generations. The need for change stemmed primarily from the hackneyed and jaded dominant poetic conventions, but also from the changes society was undergoing. A post-war society, disillusioned by the impossibility of realizing lofty ideologies in its no longer euphoric daily existence, had no room for elevated language and sentimental rhythms. The change in poetic conventions and norms is also rooted in different sources of influence, that is, in two leading poets who dared to initiate and execute a stylistic revolution despite the stylistic and thematic differences between them.[23]

As early as 1953, Zach voiced the need for an artistic revolution. In his critique of an art exhibition he writes about the generation's taste in art:

> I visited the exhibition on Saturday; the tiny hall a refuge from the hot winds outside. Dozens of people wander in and out. I eavesdrop on their comments. The "man in the street's" lack of understanding in art is quite astounding. At times it may seem to you that his only criterion for distinguishing between a good and a bad picture is its "likeness to nature". Various levels of competency, a different "spirit" or style—of this he is clueless. In this, we are still way behind other progressive countries, and we must consider taking serious action to impart basic principles of art to the interested public.[24]

Before we embark on our examination of Amichai's entrance into Hebrew literature, I would like to turn the reader's attention to an early poem by Natan Zach, Amichai's cultural "twin". Zach's first book of poems, *Shirim rishonim* (First poems), appeared in the same year as Amichai's first collection of poetry (1955); his second book, *Shirim shonim* (Different poems), came out some years later, in 1961. Zach and Hrushovski were the two leading figures in the *Likrat* group and were its critical and cultural mentors. Zach, who began as a cultural critic, composed the group's manifesto and was its most outstanding poetry critic. The first poem we will examine here is taken from the first edition of *Likrat* (July 1952, p. 20):

"Mesaviv lashir ahavah" (Around a love song)

Elisheva isn't here
and I don't know where she is.
And I don't know if she was ever here.

(memories of a wonderful past; no-one knows if
   there was a present.)

Go and ask my mother. She will remember her son as
   if in a distant dream
that faded for not being understood.
(and every dream fears misinterpretation)
she will smile, she will welcome:
my son was born in nineteen thirty.
(my son—you've grown absurdly).

Everyone has a right to Elisheva.
But from whom, from whom must it be sought?
Again I'm naked (the night is cold)
If only I could lie a little in my poem like everyone else
   (perhaps it'll warm up);
Poems like mine should not be written.
Poems like mine should not be sung in the streets.
Every sentence in them flees to its writer out of fear.
—who would see himself in the mirror and not be afraid?
(They say: each reflection—a souvenir in the hands of time
you part from it and fear . . .)

Everyone has a right to Elisheva.
Particularly if he loves her so.

Albeit juvenilia, one can already discern the changes taking place in the genotype that will pave the way to a new genotype. "Around a love song" is a romantic love poem about unrequited love; in other words, both a poetic manifesto and a poetic confession. Zach frequently combines these three experiences in his poetry, as he does also in the sequence *Tarnegolei shokolad* (Chocolate cockerels) that appeared in the *Beshlosha* collection,[25] and subsequently in *First poems* and later in *Different poems*. By way of an initial insight, one can immediately see that the language in this poem differs completely from the poetic diction of the native-born poets.[26] Zach's poetic diction is on a lower register in comparison with the poems of the *dor baaretz*. The rhythm is free and although the poetic voice occasionally uses rhyme, it is not formal but functional (*likhtov/barehov* [to write/in the street], *yireh/yira* [will see/will fear]). The narrator also uses anaphoric rhetoric and a refrain, but again, these rhetorical tools are more functional than formal. Moreover, some of them fulfil an ironic function that negates, rather than intensifies, the pathos. These self-effacing ironies stress the fact that this is self-referential poetry showing itself in an ironic light.

The ironies appear throughout the poem, the parentheses being their formal frame. The idea conveyed is equivocal and is founded on a blending of self-negation as a poet (which is simultaneously a self-affirmation) and existential frustration—the very source of inspiration for the poems that should not be written. The addressee is called on to fill in the gaps between the poem's directness and its simplicity, and the ironies referring back to this directness. This essential characteristic of the poem is very different from the poems of Dor, Ben-Shaul, and Sivan. Like Amichai, Zach also shattered the conventions of his generation. Both are rebellious sons who became fathers of a new era, effecting the opening line of Popov's poem used as the epigraph for the first edition of *Likrat*: *"Look ye for a new way!"*

VI

Likrat published Amichai's first book of poems, *Now and in other days,* in 1955. He joined the group with its second edition, wherein he published *Mashakhta oti kmo sefinah* (You drew me like a boat) and "Autobiography for 1952". The general response to his book was positive and it became his official visiting card. There were other poems, however, that preceded the collection (some were included in the book) and which may help sketch his unique status as a figure who transported Hebrew poetry from one genotype to another and broke the traditional horizon of expectations.

I will focus on several poems, some of which appeared in the collection, to illustrate the tension between tradition and innovation in Amichai's poetry. Like many other poets, Amichai did not start out in an avant-garde or oppositional journal, but rather was linked from the outset with the political trend that groomed young poets and writers. Avraham Shlonsky was patron to most of these poets, most of whom published in the *Mishmar* (subsequently *Al Hamishmar*) daily.

Mishirei Tveria (Poems of Tiberius), one of Amichai's first sequences of poems, first appeared towards the end of the War of Independence in *Al Hamishmar* (1 July 1949). These sonnets corresponded to the likes of Rilke and Leah Goldberg more than they did to Shlonsky's or Alterman's poetry. Leah Goldberg, in an article she published after Amichai received the first Shlonsky Prize, grasped his unique status in the development of Hebrew poetry:

> This generation no longer seeks to cling to the ready-made forms—with their sophisticated rhythms and rhyme-schemes—passed down by their ancestors. They don't want to relinquish what has been achieved in living po-

etic diction. They want to develop it in another way without renouncing the entire legacy.

Hence, at times, their rugged rhyme-schemes, the use of new expressions and the tendency towards prosaicness ... added to all these is the influence and experience of foreign literatures (Rilke and the new English poets in Amichai's poems) and their crystallization when they find their way as vital elements into a poetry that is, in quality and essence, so very different.[27]

With characteristic simplicity and clarity (and without Gideon Katznelson's bias) Goldberg points out that the shift from one genotype to another (from one repertoire of possibilities to another) is characteristic of Amichai's poetry. She attempts to explain the nature of this change, its roots, and its external influences.

Let us return to Amichai's poetry. Of the three sonnets published as "Songs of Tiberius" in *Al Hamishmar*, two appeared later in the sonnet sequence *Ahavnu kan* (We loved here) in *Now and in other days*:

"Shirei Tveria" (Songs of Tiberius)

A

The boathouse is without a boat,
water laps at its walls like sad weeping,
anger but not murder, print drips from a note,
steps lead down to memory, fleeting.

A ring holds a rusty chain
with nothing at its end. Like the empty hand
of Tantalus that didn't know
that nothing's there ... but holds on, and

inside we alone spoke softly
like one whispers in a cemetery.
Then, without a backward glance, we went away.

Cars pass by. Here's our day!
But something would not return, this we know
a boat, we, another world's echo.

B

We read Eulenspiegel,[28] we lit the light,
we read of lovers, of nations—their fate
*   and chance.*
Those were "days of airplanes in flight"
and an ancient festival rose up to the dance.

Then we went to watch the fishermen on the shore.
We wished still to learn from everyone
but they said: teach us, teach us more.
All lacked something, something was gone.

White and dead, distant, replete,
Hermon winked, it knows it all!
we don't know; we are living still.

See, the water making electricity
suddenly, after a whirlpool, is calm now.
This was death, without knowing how.

C
My mother is yellow, yours is black,
on our mothers' backdrop, night and day,
we acted our love until it strayed
on the road to truth, tangled in wire on the way.

Her clothes are ripped in the storm ahead,
winters come upon her, whose king is dead,
and in the nights without the child at our breast
our heart's wine is burning and red.

Our heart's wine is red and old;
to copy his strange biography
someone, passing, made it cold.

We copied and read, we didn't comprehend!
Grass by the roadside won't understand the car,
but from then our love was wondrous, without end.

The first two sonnets, as I have said, were included in the "We loved here" sequence (in reverse order).[29] Dan Miron, in a critical essay that was an initial response to Amichai's book, refers to these sonnets as part of this sequence. The principal tension in these sonnets, according to Miron, is between past and present: an unknown and inanimate past and love which is a way of overcoming the past. The contrast is apparent, he notes, in the polarized descriptions: the "electricity" and "Eulenspiegel"; the opposing of "days of airplanes in the sky" with "the ancient festival".[30] The structure in these sonnets is traditional: the rhythm is generally iambic pentameter and the rhyme-scheme in the first and last sonnets is fixed. It is the second sonnet that defies, both in its quatrain and its two tercets, rhythmic dictates, and breaks the rhythm much like in popular children's verse ("the days of airplanes in the sky").

The narrator tries to create various internal rhymes (*mikhtav / zelof katav / shetzef* [letter / dripping print / anger]; *madregot / yordot* [steps / going down]) as well as alliterations (*shelo lamdah ladaat* [didn't know]), along with other contrivances of versification and sound. There are no Shlonskyisms in Amichai's language: he hardly ever uses neologisms, nor does he attempt to transform ordinary words into *segolate* words. Only two digressions are made for the sake of metre and rhyme: *zelof-ktav* and *tofsa* (instead of *tofeset*). Amichai generally uses a lower register than that of his biological and literary peers. The lowering of the register and the ability "to talk poetry" in everyday language is a definite achievement in his shaping of the new genotype.

The change in genotype is not marked only by the existence of new phenomena but by *the absence of old ones* as well. The framework of the Tiberius sequence is missing in the "We loved here" sonnet sequence in his book "Now and in other days", and it constitutes an overall backdrop of sorts, an intertextual connotation for the reader, giving the various paintings local and spatial significance.

Once these sonnets become part of the sequence, Amichai relinquishes this framework and the sonnets exist outside their implied concrete context. The reader is invited to create a new context for himself or herself. In the quatrains of the first sonnet, and in the quatrains and tercets of the second, the speaker relies on concrete details of the Tiberian landscape: a boathouse (at Deganya?), descending stairs, a rusty chain, fishermen on the shore, Mount Hermon, the electricity-producing water (the Routenberg hydroelectric plant). These elements are personified in the first sonnet, each contributing to the atmosphere of the overall pattern. In the picturesque, perfectly designed boathouse there are hints of lack, sadness, privation, loss of memory, and ultimately—in the image of the chain likened to Tantalus' punishment—frustration.

The tercets are set in opposition to the quatrain. The lovers can sense the aura that pervades the setting: the empty boathouse creates a world of need. The tension in the second sonnet is also between the lovers and the outside world. The "we" refers to the couple, not to the "first person plural" so frequent in the works of Amichai's biological contemporaries.

Eulenspiegel and the interior landscape give form to the ancient festival: the outside world of the fishermen and the natural landscape are unable to provide them with the things they can provide for themselves. The menacing exterior threatens to bring turbulence, death, and paralysis. Only the lovers' combined inner world can confront these outside forces, which are an internalization of hostile forces (death) that jeopardize the lovers' vital life-force.[31] The pictorial elements in the sonnets are sufficiently integrated, despite a certain fragmentation of the figurative units.

The sonnet forms a classic unity of fragmented pictorial units that converge on an emotive level of meanings that transcends each unit's explicit meaning. The sonnets' low register undermines conventional poetic values of rhythm, rhyme-scheme, and so on. Amichai's poem is important in that it was written in complete identification with the left-wing political consensus (*Hashomer hatzair*), although he, like many others, began drifting away from this trend in the mid-1950s.

This poem was written only a few months before Amichai published in *Likrat*'s second edition, and is evidence of the thematic-ideological link that still existed between him and his left-wing political reference group. However, even in this poem there is a structural deviation from tradition.

One of the Israeli Left's most problematic political alliances was its link (and *Hashomer hatzair*'s in particular) with Stalin's USSR. It maintained this trend to a certain degree until the Twentieth Convention, and only subsequently did its allegiances and dogmas begin to dismantle.

Despite the execution of almost all great Yiddish writers on 12 August 1952, and the Soviet authorities' claim to having exposed a conspiracy of Jewish doctors in Russia and America (accusations that were revoked after Stalin's death), the Israeli Left continued to swear allegiance to the second homeland. Throughout the world, and amongst Israel's Left, the death of Joseph Vissarionovich Stalin on 5 March 1953 was considered a cosmic catastrophe—"the setting of the sun of nations". Yehuda Amichai provided his own elegiac contribution on the death of "the sun of nations". I quote from Amichai's poem *Moto shel Stalin* (The death of Stalin), printed in *Al Hamishmar* on 13 March 1953, at the end of the *shiva*, one might say:

The Death of Stalin

What movement ceases when these limbs
fell silent. Think of it. Now
they have been stopped forever—calcified,
and like the lime in Russia's kettles—his veins

like a network of rivers,
so great and sad in their blessing,
and how his body, like a map, bore the features of his land,
mountains, roads—all was placed on him!

> *And, how in the end, his heart, as always*
> *like soldiers marching to the front,*
> *how, as then, in days of alliance,*
>
> *his blood, red and fretful, flowed*
> *like a trumpet-call into his proud death -*
> *how it flowed never to return.*

This ode, or elegy, is written in the classical sonnet form:[32] it is mostly iambic pentameter or hexameter, and the rhyme-scheme is *abab cdcd eee fff*. The rhythm in the poem overpowers the metre. The caesuras are frequently surprising as are the transitions from one stanza to the next. The tercets are linked by extending the metaphor in the first tercet over into the second. The poem's picturesqueness is the internalization of a landscape that has become part of the individual's body: one's body is a part of his or her homeland, or the homeland is a part of one's body.

The metaphors lure each other and give an unexpected description of the figure: the blocked limbs like limed kettles, the veins like the rivers of Russia, the body like a map of the land, the heart like a battle march, and the red blood charging towards the brain as in the war by virtue of which the poet remembers the character.

The poem merges the individual and the landscape (and the landscape's history). The individual becomes the landscape and the landscape—the individual. The heterogeneity of the descriptive elements merges with the theme. The moulding of the image through a sequence of metaphors is both surprising and typical of other poems in "Now and in other days", such as *Yehuda Halevi* and *Ibn Gabirol*. The metaphorical homogeneity and the merging of thematic elements so characteristic of Amichai's poetry are once again evident in this pseudo-political poem, and are akin to the themes of Amichai's political reference group at a specific point in time.[33] Amichai adapted to the group's political line, despite the dissimilarity between his poetic form and that of the other poets in the group. In other words, the variation in form existed despite the thematic identification.

This poem was not included in his book as it went against the book's ideological grain, just as "You drew me like a boat" that appeared in the second *Likrat* was kept out of the first book owing to its proximity (more so than the other poems) to the traditional form of the Alterman— Shlonsky generation and its successors.[34]

Aravim aherim (Other evenings), another important poem, was not as far as I know included in any collection, but appears in *Gilyonot* (edited by Izhak Lamdan), a literary journal outside the conventional boundaries of

Amichai's political and literary reference group. S.Yizhar also started out in this journal in 1938. "Other evenings" preceded the poems of Amichai published in *Likrat* (he was nevertheless identified with the young group of poets publishing in *Likrat*, even though he was some five or eight years older than them). This poem also differs from those of his biological contemporaries and stresses the singularity of a poet who deviated from the existing repertoire of possibilities to create a new one:

Other Evenings

I remember other evenings. Entirely different:
evenings of you.
Evenings of your eyes in a room with other eyes
amongst friends and curtains (the frame of your hair over your eyes)—
I loved them all, all of them, for you were amongst them.
Our love is embroidered on the room and on them,
and your blue dress and your red dress strewn with white dots,
By virtue of these evenings there will be eternity in our short lives,
and by virtue of these evenings I know that death is not unkind.

The footprints in the sand!
Fine, trembling footprints, like a Yemenite curio,
the footprints of fieldmice, the lizard, the gecko and the crab
on smooth sand: the new books exuding glue and binding.
And I know today that the bright dripping sands
are not a good shelter from fire,

and I know how to appreciate the dark bodies,
coarse and sturdy,
I know the books are still in my room.
By virtue of all this there will be eternity in our short lives,
and by virtue of all this death is not unkind.
(Gilyonot, vol. 25, no. 12 [1951], p. 350)

Although I do not see this as one of Amichai's better poems, it does have certain features characteristic of the genotype he created. Its rhythm is free and fairly difficult to describe in clear meter (it was easier to define the iambic sonnets in these terms). The poetic narrator foregoes any organized rhyme-scheme; the register is not high, although the poet does use rhetorical devices to stress the poem's dialogical nature. The poem is the lover's invocation of his beloved. The primary rhetorical device is the refrain (which is also based on an extended anaphoric opening), which also links the two figurative systems in the two stanzas.

Several key-words reappear throughout the poem in different variations (evenings, eyes, your eyes, them all, them all, your dress, and the footprints, the sands, etc.). These repetitions have an emotive function; they stress the significant units and have a poetic function in that they transfer units from the axis of choice to the axis of sequence. The poem is organized around the refrain and its explicit statement: the situation described in both stanzas bestows eternal life and enables the individual to overcome death. The hermeneutic refrain thus determines the reading of the two stanzas. In both stanzas a detailed picture of the character is shaped by his environment; he is a synecdoche of the metonymies around him. The tiny details, which could be seen as either humorous or sentimental (the frame of your hair around your eyes, your blue dress and your red dress strewn with white dots), create the picture and the evolving emotive concreteness, despite the absence of a concrete figure.

The second part combines the footprints in the sand—concretized by a catalogue of creatures—with the books. There is no immediate situational link between these books and the footprints (specified also by a distant image such as the Yemenite artefact), neither is there a connection between them and the dark masses the narrator has "learnt to appreciate". The associations between the figure, the friends and the dress, and between the footprints left by various insects in the sand, and between them and the new books and the dark masses, do not create an integrated picture. The link between them is obscure, but there a certain atmosphere takes shape in which these heterogeneous elements form an emotive whole cemented together by the closing phrases. This figurative heterogeneity is typical of Amichai's later works, much like his characteristic phrases that hover between profundity and a joke.

In conclusion, the principle components of the poetics of the genotype which Amichai created are the following: abandonment of metre, open rhyme-schemes, an almost prosaic register, abstinence from figurative and "poetic" materials, and, in contradistinction to the above, the utilization of the effects of repetition as an emotive element, and a poetic, heterogeneous and catalogue-like language which borders upon the comic in that it enlists unexpected combinations that do not easily mesh.[35] By employing these literary devices, Amichai differed right from the start (in 1951) from the majority of both generations of his contemporaries. Zach shifted the genotype to a different form, and we have alluded to this, but this is not of central concern to our present discussion. Indeed, Zach, who was in one way or another the outstanding theoretician and principle critic of the generation, described well a number of these phenomena of Amichai's poetry in an initial reaction to Amichai's first collection of poetry. Zach writes: "Amichai's language is also personal and provides a most pleasant surprise for the reader of young Hebrew poetry. The language is free of figurative flourishes; it flows, has the rhythm of speech, but is not gray prose. And most important, this is immediate language without the 'stylistic embellishments' of experience."[36]

The poem "Autobiography 1952" was published twice, first in *Likrat* 2 (August 1952), p. 13, and in *Maavak* (9 January 1953), and was then collected in *Now and in Other Days*. In the version published in the collection, there are minor changes from the original:

> *My father built over me a worry big as a shipyard*
> *and I left it once, before I was finished,*
> *and he remained there with his big, empty worry.*
> *And my mother was like a tree on the shore*
> *between her arms that stretched out toward me.*
>
> *And in '31 my hands were joyous and small*
> *and in '41 they learned to use a gun*
> *and when I first fell in love*
> *my thoughts were like a bunch of coloured balloons*
> *and the girl's white hand held them all*
> *by a thin string—then let them fly away.*
>
> *And in '52 the motion of my life*
> *was like the motion of many slaves chained to a ship,*
> *and my father's face like a headlight on the front of a train*
> *growing smaller and smaller in the distance,*
> *and my mother closed all the many clouds inside her brown closet,*
> *and I walked up my street*
> *the twentieth century was the blood in my veins,*
> *blood that wanted to get out in many wars*
>   *(and took every opportunity)*[37]
> *and through many openings,*
> *that's why it knocks against my head from the inside*
> *and reaches my heart in angry waves.*
>
> *But now, in the spring of '52 I see*
> *that more birds have returned than left last winter.*
> *And I walk back down the hill to my house.*

And in my room: the woman, whose body is heavy
and filled with time.

(Tr. Stephen Mitchell; Maavak,
9 January 1953; Now and in
Other Days [1955], pp. 13–14)

I suggest that this poem should be regarded as a key text. The characteristic features of Amichai's poetry are already fully present here. Rhythm overrides the measured stress (which is iambic only to the degree that Hebrew tends toward accenting on the ultimate syllable). The speaker in the poem abandons formal rhyme and relies upon what is termed "white rhyme" and also on other resonant tones; and when rhymes or internal resonances do appear they seem almost unintended.[38] The rhythm is set largely in accord with the length of the lines, and is determined by ellipses which create a contrast between the caesura determined by the line and the natural continuation of the sentence ("in many wars", "many openings"). Rhythm is also established by various uses of repetition which create an emotive structure, as, for example, the anaphoric language which determines the year of life of the poem's narrator ("and in [the year of] . . . "), or recurring leitmotifs such as "my father" and "my mother".

Also typical of Amichai's poetry is the absence of elements of form, and that which fills this absence. This created the repertoire of possibilities that he and those who have followed in his footsteps have developed into various forms.

The autobiographical declaration is important in this poem, which is pieced together in stages and which is at one and the same time a thematic and a poetic manifesto. The narrator declares incidentally that autobiography is the source of poetry and its form is the way in which it is absorbed.[39] Autobiographic factors as poetic material recur in various combinations in Amichai's poetry: father and mother, variations on the topic of love and the antagonism between love and history, as well as the significance of the fateful years of his life.

The narrator considers the year 1931 the first terminal in the course of the poem and of his life. The years of his youth are lost. Immediately afterward 1941 appears, the year of maturation, pregnant with war, in which the dream of love as a romantic picture stood in contrast to historical forces pressing war down upon the hero. 1951 is the next stage, and it is marked by the death of childhood and the departure of the father and mother motif from life's horizon, as they are transformed from an autobiographical source itself to an elegiac source of memories. Further on, the narrator becomes a kind of instrument through which his century sings its anxieties, and, in 1952, opposite such worries recur and stand the love and the beloved, as they stood opposite them in 1941.

In brief, the main topics of Amichai's poetry are the following: lost childhood and longing for parents, "make love, not war", and the destructive force of the twentieth century, opposite to which also stands the power of love. Moreover, the pattern of the treatment of these topics is set in this poem. He refers to various stages in his life and transforms each stage into a poetic image, rendered poetic by means of a chain of illustrations which bestow significance the moment they are perceived.

The continuity determines the story. The narrator is central, while each stage is fashioned by increasingly expansive metaphors and stands in its own right. In the first stage the narrator relies upon the picture of the port (shipyard, shore, departure).[40] The second stanza is marked by the image of hands (hand of the child, balloons in the hands of a young girl, and the flight of the balloons).

The third stanza returns to the image of the ship and the train, and the increasingly great distance of the slow boat or the train from the shore of the father and mother (the clouds acting as elements attempting to overcome the slow passing of time into the distance). In the second part of the stanza the narrator ties his time to his blood, as the time, which has become internalized, acts from within and destroys the body from within, because it wants to explode from its confinement to the outside. In this section the image of the sea returns, this time as a part of the image of flowing blood (waves). The third section is the most concrete of all. The birds are captured as a positive mantic sign which leads to the stability of room and house.

The last section also ends the poem. This poetic completion bestows a sort of closure to the continuity of the story, which begins with the departure from the port of the house (in which the boat was created as an object which symbolizes the poetic narrator), and concludes in a house which may remove the worry that originated in the "shipyard" of the first house. The closure also hints at a stoppage in the passage of time "in the heavy body of the woman who is full of time". The poem is almost a description of a circle of a woman leaving and returning. The hero embarks from the port of the house and arrives at the port of "a house".

Amichai's later poetry is marked by expanded metaphors and a poetic continuity which creates a plot which has beginning, middle, and end. The closed plot, which links the heterogeneous graphic elements and endows them with unity, asserts the integrity of the narrator as well. The poem we have considered, in its structure, style, and subject matter, is a basic model of Amichai's poetry and more or less epitomizes his range of possibilities which would develop further in different forms and incarnations.

VII

If we now return to a comparison of the poetic features of the early poems of some of Amichai's contemporaries, there is a bold contrast between the range of possibilities that they realized and the new repertoire that Amichai created (I will not here delve into the history of the variations of this repertoire). I conclude with a reiteration of the findings in the poems of Moshe Ben-Shaul, Aryeh Sivan, and Moshe Dor. The metaphorical material in Ben-Shaul is literary, with a tendency toward *segolate* nouns (*keret* in place of *kiryah*) to allow for a trochaic "feminine" ending, a device common in Shlonsky.

The influence of Alterman and Ratosh is evident in Sivan's poetry in quite a number of literary layers, including the meter, archaic and "literary" linguistic elements, and also the theme which stresses the link between love and jealousy, which is not far from Alterman's legacy.

Prominent in Moshe Dor's poetry are a number of characteristics typical of Shlonsky's generation, including metre, the inclination toward the interlacing of masculine and feminine endings, rhyming of resonant tones, and especially the preponderance of artificially created *segolate* nouns with the aim of "enriching" the language with rhythmic combinations which lay stress on the final syllable. The realization of "incomplete" pictures was also typical of the poets of the previous generation. The thematics of fear in "Shirei hapahad haribua" (Poems of square fear) and its shaping by means of its realization in the landscape was also drawn from the same literary source. As already mentioned, Zach's poetry had a uniqueness all of its own and constructed a genotype which opens different possibilities from those that were created in Amichai's poetry.

The description of these poets' typical trends emphasizes Amichai's distinctiveness and the turning point that his poetry constituted, as one who entered an existing system and struggled with it. He tried to struggle with this system by means of an internal change of the existing classical structure (the sonnet); but he overcame the chains that he cast upon himself and arrived quite quickly at open, liberated poetry which required its own themes and forms of expression.

The first book of Amichai's poetry was received warmly by the majority of critics (the novel was met with greater reserve).[41] Amichai's influence over modern Hebrew literature has been unmediated and a large part of the new development of the "old school" of realism and the old school of poetry can be linked with the daring appearance of Amichai (and similarly of Natan Zach and Pinchas Sadeh). A long line of poets appeared simultaneously with Amichai. Most important among them were Natan Zach, David Avidan, and Dalia Rabikovitz, and later Yonah Wallach, Meir Wieseltier, and Yair Horowitz, authors, playwrights, and critics whose work also gave expression to values opposed to the social and artistic values of the old establishment. These "countervalues" eventually become dominant.

Narrative fiction entered the scene still later, and it also enabled the new generation to establish pre-eminence over the previous one. This new generation included Sadeh, Amichai, Shahar, Orpaz, and Kahana-Carmon (who were somewhat older), and especially Appelfeld, Yehoshua, Oz, Kenaz, Shabtai, Kaniuk, and others. Most important of all, on the heels of Amichai there was an extreme change on the literary horizon of expectations in Israel.

The process of change did not pass over the "veteran" poets and authors. They also absorbed new external influences. A large number of them established a linguistic and artistic link closer to Anglo-Saxon and French culture. Many of them were sent abroad or travelled overseas (Guri, Shamir, Meged, Bartov, Shaham, Tammuz, Ben-Amotz, Mossinzon) and the sources of their influence were varied and altered. On their own initiative, they familiarized themselves with modern poets and authors in both Hebrew and general fiction and poetry. One must remember that Natan Zach made an important contribution in changing the canon of poetry and in the restoration of Vogel, Steinberg, Avot Yeshurun, and Lenski to poetic currency.[42] Many critics have followed in their footsteps, and Miron, Peri, and others have placed the poets that have been mentioned, especially Avot Yeshurun and Gabriel Preil, at the centre of the movement. An outstanding example of the change in norms that occurred in the poems of a veteran is that of Haim Guri, who in his book *Shoshanat haruhot* (1960) departed from the Alterman–Shlonsky legacy and created his own modern style.[43]

It is reasonable to assume that this turning point in Guri was encouraged *also* (but not only) by the catalyzing role of Amichai's poetry. Not only was this poetry a turning point in the history of modern Hebrew poetry, but its positive reception meant that the poets who continued in the accepted tradition were pushed into the background and those who set out on the new path were given the place of honour.

To a certain extent, Amir Gilboa achieved centrality in the poetry of his generation, since from the 1950s onward he diverged from the tradition of Shlonsky and his generation.[44] His central position was accepted only after modernism as a whole took its place in the history of literature. In my opinion it is no coincidence that Amir Gilboa and Yehuda Amichai were awarded the Israel prize in the same year and with the same status (1982). Amichai and Zach paved the way for a revolution which supported the central position of Gilboa, who was their senior (1917–1984), in the literary community.

Thus Amichai filled a dual role. While his work itself constituted a literary revolution, that same work gave birth to a literary revolution, becoming the accepted norm of the generation. The appearance of interesting poets such as Horowitz, Wallach, Wieseltier, and after them Aharon Shabtai, Laor, Bejerano, and Yossi Sharon, changed this norm. The characteristics of the new norms have not been fully explicated, and scholars are left with the task of investigating how and by which path these poets have constituted a dialectical reply to the norms that have been established by their elder brothers, Amichai and Zach.

Translated by Shaun Levin
Robert Harris
Glenda Abramson

Notes

1. Janusz Slawinski, *Literatur als System und Prozess* (München, 1975). Literary theory uses the term "phenotype" to describe the one-time manifestation of repertoires of possibilities in the literary text.

2. Gideon Katznelson, *Hameshorer shel dor sheheikhalo nitroken* (The poet of a generation with an empty temple), *Haaretz,* 18 July 1956. Natan Zach, on the other hand, praises the breaking of conventions: "Notwithstanding, there is no doubt that his sonnets are liable to shock anyone unaccustomed to the classical form of this aristocratic genre: there are not many rules here that Amichai does not gush over with an apostatic outpouring" (Natan Zach, *Shirei Yehuda Amichai* (The poems of Yehuda Amichai), *Al Hamishmar,* 29 July 1955). David Aran, a distinctly Marxist critic, agreeing with the presupposition that Amichai broke through the conventions to create a new poetry, adds: "I believe I am not alone in saying that Yehuda Amichai's 'Now and in other days' is one of the most interesting books to appear amongst our younger poets. To the extent that it is at all possible to talk about the 'conquest' of poetry—for the poetry-reading public is not that large—when it comes to Amichai this term is no hyperbole. A young poet conquers because he answers to the psychological needs of our generation more than any other" (David Aran, *Kavim leshirato shel Yehuda Amichai* (Outlining Yehuda Amichai's poetry), *Al Hamishmar,* 10 August 1956). Unlike him, Shlomo Zemach, a more "conservative" critic than Katznelson, refuses to accept the revolution in the tradition and condemns it: "And so, the aforementioned images used by Amichai are substitutes for a metaphor and are a mockery and a joke . . . . After twenty-five years of doing nothing but mimic the works of others, Hebrew poetry has evolved into an ape" (Shlomo Zemach, *Matzeva veshalakhta* (A tombstone and its leavings), *Davar,* 28 June 1955). For another positive view of these innovations see also Shraga Avneri, *Shirei Yehuda Amichai* (The poems of Yehuda Amichai), *Mevoot,* 1 July 1955, which appeared after "Two hopes apart".

3. I would like to thank Rivka Maoz for bringing this poem to my attention: "On the eve after the holiday, when the day declines / we sat in our room, the time trickled, / the

days of the happiness slept, and stood still, / our heart's Sabbath had already passed. // I lit a candle in silence, a *mavdil* candle / separating the holy from the profane / a good light, a reminder of love and joy, / of festival of my soul, blessed days for all. // We also blessed the perfumes last night / the fragrance of sun-drenched hair / the smell of a tranquil pasture. // We put the candle out with a drop of wine, / dipped a finger in it, wet our eyes, and drank from the small beaker." The secularization of sacred rituals and their transformation into rites of love, so typical of English Metaphysical poetry, is discernible even in this early poem. This vein continues in Amichai's poetry.

4. Avraham Shlonsky's (1900–1973) early major works which are relevant to the generation of his successors were: *Davai* (1924), *Leaba, ima* (1927), *Begalgal* (1927), *Beeleh hayamim* (1930), *Avnei bohu* (1934), and *Shirei hamapolet vehapiyyus* (1938). Natan Alterman's (1910–1970) major works were *Hakokhavim bahutz* (1938), and *Simhat aniyim* (1941). Leah Goldberg's (1911–1970) major works were: *Tabaot ashan* (1935), *Shibbolet yerukat haayin* (1940), *Mibeiti hayashan* (1944), and *Al haperihah* (1948). Yonatan Ratosh's (1908–1981) main works were *Huppah shehorah* (1940), and *Yohemed* (1942).

5. In 1942 Sifriat Hapoalim brought out the anthology *Russian Poetry*, edited by Avraham Shlonsky and Leah Goldberg, with translations by their contemporaries of their favourite poets. Shlonsky translated A. Bloch, Yesenin, V. V. Mayakovsky, A. Bély, V. V. Halavnikov, and many more.

6. A selection of Shlonsky's translations (mainly from the Russian): Russian Poetry (eds. A. Shlonsky and L. Goldberg) (Tel Aviv, 1942); Michael Shokolov, Virgin Soil (1935); And Quiet Flows the Don (1953–58); Romain Rolland, Kolas Breugnon (Our boy still lives) (1950); Charles de Coster, The Story of Till Eulenspiegel (1949).

7. Neither did the interim writers, such as Shenhar, Arikha, Bar-Yosef, Yaari, Zarkhi, and Hameiri, who did not join the Shlonsky group and were affiliated mainly with the journal *Gilyonot*, get the same high praise from the cultural elite nor from the general readership. One should keep in mind that *Gilyonot* published a large amount of "peripheral" poets living in the Polish, Russian, and American diaspora, and other local poets taking a different course to the Shlonsky school. See G. Shaked, *Hebrew Prose 1880–1990*, vol. 2 (Tel Aviv, 1983), pp. 244–268.

8. Amir Gilboa and A. Hillel, two poets who tried to escape from this tradition, hitched their wagons to other sources (Uri Zvi Greenberg and Walt Whitman).

9. The traditional genotype has been described to a certain extent by Natan Zach in *Zeman veritmus etzel Bergson uvashirah hamodernit* (Alef, 1966). He has also described the opposing genotype in his article "Leakliman hasignoni shel shnot hahamishim vehashishim bashiratenu", *Haaretz*, 29 July 1966). See also his article "Hamevaker kemegaleh", *Haaretz*, 22 July 1966. In this article he describes himself as the founder of the school that paved the way to the future by rejecting the past.

10. David Perkins, *Is Literary History Possible?* (Baltimore and London: Johns Hopkins, 1992), p. 23.

11. Amos Levin, "Bli kav: ledarkah shel Likrat basifrut haivrit hahadashah" (Tel Aviv, 1984). As one who was a member of *Likrat* I do not agree with all the arguments and descriptions in Levin's instructive book.

12. In the early 1950s the composer of these lines published poems in *Bamaaleh, Bashaar, Likrat,* and *Gilyonot*. His poetry is of no importance; in the mid–1950s he turned to literary criticism.

13. Pinhas Sadeh-Feldman, born in Lvov 1929, immigrated 1934, died 1993, whose first book of poetry *Masa Duma* came out in 1951, was influenced by Uri Zvi Greenberg and did not identify with any group.

14. S.Y. Penueli, *Pamalia* (Writings of young authors edited by Yisrael Cohen) (Tel Aviv, 1953); *Gilyonot*, vol. 29, no. 7 (June–July 1953), pp. 40–41.

15. One of the examples, Jerusalem, 18 January 1960: "Dear B.Y. Michali: Thus you almost spoke and I shall reply. I am appending two poems and I will be grateful if they could be placed in our journal. Is it customary to send a proof? If so I would request that you send me one. With a friend's greeting, Yehuda Amichai." *Genazim* A-67615.

16. Israel Cohen, "Im hasefer", *Pamalia* (1953).

17. In the celebration for the fifteenth year of the appearance of *Likrat*: "I am certain by the way, that the division and the internal conflicts were a kind of curse that has clung to the people of *Likrat* and *Akhshav* of all kinds. Much more than splits that were always part of any literary groups."—"There is also the chronological paradox. The poet Moshe Dor, one of its members, bent the ears of all those who came by saying that actually the beginning of the activity around *Likrat* was not in 1953 but already in 1949–50 with the coming of the young students and longing for criticism and creation in the new style" (Gabriel Moked, "Al mesibah veyovel batzidah", *Davar*, 13 December 1968). As one of the participants in the first two issues, I can confirm that indeed there were a certain number of sporadic meetings during these years, but only with the appearance of the first issue was the group established as a group.

18. Benjamin Hrushovski devoted the central article in the first issue of *Likrat* to Moshe Dor: *Likrat*, no. 1 (July 1952), pp. 8–15, 28.

19. See for example Shlonsky's poem "Kiriyat namal", from *Avnei bohu, ketavim* 3 (1971), p. 20.

20. Compare for example with Tani Tani's pastoral-bucholic poem, "Batzoret", printed in *Al Hamishmar's* literary page, 10 March 1944. This shows that in both cases the poets rely on literary materials that lack direct contact with the concrete.

21. See note 19.

22. In A. Shlonsky, *Avnei bohu, ketavim* (1971), p. 92. It seems to me that the existential urban "fear" in Dor's poetry has literary sources as it probably has experiential sources as well.

23. Zach formulated the thematic and structural platform of the new generation and was one of the rebels against the previous generation. Zach's most programmatic and anti-Alterman article appears in *Akahshav* 3–4 (Spring 1959), pp. 109–122. See also note 9.

24. Natan, *Maavak*, 9 January 1953.

25. Later Zach published "Tarnegoli shel shokolad", *Likrat* (1953), p. 21. This is more accomplished and complex than his earlier poetry and is not very far in its technique and existential character from one of his early poems.

26. We have to repeat and emphasize that in the first generation there were always outstanding poets, like for example Amir Gilboa, who proved the rule; while in the second generation, Zach, Amichai, and Sadeh, afterwards also Rabikovitz, Avidan, and Pinkas, quickly became outstanding, became a norm, and left their mark on their generation and on the generation that followed them.

27. Leah Goldberg, "'Ad barzel', on Yehuda Amichai—on receiving the Shlonsky Prize" (in Hebrew), *Al Hamishmar*, 26 July 1957. See also note 2.

28. *Till Eulenspiegel* in Shlonsky's translation was first published by Sifriat Poalim in 1949.

29. Many scholars have correctly noted Auden's influence on Amichai in the choice of the sonnet form and the sonnet corona. See for example G. Abramson, *The Writing of Yehuda Amichai* (Albany, 1989), pp. 103–105.

30. Dan Miron, "Hoveh hamashkif el hayamim haaherim", *Zemanim*, 17 June 1955.

31. In his first article of response, Natan Zach noted a number of central phenomena that we have stressed here. Zach notes the "personification of the individual world", domesticity, and love as a high value: "The single fundamental experience is revealed here dressed in various new guises" (Natan Zach, "Shirei Yehuda Amichai", *Al Hamishmar,* 29 July 1955).

32. Following Stalin's death a fair number of poems were written, most of them in emotive and flattering Mayakovskian style. The comparison of the various Stalin poems is the subject for a separate study.

33. In the same issue of *Al Hamishmar,* a programmatic article appeared on the topic of "socialists" and cultural matters from which I shall quote: "Therefore *Pravda* calls first and foremost for the unity of the class war of the proletariat. Unity above all. To the degree that we are not obliged to compromise with our enemies to this extent we must apply consideration in the relationships with our fellows. A war with the enemies of the workers' movement, peace and labour within the unity within the movement—these will be a candle to *Pravda* in its daily function."—"Worker-writers do not fall ready made from heaven, they develop slowly within literary work. We must approach our work with courage: from time to time you will fail but at the end you'll learn to write. Therefore together to labour!" (*Al Hamishmar,* 13 March 1935).

34. "Mashakht oti kmo sefinah": "You drew me like a boat / into the harbour of your secret / . . . " (*Likrat,* 2 August 1952, p. 9). The poem uses old, worn-out conventions. At the conference on 27 June 1994 in Oxford to honour Yehuda Amichai on his seventieth birthday, I was told that this poem was included in a much later collection.

35. A number of the conclusions that I have arrived at in my research on Amichai's first works have been treated extensively in Boaz Arpaly, *Haperahim vehaagartel. Shirat Amichai 1948–1968* (Tel Aviv, 1986).

36. Natan Zach, "Shirei Yehudah Amichai", *Al hamishmar,* 29 July 1955.

37. The words in parentheses appear only in the first versions and do not occur in the final text of *Now and in Other Days*.

38. In later poems Amichai often intentionally employs internal resonances as structuring elements.

39. See Boaz Arpaly, *Haperahim*, especially pp. 140–172. Glenda Abramson emphasizes that the poem expresses more a collective autobiography of the generation than a personal one (G. Abramson, *The Writings of Yehuda Amichai* (Albany, 1989), pp. 22–23). Seventeen years earlier I gave the label *tahanot* (stages) to this technique, which transforms each autobiographical event into a source of figurative development (Gershon Shaked, "Masa al tahanot, al *Meadam atah veel adam tashuv* shel Yehuda Amichai", *Haaretz,* 27 December 1985).

40. At the same conference in Oxford on the occasion of the poet's seventieth birthday, in her brilliant lecture Nili Gold described these metaphors ("shipyard" and "port") as feminine metaphors and stressed the "feminine" expressions in Amichai's poetry.

41. See above, note 2. See also the essays of Miron and Zach cited above, notes 27 and 28.

42. On this topic, see Natan Zach, "Hamevaker kemegaleh", *Haaretz,* 22 July 1966. In this article he describes himself as founding the school which paved the way for the future by exiling the past.

43. Gershon Shaked, "Hapegishah im haproza (al *Shoshanant haruhot* leHaim Guri)", "Masa", *Lamerhav,* 15 November 1960.

44. His third book, *Shirim baboker baboker,* which was published in 1953, about two years before the books of Zach and Amichai, was a turning point and was received warmly by the literary community.

Part Two

Drama

10

God, Jonah, and the Drama: The Actualization of a Myth

Gabriella Moscati Steindler

In spite of its title, *Masa leninveh* (Journey to Nineveh) by Yehuda Amichai, performed at the Habima Theatre in 1964, is not a simple journey. This drama, clearly prompted by the famous biblical tale of Jonah and the whale, is unlikely to be listed in the effective and wise classification of biblical dramas suggested by Shaked.[1] Indeed, each reader or spectator is surprised by a radio introduced among the characters of the drama. The radio in the second scene of the second act transmits God's voice calling "*ayyekka*", "where are you?" (Gen. 3:9), while Jonah is hiding. In this way it reproduces the same situation as Adam's. The divine call echoing behind the scenes can also be found in other Hebrew dramas of biblical themes. As an example I shall quote *Yaakov verahel,* performed by the theatrical company Ohel in 1928. Yet the divine word transmitted through a popular and humble household appliance allows us to understand Amichai's poetics and define his dramatic language. In fact much of Amichai's poetry uses biblical materials since they reflect his cultural background rather than his religious feelings. Thus Amichai takes pleasure in speaking to God through a sort of filial relationship, as he himself has told me.

In her study of Amichai, Abramson stresses, "Amichai's usage of biblical and liturgical sources . . . is one of the fundaments of his poetics."[2] From this point of view Jonah too, the hero of this drama, is described in modern terms as "the prototype of modern metropolitan man", according to Abramson's analysis.[3] This superimposition of ancient and mythical elements on those linked to our reality gives us two levels of reading: the former closely related to the text, and the latter to the technique of the scene-structure. The two different levels of interpretation will define the meaning of this theatrical event from an anthropological point of view.

The connection between the drama and the biblical text emerges clearly. In fact the opening scene of the play is a dining room with no actors; only a radio transmits the verses in the book of Jonah where God asks the prophet to go to Nineveh. Soon after, the dramatic dialogue grows richer as the main character, Jonah, and two women, his wife and an *isha zara* (strange woman), start speaking. Our hero looks like a bewildered soul, as his wailing proves: "Have I lost my wits? People have recently been addressing me; they send me some letters. While I'm having lunch I find letters under my plate where I read 'Go to Nineveh'."[4] The mysterious *isha zara* (the strange woman) too invites Jonah to begin the journey. She tries to use her own charm; at first they argue, then they embrace. It is clear that the introduction of this woman gives the drama a new interpretation, different from the biblical narrative. In addition to the temptation and the desire to break with the past, the possibility of having new freedom emerges as well: "So, at last, you'll be able to do what you have always wanted."[5]

The drama is embellished by characters and scenes which complete and comment on the holy text and help Amichai to define both the substance and the form of his conception of reality. So we witness the sailing of the ship to Tarshish; this time the scene introduces a harbour in the night, when Jonah is taken on board and almost secretly locked in a case. The increase in the number of characters who have a modern job, like the radio operator, does not stop Amichai from following the order of the biblical narrative. He repeats the scene of the storm and the famous hero's dive into the sea where at once the eager whale gulps him down.

The novelty introduced by Amichai appears in the scene where we meet Jonah once again, this time in the belly of the sea-monster. Although the drama is rebuilt in modern terms, the hero must spend time in the whale's belly while going to the mythical Nineveh. At this point the theatrical content and language obtain a new meaning thanks to the radio, a mouthpiece of the divine will with which we have already dealt, and to the presence of a triplicate Jonah: in the belly of the fish we find two more characters, Jonah 2 and Jonah 3. As Harold Fisch points out, "Jonah's 'descent' into the belly of the ship and his further descent into the belly of the fish, where *tehom* (the abyss) is said to be all around him, is of a piece with all the ancient stories that involve the hero's descent into the netherworld to overcome the forces of chaos."[6] Besides, according to Fisch, quoting A. Lacocque and P. Lacocque: "Moreover the fish, with its connotations of life and fecundity, adds to the analogy in representing the motherly womb and takes on a significance that is rooted in the mysterious origins of life. Thrown into the ocean by the sailors Jonah returns to the very sources of his existence."[7] Carl Gustav Jung, too, gives the same interpretation of the biblical archetype. In his opinion, two parallel impulses coexist: the desire to go back to childhood and to rediscover "the maternal vessel of rebirth" in order to "renew his life".[8] It is from these reliable allegorical interpretations that we can give meaning to the many female characters in Amichai's drama, which follows an almost Faustian conception of the return to youth. The *isha zara* at the beginning, and then the other nameless woman in the third act who accompanies Jonah during his wandering about Nineveh, symbolize the deep desire to restore the stage of existential happiness through love. Yet the descent into the monster's belly, containing the spiritual and symbolic principles of new life, is a difficult and dangerous goal. There we can find, as Jung says, "Treasure hard to attain".[9] In this context a sort of struggle within the human unconscious takes place, and as Jung writes: "The hero is a hero just because he sees resistance to the forbidden goal in all life's difficulties and yet fights that resistance with the whole-hearted yearning that strives towards the treasure hard to attain, and perhaps unattainable, a yearning that paralyses and kills the ordinary man."[10]

These contrasting aspects, so graphically described, seem to me to justify the grotesque separation of the mythical Jonah into three different parts by taking into account the fact that Amichai's character is simply a contemporary man with a complex personality, full of anxiety and fear. My interpretation seems to be partly confirmed by Gideon Ofrat's article where Jonah's split personality is defined as the projection of the poet in two more persons "who aim to change the society".[11] In the play Amichai seems to mould different faces and aspects of one single character. Yet the biblical tale of Jonah introduces another myth which, in Fisch's opinion, "beholds it critically, balances it, and, in an important sense, controverts it".[12] The biblical hero, after obeying the divine will and carrying out his mission in Nineveh, waits for the unavoidable results. In fact, "Jonah takes shelter now in a *sukka* to shade himself from the heat of the burning sun . . . . The *sukka* here . . . symbolizes extreme vulnerability but also miraculous protection."[13] In addition to the myth connecting the biblical hero with the whale, the myth of "Jonah-and-the-*sukka*" appears as well, evoking the desert, "a place of trial, the trial associated with history and the tensions of history".[14]

The third act of *Masa leninveh* proposes the two symbols of *sukka* (hut) and the desert in an imaginative and modern way by transforming and explaining them. A clear analogy of the hut as a means of refuge and protection has already emerged in the second act, when the hero hides in the case in which he will be deposited on the ship. The case performs the same function as a house, as Abramson has noted.[15] This conception becomes stronger when, in the third act, the hero lands on the beach and runs to a telephone booth to inform people that he has completed his mission.[16] In fact, at first sight, it seems to be difficult to find a link between the desert in its biblical meaning and the town of Nineveh as Amichai sees it, full as it is of strange and often mysterious characters such as a woman, two men, an ambiguous barber, three surgeons, and a journalist, each of them not easily identifiable as they have no names, no realistic features, no precise roles. By following Fisch's theories, I find that the biblical archetype of the wasteland is structured in different ways of writing and makes several realities concrete, thus defining an aridity and a metaphorical desolation. Fisch describes the ways of this myth: "The wasteland too may be traced back to premodern sources, but it reaches its apogee in the nineteenth century, when it serves as a way of dealing with the crisis of that age, and it reaches its dreadful consummation in our time, when we awaken from the nightmare to find the truth."[17] The myth of the desert is perceived as a temporal category. Jewish poets often "feel the weight of history past as well as present".[18] Amichai's drama recovers the spiritual desolation by the overflowing presence of grotesque and sometimes alienated characters on the stage, who allow us to look at reality from a different point of view. The writer has chosen such a device in order to practise the artistic process of estrangement.

The last scene of the third act seems almost to synthetize the two myths of "Jonah-and-the-Whale" and "Jonah-and-the-*sukka*" by proposing them again. In fact on the stage they restore the opening scene in our hero's house, his shelter, his *sukka*. Yet he is not alone. Threatening characters crowd the stage, thus recovering the meaning of desolation used to explain the previous scene. These characters are one general, two soldiers, and a woman-soldier, with no identity and no name. They break into Jonah's privacy and inform him that he has not succeeded in his mission. His house will be slowly transformed and he will fall into the whale's belly again.[19] Jonah's despair is useless; he is ready to try again. The character forcefully stops the curtain from descending on the scene, while the young woman-soldier repeats like a robot, "May everything be fine, really fine".[20] We can again find the symbology of the motherly womb (belly) and water as sources of regeneration. The drama ends with a link with the opening, and intensifies the dramatic narrations' cyclical nature, as in a mythical fable.

In this interplay of myth and modernity, where several extravagant characters appear and sometimes split into two or three parts, we can understand the writer's theatrical language, which helps to integrate and explain some of the elements on the stage which are not always clear. Amichai is linked with Jean Cocteau's dramatic art, which is ahead of the Theatre of the Absurd in some of its scenic devices. In his article of 1973,[21] Gideon Ofrat, reflecting about the content, proves the link between *Masa leninveh* and Cocteau's one-act drama *Orphée*, performed in Paris in June 1926. Ofrat discovers some common elements in the poetic language used by both dramas: in the mythical narration merging into reality, in Orpheo's fall into hell and Jonah's fall into depths. Another Israeli critic, A. Otniel,[22] considers Cocteau's will to destroy some myths as analogous to Amichai's. However, Otniel strongly refutes the use of radio as a means to let the God of prophets speak. Almost by contrast, reflecting on this means of modernity and everyday life, I have managed to return to Cocteau's dramatic art through his *pièce Orphée* and to the homonymous film, the script of which is by the French writer himself. On this subject, the use of objects not directly related to the particular context of the drama, it is enlightening to quote the French scholar Jacques Guicharnaud, who theorizes on Cocteau's artistic aims: "The objects often acquire their powers from disorder. Out of their usual places they seem stripped of their usual functions, diverted from their roles in this world, and free therefore to assume new functions. The incongruity of an object not in its proper place creates an uneasiness in the spectator which comes from consciousness of pure unjustified being."[23] Guicharnaud reaffirms Cocteau's almost grotesque view of theatre by defining it as "the double game".[24]

In fact in the drama *Orphée*, too, the device of a horse which, beating its hoof, transmits the Morse alphabet to *Orphée*, is a striking expedient aimed at surprising the audience. These unusual and strange connections between consolidated and known mythological texts and our everyday life make both writers similar. Besides, the increase of minor characters clearly reflecting our technological and alienated reality outlines some undeniable analogies. Cocteau's decision to portray Death accompanied by two servants dressed as surgeons with rubber gloves while taking Proserpine again,[25] and the conclusive scenes of the drama showing a policeman helped by a scrivener who questions Orpheo, can be compared in their theatrical structure with Amichai's work.

Yet I believe that these scenic devices and the progressive presence of characters who stress the estrangement of the main character, even if they involve some analogies at the structural level, do not specify any common subject matter. If, at first sight, the symbols of the two myths can appear homologous in some of their aspects, we must stress that the cultural codes they refer to are completely different. Cocteau avails himself of a Greek myth, to which he is bound from a purely cultural point of view. He recovers, on the creative level, a typical trend in literature. Amichai, on the other hand, goes back to a biblical text full of religious meaning. It is useful to remember that the Book of Jonah is read in the most solemn day of Yom Kippur and it aims at the exemplification of divine mercy, God's complete acceptance of penitents and his deep and paternal relation to mankind. So Amichai's choice of recovering the character of Jonah and his text taken from the biblical canon is not accidental, and it influences the dramatic performance of the play. Amichai's poetics clearly proves his ambivalent relation to God and his worried, tormented, and sceptical perception of divine mercy. Therefore at the root of this biblical drama there is a symbology which takes its origins from a precise cultural background.

At this point I would like to extend my analysis toward an anthropological framework to explain the semiological and symbolic methodology of this drama. As Victor Turner notes: "Religion, like art, lives insofar as it is performed, that is, insofar as its rituals are 'going concerns'. If you wish to spay or geld religion, first remove its ritual, its generative and degenerative processes. For religion is not a cognitive system, a set of dogmas, alone, it is meaningful experience and experiences meaning. In ritual one *lives through* the alchemy of its framing and symbolizing, relives semiogenetic events, the deeds and the words of prophets and saints . . . ."[26] Yet the English anthropologist adds that when faith and "where historical life itself fails to make cultural sense in terms that formerly held good, narrative and cultural drama may have the task of *poiesis*, that is, of remaking cultural sense, even when they seem to be dismantling ancient edifices of meaning that can no longer redress our modern 'dramas of living' . . . ."[27]

We can outline a macroscopic manifestation of this trend in Hebrew dramaturgy from the beginning of the century to the present day. The biblical texts are used to communicate the extra-literary, social, and ideological messages specific to the modern context. However, *Masa leninveh* is detached from this particular Israeli trend, because of the use of the symbology I have tried to demonstrate. The choice of the particular mythical area attached to the religious ceremony of Yom Kippur, which the drama analyzed here refers to, by applying Turner's conclusion can be related to a wider cultural context. The message contained in the detailed report of Jonah's adventurous journey exemplifies and defines a precise ritual, a *rite de passage*, still practised in some tribal societies.[28] These rites can involve either a particular group or all the members of the society. In this case, ". . . it implies collectively moving from what is socially and culturally involved in an agricultural season, or from a period of peace as against one of war . . . from a previous socio-cultural state or condition, to a new state or condition, a new turn of the seasonal wheel".[29] This time of transition from one to the other one is called liminal, from the Latin word *limen* (threshold).[30] Also, in the most complex societies, "Liminal phenomena tend to confront investigators rather after the manner of Durkheim's 'collective representation', symbols having a common intellectual and emotional meaning for all the members of the group. They reflect, on probing, the history of the group, that is, its collective experience, over time."[31]

The celebration of Yom Kippur must be seen from a double point of view: on one hand, as the process of renewal of individual and community through a complex and even symbolic system of actions for spiritual purification; on the other hand, as a celebration merely associated with the seasonal cycle of the year which defines the start of agricultural work. Both trends allow us to consider this celebration as a *liminal phenomenon*. After all, the book of Jonah is inserted into the ritual of celebration with a double meaning: scenic and textual. The reading aloud of the text achieves its own precise temporal order and is connected with the practice of religious performance. At the content level, the book offers a symbolic message structured on liturgical function.

So Amichai stages a *performance* linked with the emotional and spiritual world of his childhood. He revises it by following his imagination, in this way calling up a new ritual in greater accordance with the sensibility of a secular person. Yet in this artistic interplay the *liminal* condition, that is an intermediate position between two cultural contexts, can be seen within the expressive means he chooses. The theatre, the roots of which are in Greek tragedy and in the celebrations in honour of Dionysus, was forbidden by the Jewish sages because of its pagan origin. Besides, in our society, modern theatre, with its ambiguous characters, is in a *liminal* position in relation to the living social order.[32] On the interaction between different cultural contexts Amichai builds his ritual to perform his myth of Jonah, which goes beyond the precise Jewish myth and is connected to our reality.

Notes

1. Gershon Shaked, "Hasikkui vehasikkun (Le baayyat haibbud shel homarim mikraim ba mahaze haivri)", *Bamah*, vols. 79–80 (1978–79), pp. 125–131.

2. Glenda Abramson, *The Writing of Yehuda Amichai: A Thematic Approach* (New York: SUNY, 1989), p. 203.

3. Abramson, p. 208.
4. Yehuda Amichai, "Masa leninveh", *Paamonim verakkavot* (Tel Aviv: Schocken, 1968), pp. 88 ff.
5. Amichai, p. 96.
6. Harold Fisch, *A Remembered Future: A Study in Literary Mythology* (Bloomington: Indiana University Press, 1984), p. 134.
7. Fisch, p. 34, note 6.
8. Carl Gustav Jung, *Symbols of Transformation: An Analysis of the Prelude to a Case of Schizophrenia* (Princeton University Press, 1956), p. 408.
9. Jung, p. 330.
10. Jung, p. 331.
11. Gidon Ofrat, "Hakiyyum, haani, hameshorer vehahevra hayisraelit (al mahazotav shel Yehuda Amichai)", *Shadmot*, vol. 55 (1973–74), pp. 84–98.
12. Fisch, p. 134.
13. Ibid.
14. Fisch, p. 135.
15. Abramson, p. 211.
16. Amichai, p. 144.
17. Fisch, p. 144.
18. Fisch, p. 149.
19. Amichai, "Masa leninveh", p. 155.
20. Amichai, p. 157.
21. Ofrat, pp. 84–98.
22. A. Otniel, "Hanavi beal korho. 'Masa leninveh' le Yehuda Amichai beteatron Habimah", *Moznayim*, vol. 19 (1964), pp. 342–343.
23. Jacques Guicharnaud, *Modern French Theatre from Giraudoux to Genet* (New Haven and London: Yale University Press, 1967), p. 49.
24. Guicharnaud, p. 24.
25. Jean Cocteau, *Orphée* (New York: Hill and Wang, 1961), p. 23.
26. Victor Turner, *From Ritual to Theatre: The Human Seriousness of the Play* (New York: PAJ Publications, 1982), p. 86.
27. Turner, p. 87.
28. Turner, pp. 20–27.
29. Turner, p. 24.
30. Turner, p. 55.
31. Turner, p. 54.
32. Turner, p. 201.

Part Three

Fiction

11

Home and Abroad: The Case of Amichai's *Not of This Time, Not of This Place*

Risa Domb

In this paper I would like to focus on one theme from Amichai's rich and expansive novel, *Not of This Time, Not of This Place*. The theme, indicated by the title of my paper, is "home and abroad" and is particularly dominant in Israeli fiction written since the 1980s. Interestingly enough, it is as dominant in Amichai's novel, published as early as 1963. In this respect he was breaking the poetic norm, something which is evident in all other aspects of his writings. Since I regard this theme to be central to contemporary Hebrew writing, I would like to introduce it in general terms before examining its manifestation in Amichai's novel in particular.

The geographical shift of Jewish existence from West to East with the establishment of the State of Israel entailed a shift from an existence outside time and space to an existence within space. From that time onwards a dialectical tension existed between Israel and Europe, between home and abroad. National concerns have traditionally been the principal locus of the imaginative work of Hebrew writers. But, finding the geographical and cultural limits to their fictional worlds constricting, many Israeli writers strove to escape by maintaining connections with the outside world, with the horizon.

This fate is of course not new in the development of Hebrew literature. It has been noted that the inside/outside dichotomy introduced an important thematic opposition during the Jewish Age of Enlightenment: "inside/outside" would automatically be taken as relating to the conflict between Jewish values and secular European values, between what lay inside the "camp" or the "home" and what lay beyond it.[1]

Although still keeping up with European literary genres, the literature of the first generation of Hebrew writers in Israel in the 1940s and early 1950s, for various reasons which are beyond the interest of this paper, became insular and regional. In Hegelian terms of action and reaction, it is not surprising to discover that the writers who followed, the "New Wave" of the mid-1950s and 1960s, reacted against their predecessors and turned away from regionality towards universalism. They felt that the actual geographical limits to the fictional world had restricted the imagination of their predecessors. Once again, Hebrew literature looked outwards, towards Europe. This shift coincided with the political and economic circumstances which enabled Israeli writers to travel abroad more easily.

The dominant oscillation had become between home and abroad, rather than home and away, as Gershon Shaked has pointed out:

> The Exile was no longer abhorred and negated. It ceased being a source of nightmare or an object of nostalgia and instead it became a source of attraction and magic; no longer an enigma, but, rather, a wonderful and open world seductive with its magic. . . . the protagonists of the 50s and 60s were amazed by the strangeness of the world, its openness and the unlimited possibilities of expanse and freedom on the one hand, and the negative and demonic forces awaiting the Jew and the Israeli in this strange world, on the other.[2]

Thus the renewed encounter with Europe triggers admiration and attraction as well as hostility and repulsion. Some protagonists escape to Europe and others from Europe, but in both cases Europe never serves as just a tourist's sightseeing spot abroad but as a world which stands in total contrast to Israel. As we shall see later on, this is the case in Amichai's novel under discussion. Europe can also be presented as a challenge, which puts the culture of the *sabra* under scrutiny. It is easier to ask fundamental questions about the nature of the whole Israeli national enterprise when placing the fictional characters far off. From this vantage point it is also easier to rediscover the lost conceptual paradise of home. As suggested by A. Rubinstein,[3] A. B. Yehoshua commented about his own stay in Paris between 1963 and 1967: "The distance seemed to help me accept Israeli reality."[4] Distance in this case serves not so much the purpose of discovering the "other", as of examining the self, as is the case in Amichai's novel. This is testified by Amichai himself in an interview after the showing of the television programme "The Language of Images", where he says: "Sometimes you [need] to get out and to look at yourself from outside."[5] The Israeli characters who go abroad are seeking not only to examine their self but also to examine the collective. This, to my mind, is what distinguishes Hebrew literature from most of twentieth-century European literature.

Every period in history has its real and imaginary journeys. The protagonists of Romantic travel stories sought adventure, something alien and exotic, as well as solitude. The journey itself was often the aim, not necessarily its destination. At times it was seen as a journey into the mind, blurring the distinction between actual and ideal reality. Many leading twentieth-century authors also wrote about the "big voyage", an escape from the deadly humdrum routine in which their protagonists were trapped. Their search for redemption during the 1920s and 1930s, the journey, and life as a journey, became dominant themes in English literature.[6] All these endless and often meaningless journeys can be seen as a warped reincarnation of the Odyssean epic. Nevertheless, they all involve promise, hope, and renewal, despite the sorrows incurred. The Israeli poet Natan Zach has pointed out that these Odyssean characteristics continued throughout the long history of European culture and far beyond:

> The symbol of the journey and all that it involves—the sense of mission, of yearning for revelation, for renewal, for the improvement of the world and of the soul, for reacquaintance with all that had been and was now lost, or that which never was, everything brilliant which had tarnished or had been concealed in the wearying routine, the intoxicating charm of the big adventure with all its dangers, as well as the prospect of self-fulfilment—all these have long become archetypes in our private and collective consciousness and are repeated motifs and structures in the history of culture and literature.[7]

Along the same lines, Dan Miron has argued that protagonists in Israeli cultural life are continuously seeking some sort of a locus, a definite place in time and space, which might reveal authentic reality.[8] But, he points out, the "locus" moves around several places so that it can suit the desired self-image of the characters. Consequently, the place is perceived subjectively. The idea of a constant search for the one place underlies Yizhak Orpaz's idea of the "secular pilgrim".[9] He compares many characters in contemporary novels with pilgrims, except that being secular, they lack a holy place. Like pilgrims, they are in a state of unrest, in constant movement. The characters are inherently strangers wherever they are found, forever seeking the unattainable, and forever unable to settle down in any one place.

Amichai's novel *Not of This Time, Not of This Place*[10] deals with this state of unrest. It demonstrates some of the poetic uses of the place, and explores unusual and original literary possibilities using the dialectics of home and abroad. Amichai places Joel, the novel's protagonist who is in his late 30s, in two different geographical locations simultaneously. This tension between the alternatives of home and abroad can be seen as a tension between "inside" and "outside", to borrow the French phenomenologist Gaston Bachelard's terminology.[11] Bachelard observed that inside and outside form a dialectic of division, and that beyond their formal opposition lie alienation and hostility. Yet they are always ready to be reversed, to exchange their hostility. He postulates that inside and outside are not abandoned to their geometrical opposition and that human beings are composed of both. This being the case, the board or distinction between these two oppositions is ambiguous.

Jerusalem and Bavarian Weinburg are the two juxtaposed cities where the two parallel stories of Joel's life simultaneously take place, representing two aspects of his character. The two parallel stories, which are marked with surreal elements, are presented significantly from two different viewpoints: the story of Joel in Jerusalem is narrated in the third person, whereas the story of Joel in Weinburg is in the first person. This emphasizes the psychological split in Joel's life, where Jerusalem belongs to the present and Weinburg belongs to his past. The two are irreconcilable parts of his personality. Yet they constitute not only Joel's personal biography, but that of a whole generation which survived Nazi Germany. Although his voice is the voice of the individual, it is a voice which cannot disassociate itself from the collective: "I stood there and I cried within myself about the destruction of my life and the destruction of Jerusalem" (p. 52).[12] In this novel Amichai emphasizes that man is never on his own but always part of a whole generation, and that the two are intertwined (for example pp. 416, 597, 607). Significantly, Joel is an archaeologist whose aim is to unearth the mysteries of the past. The linking in the story between the earth, or the place, and the past is based not so much on some hidden resemblance or analogy between the Time and the Place of the novel's title, but rather on external relation, and thus the place functions as a metonymy for the long history of Israel. The biblical period, the second Temple, the Roman and the Crusaders' invasions, the long wars between Jew and Arab, have all left their mark as layers of the very earth which Joel has been excavating. In addition, the constant presence of a no-man's-land which has split the city into two is a constant reminder of the blood spilt by man in futile wars, as well as creating a sense of an inescapable siege. Joel was attracted to the no-man's-land, that dangerous area which receives special mention throughout the story, and which is where he and Mina eventually find their deaths (for example pp. 147, 157, 500–501). It was an area saturated with the blood of many generations (for example pp. 28, 90). Jerusalem and its history, Place and Time, are thus seen as full of blood and destruction, and even the onslaught of the summer is perceived by Joel as the arriving armies of Titus and Nebuchadnezzar (p. 141). It is a hard, stony city (for example pp. 220, 571), dried up and full of despair, cemeteries, funerals, and death (pp. 263, 325, 377). Nevertheless, after each destruction a new era emerges (p. 550). Contemporary Jerusalem, with its different houses and neighbourhood (for example pp. 26–7, 36, 91–92, 105, 114, 115, 169, 498–499, 502, 604), the sensuous smells of its trees (for example p. 101) and its mesmerizing fascination, is a place pulsating with life. The native-born and immigrants, the cultured and the uncultured, orientals and occidentals, Jews, Christians, and Moslems, all create a colourful, if complex, tapestry of daily life.

Set against Jerusalem, the parallel plot of the story takes place in Weinburg. The comparison between the two cities serves as a poetic tool in the structure of the novel. This is but one of countless apparent analogies upon which the story rests, as pointed out by Gershon Shaked in his analysis of the story.[13] I would like to argue that the endless analogies in the story are not its weaknesses, but its strength, and that they have a similar function to that of the analogy which binds together the different units of his poems. Amichai is teasing the reader with suggestions and hints of analogies, but in the final analysis they do not all hold their ground. There is no analogy between Jerusalem and Weinburg, any more than there is between the Holocaust and other catastrophic events in history.

The strange, irrational idea of going back to Germany and yet remaining in Jerusalem at the same time was suggested to Joel by his mentally ill friend Mina, a Holocaust survivor. The purpose of returning to Weinburg was to take revenge for Ruth, his childhood girlfriend, who perished in the concentration camps. Bearing in mind the strong autobiographical aspect of Amichai's prose and poetry, Joel's journey thus assumes an added dimension. His journey abroad serves a very specific function: it is the particular case of his confronting the memory of the Holocaust. He believes that revenge will cure his sorrows, and the importance of revenge in the scheme of events is indicated by the motto of the novel: "He saw a skull floating on the waters and he said to it: 'because you have caused others to drown, you will drown'" (*Pirkei Avot* B, 6; also pp. 156, 157, 277, 364, 422, 518, 533, 541, 550, 552, 584, 592, 612). However, Joel discovers that erasing memories of terrible events is a better and more effective cure. The way forward in life is to be able to forget. On his journey abroad, Joel stops for a few days in Zurich. He needs to detach himself from Jerusalem and to get used to the thought of being in a German-speaking country once again (p. 53). Similarly, he needs a few days in Paris on his way back home to Jerusalem. But above all it is Weinburg which creates the dialectics of home and abroad, inside and outside, discussed earlier in my general introduction.

Weinburg is a city with a river, bridges, and fountains (pp. 153, 155, 174, 175), by contrast to Jerusalem, which is dry. Like Jerusalem, it is stony, but here the stone indicates civilization, not destruction: the stone has been made into carvings, statues, and sculptures of angelic and saintly figures and of medieval heroes (for example p. 560). The irony is that it is in this seemingly cultured city that Jews were so savagely murdered (pp. 580–1). Although there is some evidence of destruction in Weinburg, most of the city has been completely rebuilt after the war (for example pp. 105, 153, 180), and it remains a city of towers, churches (for example pp. 97–8, 149), and wine cellars, as it always was. Whilst parts of Jerusalem have also been rebuilt, the evidence of the past could never be erased there.

Joel is excited to see again the familiar landscape of his childhood and he enjoys the natural beauty of the surroundings of Weinburg (pp. 76, 86, 492). Sentimental memories and childhood attachments intermittently obscure his hatred of the place. His visit to Bachfield, his late grandparent's village, further emphasizes his ambiguous love-hate feelings towards Germany. The familiar landscape has not changed here despite the terrible war, and the destruction has not left its mark in the earth for an archaeologist to discover.

The story set in Jerusalem is the story of Joel's sensuous love for a strange Christian woman. His love helps him escape the conventions of family framework and social expectations. The end of the relationship seems to illustrate that it is possible for love to leave no traces. The story set in Weinburg is the story of Joel's journey for revenge and it appears to illustrate that, unlike love, war and revenge do leave traces. However, typical of many of Amichai's teasing analogies in this novel, love and revenge are ironically no different from one another: both leave traces.

It is interesting to note the close relationship between Amichai's prose and his poetry, which can be exemplified in this particular case by one of his poems. In "The Travels of the Last Benjamin of Tudela", the speaker announces: "Come, my bride, in your hand hold something made of clay / At sunset, for flesh melts away / And iron is not preserved. Hold clay in your hand, / So that future archaeologists should find and remember. / They don't know that even anemones, after the rain / Are an archaeological find and a great attestation."[14] The poem contains many poetic and thematic elements which have been transferred from Amichai's poetry and extended further in his prose, a poetic feature which has been discussed at length elsewhere.[15]

Through Joel's endless wanderings in all parts of Weinburg in search of his childhood, he records the minute details of buildings and neighbourhoods in the town. The cumulative effect is achieved through the use of the "catalogue" technique, discussed at length by Boaz Arpaly in his book about Amichai's poetry.[16] Joel is particularly attracted to the central railway station, which epitomizes the "big voyage" mentioned earlier in my introduction: "A railway station is the native land of wanderers the world over. Railway stations are the embassies of all the homeless, or of those who have left their homes by choice and are in a state of complete oblivion. This is comparable to the 'big voyage'" (p. 96). As already mentioned, many leading twentieth-century authors write about the journey as a temporary solution for their protagonists in their search for their place in the world. This coincides with the state of mind of modern humanity, which has lost its sense of belonging. We find that the idea of place has become empty and our modern consciousness has become a "homeless mind", never quite finding its place. This is the case for Amichai's protagonist (for example pp. 278, 345, 489). His version of the "big voyage" is in being compared to Lot's wife, who turned into a stationary pillar of salt yet always trying to run away (p. 549). Similar to the secular pilgrim mentioned earlier, Joel too is in a state of unrest, constant movement.

Joel's problems are specific to a Holocaust survivor, but at the same time they also represent some of the problems of modern human consciousness. The dialectics of home and abroad are an interesting poetic device through which Amichai chose to convey these problems. Joel's endless and often meaningless wanderings are a warped reincarnation of the Odyssean epic. They often involve pain and suffering, but they also involve promise, hope, and renewal, as is the case in the novel. Joel missed home and began his big journey back commenting: "When one is away from home, home hurts like a tooth; as if home is part of one's body" (p. 462).

Joel's process of personal and collective reconciliation and renewal had begun to take place. He left Jerusalem, yet wanted to return (pp. 496, 584, 618), reflecting: "I suddenly understood why God is called the Place" (p. 591). This idea refers to the Bible's attitude towards wandering, which is seen as a movement towards the right place, towards God who Himself is subsequently referred to as "the Place". However, unlike the wandering of modernist protagonists who are in search of their personal solutions, Joel's are also in search of solutions for the collective (p. 272), which is one of the distinguishing features of contemporary Israeli literature. Through the dialectics of home and abroad, inside and outside, Amichai's protagonist can confront his past so that he is able to live in the present. A certain degree of harmony can be achieved only when the memory of his past has been confronted, and when the tension between home and abroad has been clearly defined, yet diffused.

Notes

1. Alan Mintz, *Banished from Their Father's Table: Loss of Faith and Hebrew Autobiography* (Bloomington: Indiana University Press, 1989), p. 96. Professor Werses, in his illuminating paper "The Houses of Berdichevsky", published in *Mehkerei Yerushalaim basifrut* (Jerusalem Studies in Hebrew), no. 5 (1984), pp. 63–94, pointed out that this tension can already be found in early writers such as Mendele, H. N. Bialik, and M.Y. Berdichevsky. In the case of Berdichevsky, the dichotomy is indeed between the secluded Jewish village and that which is "beyond the river", the alluring wide horizon of the enlightened non-Jewish world outside the village.

2. Gershon Shaked, "Besof maarav" (At the end of the west), *Hadoar* (31 October 1986), LXV: 40 (2831), p. 16.

3. Amnon Rubinstein, *Lihevot am hofshi* (To be a free people) (Jerusalem and Tel Aviv: Schocken, 1977), p. 112.

4. Cited by Joseph Cohen, *Voices of Israel* (Albany: State University of New York Press, 1990), p. 47.

5. *Yediot Aharonot*, 21 January 1994.

6. Paul Fussell, *Abroad: British Literary Travelling Between the Wars* (New York: Oxford University Press, 1980), pp. 52–5.

7. Natan Zach, "Hamasa hagadol" (The big voyage), *Igra, Almanac for Literature and Art* (Carmel, 1990), pp. 149–200.

8. Dan Miron, *'Im lo tiheve Yerushalayim* (If there is no Jerusalem) (Tel Aviv: Hakibbutz Hameuchad, 1987), pp. 227–8.

9. *Hatzalyan hahiloni*.

10. *Lo meakhshav lo mikan* (Jerusalem and Tel Aviv: Schocken, 1975; second edition).

11. Gaston Bachelard, *The Poetics of Space* (Boston: Beacon Press, 1969), pp. 211–16.

12. All translations are my own, and are literal rather than literary. I could not rely on the English translation of the book (by Shlomo Katz, published by Vallentine, Mitchell, London, 1973), since it has been heavily edited.

13. "Ho dori heatzuv vehamukeh" (Woe to my sad and stricken generation), in *Yehuda Amichai, mivhar maamarei bikkoret al yetsirato* (Yehuda Amichai—a selection of critical essays on his writing), selected and introduced by Y. Tzvik (Tel Aviv: Hakibbutz Hameuchad, 1988), pp. 191–213.

14. Y. Amichai, *Akhshav baraash* (Jerusalem and Tel Aviv: Schocken, 1968), p. 129.

15. For more on the correlation between Amichai's prose and poetry, see Dr Abramovitz-Ratner's forthcoming paper entitled "Between the narrator and his poem".

16. Boaz Arpaly, *Haperahim vehaagartel, shirat Amichai 1948–1968* (The flowers and the urn: Amichai's poetry 1948–1968 (Tel Aviv: Hakibbutz Hameuchad, 1986).

12

A Home Within: Place and Time in Amichai's Fiction

Leon I. Yudkin

The procedure of the author, in his narrative as in his poetry, whether adopting the position of first- or third-person narrator, is to pose a search for a narrative past to link with the present by a string of associations. We will see how this works in the three principal sources of Amichai's fiction: *Baruah hanoraah hazot* (In this terrible wind, 1961), a collection of stories deriving from the 1950s, *Lo meakhshav lo mikan (Not of This Time, Not of This Place,* 1963), a novel, and a further novel, *Mi yitneni malon* (O that I had a resting place, 1971).

Here, it is not so much that what is remembered is objectively a source of comfort, but that the act of remembering testifies to a positive spirit, and that the action itself bears its own fruit: "To remember is a kind of hope."[1] In the story "Hakrav bagivah" (Battle on the hill), the narrator gives voice to the authorial procedure, asserting that command over words is a itself a source of power; the one who uses them, the author, can do what he wills, change bad into good, the dead to the quick. He reflects on his friend, the potter, which leads him to associate from the well-known Hebrew phrase: "I thought, this is like the creator in the hand of the material. I reversed every proverb and found that nothing ever changes. You can change the live to dead and back again, and nothing ever changes."[2] A phrase comes to mind, a thought is associated with it, the image is reversed, and then a new confrontation emerges from the recharged arrangement.

This seems to be Amichai's main theme. The past must be recovered, because, in essence, it belongs to the present, and it is together that they constitute a whole. One without the other is necessarily incomplete, and is conscious of the lack. A parallel is established, as in Plato's *Symposium*, with the yearning to return to the womb, the source of our being. In the same story, he expresses this fantasy to the girl:

> Your navel healed up, but not your eyes. Your eyes will never heal up after the breach. Once you were in the world's womb, and when you were taken out, they cut the cord. You were broken off from the world, and you no longer belong to it. That is why you long for it and your eyes have not healed.

Images of realia become generalized into this primal situation of breach and need for repair, where the language of the poem or story bears the expression of this imperfection. In actual life, the repair is not made good. The image is too fleeting, the life movement too cumbersome, lagging behind the mind. In this story, the hero lunges at the past, but misses. At a barber's shop, he descries the image of his ex-commander in the mirror. But by the time he jumps up, pays for the haircut and gives chase, the figure has already disappeared. Language is the only tool of the writer in the achievement of the ambition of nailing down the object. But it can never quite get there, and the literary work becomes the expression of that pursuit and the unavoidable frustration involved.

The longing for the past does not, as we have seen, carry with it the necessary fulfilment of that longing. The longing ties together the subject and the object, the one who experiences the need and the lack with the external target. But, as pointed out by Boaz Arpaly, not only are the two interrelated, one derives from the other: "The world outside exists deep within the intimate situation, and shapes its image with Its own language."[3] The point here is that the objective "out there" does not possess an autonomous presence. In the writing of Amichai it depends for its functioning on the imposition of the narrator.

The "plot" of an Amichai narrative then takes on a somewhat different cast from what might normally be expected of the term. It is not so much a rigid, or even a flexible, shape to which the subject (which might be the author, the narrator, or even the addressee) must relate. It rather exists by virtue of the subjective tendency. And so the plot might always be subject to alteration, and is a shadow, not only in the sense that it resembles what it is shadowing, but that it follows, necessarily later, in the wake.

This process not only modifies action taking place and future movements, but the past too. History is, under this perspective, not a story of what has happened out there, but a reflection of a later way of looking back at it. In the story "Pegishat hakitah" (Class meeting),[4] the classmates of the title use each other not just to reconstruct but to create the past. They can change external reality: "Lovers act as a shield to each other, an insulating wall, an anchor and restraining material. In chemistry, you use an accelerating material known as a catalyst. Lovers slow down the world's processes and delay the coming of the end" (p. 7). To recover the past and to seek to control it is a product of love, even when that love is frustrated. By the rediscovery of his contemporaries he also rediscovers and finds himself.

In fact, it is the external reality, existing despite his imposition of a private vision on the public face, that ultimately frustrates the subject. Whatever his personal inclinations, that external reality still exists and will force its presence on him through its own reality principle. In the event, no-one wants to attend the reunion. He may yearn for them, but they, and the world, have their own agenda. As he is told: "'You are like a lamp left on during the day. Pity about the loss of fuel'" (p. 30). And in fact, the last smile, associated with nostalgia for that period, must be followed by that which is not a smile and which heralds grief and despair.

Much of the narrative derives from word association, an association that moves from sound into meaning, from single words into clusters, from separate units of meaning into images, metaphors, and symbols. Delight is taken in paradoxes, which can lead to insight. A postcard, which in Hebrew is called "a revealed thing" (*gluyah*), is just the place where the writer would not be open and reveal himself. The object of the reunion exercise is said to be "to measure time" (p. 27), which is precisely non-measurable. The reunion in fact splits people into their separate compartments, and eventually highlights the isolation and alienation of the narrator.

It is difficult to know what to do with the past. It is required, because it makes sense of the present, casts light on it, and preserves the memory of something better within the present bleakness. But it also seems to lead on to a necessary reconciliation with the recovery of that past, and on to an eventual and inevitable breach. The world, which was once wonderful, is now harsh and unassimilable. In "Haolam hu heder" (The world is a room): "The voice of the world has changed as during puberty. The voice of the world has turned rough and hoarse, a fact not yet appreciated, as they only recalled his dulcet tones."[5] Once they derived meaning from each other, and beamed light on the darkness. But now, within the new situation, this is irrelevant. What gave the war context its significance was danger, injury, and death. Those factors avoided are of no interest now, as they did not fit the bill then.

The associative drive is what keeps impinging on the novel *Lo meakhshav lo mikan*. There is not only an illuminating association of Ruths—the name of the little girl in Germany and Joel's wife in Jerusalem. It is also the source of confusion and frustration, as the hero (the narrator in the Germany section) tries to clarify the distinction for himself and break away from unwelcome association. What the coincidence of identical nomenclature achieves is to remind the hero of his inadequacy, a guilt derived from the death of the little girl and his sense of betrayal to her when he left Germany. And now a mature Ruth, in his own maturity, his wife, must constantly be posing similar issues to him of loyalty and betrayal.

We set out with the object of discovering this central theme in the prose writings of Amichai. There could be no more explicit exemplification of this than the title, the theme, and indeed the content of the novel *Mi yitneni malon* (O that I had a resting place).[6] In this novel, the atmosphere of Israel leading up to the Six-Day War is invoked: the cynicism, the disillusionment, the rather tawdry materialism of those on the make, willing sometimes to exploit the idealism and ideals of others. The invocation of the quotation of Jeremiah (9:1) suggests the sense of disengagement of a prophet willing to depart from his people who are adulterers and traitors.

But the tone is not of solemn satire, nor really of humorous confrontation with the issues. It is jokey and flippant, even uncertain. However, there is an undercurrent of tragedy, a mourning on the part of the narrator that he is not at home, neither physically nor spiritually. He is in New York, ironically working for an organization whose object is to send Israelis back home. But he has been sidetracked in his efforts and become embroiled in a "crazy metaphorical" web, which has to be unravelled by his boss. In fact, the deception becomes clearly apparent to Mr Berger, the source of the funding for the project: no-one ever returns, whilst constantly promising to. The narrator both stands within himself and on the outside, the victim of circumstances and curious about his situation. He adopts a learning posture, posing the absurdist question of how long he has been in New York: "I very much wanted to know myself how long I had been here; there are various versions, and this fact, that is, this lack of fact presents me with considerable difficulty in mapping out my territory" (p. 87).

As he poses absurd questions, he adopts an ever more absurd lifestyle. He becomes a copywriter for a ladies' underwear firm, "Stone & Son". It then begins to seem that the painful attractions of exile outweigh the difficulty of the return home. The central themes here are the sense of home, which in this case, for the Israeli, is associated with Israel, and the hotel in New York, which is both a temporary resting place for those like himself and, paradoxically, a place away that offers a retreat from precisely the place to which they are to be brought back. He, the hero of the homeland, whose function is to repatriate, is in danger of becoming one of his own cases, an expatriate in America (p. 176). New York takes on the specific and private character for him of being "a city of yearning for Jerusalem" (p. 208). He has become the very stereotype of the ageing Jew in exile, constantly yearning to return. This takes him to the point of helpless terror at the prospect of imminent war.

It is not only the hero of this novel who finds himself in this situation. Yosl, in *Lo meakhshav lo mikan*, is a similarly restless spirit: "Yosl has been in Israel many years, and he is still not at home" (p. 193). In fact, for reasons which he himself cannot fathom, he is now returning to the hell-hole of Germany. In fact, he is described as seeking "complete rest" (*menuhah nekhonah*), an attribute sought for the dead in the traditional memorial prayer *Yizkor*. This restless search for home echoes that of Joel, and casts its uncomfortable shadow over that character's life both physically and spiritually. The no win situation is expressed in the Jewish need to escape conditions of homelessness and exile, and then followed by the subsequent dissatisfaction and hankering after an abandoned source.

The central theme as described here could be seen as carrying the kernel of the major Israeli preoccupation, indeed the *raison d'être* of the very existence of the new State, that is, the search for a home. Israel was born out of a negativity, out of a perception that the world is not a home for the Jew. And so the emergent State received all manner of appelations, ascribing qualities of totality, for example "land" (*aretz*), "homeland" (*moledet*). But the physical reality of an emergent political entity, with its specific character and contours, does not necessarily sit comfortably with that theoretical object of yearning, which can begin to take on a life of its own and even become its own theatre of operations, if not a new sort of homeland in its own right. The Israeli may want to carry both aspirations within himself at one and the same time. It is for this reason that a fiction can be projected that splits the character into two, each separately acting out its own scenario. Such is *Lo meakhshav lo mikan,* which divides the central character into two parts, simultaneously remaining in Jerusalem during that fateful summer and returning to Weinburg in pursuit of revenge. Shaked has characterized the book as broadening the scope of the *sabra* novel,[7] as it takes the main character, the stage where the action takes place, and the ideational focus beyond the confines of the Israel-centrism of the typically new Israeli novel. This does of course reflect a tendency of Israeli fiction of the 1960s to set the "hero" in a situation of flight from the confines of what is seen as a limiting imposition of functions for Israeli man.[8]

The possibilities embodied in a metarealistic novel grant the situation of having one's cake and eating it. Joel can simultaneously be in Israel and in Germany, to pursue two separate and even preclusive objectives, each carrying a theory into practice. This need for splitting is also expressed in narrative stance, seeing the hero in one case as third and then as first person. What seems to irk the Jerusalem Joel, where we start, is the residue of another life in his present system of functioning and the experienced need to address that other part and finish with it. What he seeks is to close that metaphorical door, although in order to achieve that, he first has to go back, thus reopening that very door.

Joel in Jerusalem reviews his whole life, and that in essence turns into the starting point of the novel. It takes its origin in chapter 1, and immediately precedes the move into the first-person narrative, the account of a dream about being in Weinburg, before his more naturalistic account of the actual venture into Germany: "Joel stood at the edge of the roof, and his whole life was with him: all his memories, his childhood, his encounters, his wars, little Ruth and Ruth his wife . . . " (p. 14). It is of the essence of this novel that the past belongs to the present, is an inseparable component of the here and now, which is made up of a story, which is a history and a biography. The past is also a problem. It is not only part of the "I"; it is also a thing out there, and is seen from the outside, becoming therefore a "he". What Joel wants more than anything else is integration of the elements, past and present, there and here, what "I" was then as "he" with the "I" of the here and now. The ambition of the historical Joel is to achieve this integration by a resolution, by coming back totally into his own skin by being in Jerusalem, which involves separating off that other part, by closing that door. Is this possible? asks the narrator: "It is not possible to go back to the place to which I am returning. I am coming to close a door that has not been properly closed in my life. A door that dances in its frame and disturbs my sleep in Jerusalem" (p. 64). Imagination, says Joel, plays strange and malicious tricks on us. We think that we left the oven or a tap on, or perhaps, a door has been left open. This is the metaphorical door for a situation unresolved. The freedom remains for the individual to close off the options and to move into a new and more decisive phase. But this can only be achieved by first dealing with that past, and it is this effort that makes up the novel and determines its complex structure.

What seems to be the common factor in the characters of the stories and the two novels is the inability to contain the tension between the two poles of attraction in time and place. There is established a human need to be both here and there, to exist in the present and to go back to the past. In *Mi yitneni malon*, each girl, the inseparable Shosh and Losh (the interlocking duo), describes her yearnings for Israel (p. 18). This is part of a wider plan to create a nexus of psychological and spiritual connection with Israel in order to facilitate the projected return. The narrator finds himself in that situation too: "Of course, then I will be going back to Israel" (p. 52). But that seems to be his situation, at least within the narrative framework presented: always to be on the point of return. This "point" is nicely located at the juncture of here and there, here physically, but emotionally absent, there spiritually but not in body, constantly suspended between the two. Another character in the novel diagnoses his condition. He has difficulties with his own identity, and she says of him: "It seems to me that he is lost. He has been dealing with the lost, but he himself is lost" (p. 87). It is not surprising therefore that he poses the question that we noted above, reflecting uncertainty over the most intimate and familiar features of his life, and cannot even relate how long he has been in New York. His later preoccupation with underclothes also assumes metaphorical status: underwear becomes an image of the labyrinth, in its mystery and complexity. Especially for the male, these garments are perplexing and a source of entrapment: "You can't get out of every entrance" (p. 140). Likewise, he may find himself locked unwillingly in a situation in which he has been the agent of his own embroilment, and he may never be able to go back home—he, whose very function has been to bring others back home and to facilitate their reabsorbtion. For him, it is only the war, with its presentation of the fundamental issues, that can in its bleak horror renew in him a sense of hope (see p. 262).

The question originally posed still remains after all the searches have been conducted and all possible exploration carried out: what and where is home? For the her (and ultimately all Amichai's narrative movement in poem and story revolves around the psychic condition of the character/s), no ultimate, unambiguous home is discovered. Home is both whence you derive and where you feel that you belong. It is also where you return after you have made your excursions into strange territory. It is in that strange territory that you should really find the sort of "hotel for guests" that is cited by the prophet Jeremiah, invoked in the title of the Amichai novel. But the Amichai character both leaves his uncomfortable source, and finds no totally satisfactory alternative. Israeli man is perhaps by definition not at home, since the source of his being and the definition of his identity derive from a conflict of identity and attachment. That difficulty was established at some undefined point, undefined but far back. As Sister Maria pronounces (when approached by Joel in the Weinburg institution [for the aged] for more information about little Ruth): "We are all from long ago" (p. 134). That is what has shaped this group identity. The specifics of particular history and landscape are changed. What remain are the longings and the obsessions. As Amichai wrote in his poem "Bezavit yesharah" (At right angles): "My fate has not grown with me." The individual has changed his external circumstances, but the defining shape remains as it was. That is his Fate.

The building of a home within is the object, conscious or unconscious, of every human being. The difficulties in achieving this apparently simple but deceptive goal are paramount. We suffer from illusion and delusion. For Melanie Klein, human creativity can be achieved only by the realization of externality, something akin to Freud's reality principle. This is a goal that can only be reached in the so-called "depressive position", when mourning the loss of a loved one has first been experienced, and then the fact absorbed into consciousness.⁹ Mourning has to be experienced for otherwise we would not have loved and we would not be human. We would otherwise be machines or monsters. Amichai's writing is about the experience of loss on the part of the individual, and the methods contrived to confront, absorb, and transmit the experience. The work of art, and in this specific case the literary artefact, the story, is clearly not just an imitation of life, for all the apparent similarities. Life is already there, so why imitate it in ways unavoidably inferior to the model? The artefact is not a pale imitation, but a life equivalent. It is this intersection between life and fiction, the crisscrosses, that creates the tension. This sort of writing is constantly looking back at life, and then transforming bits of what remains. Proust, at the end of his massive novel, tried to explain what he had been doing in the book. What is a book? "Un livre est un grand cimetière ou sur la plupart des tombes on ne peut plus lire les noms effacés" (A book is a large cemetery where on most of the tombs one cannot read the defaced names).¹⁰ Amichai, with his interest in the individual soul exemplified in the heroes of the narratives examined here, is the sort of writer about whom the great French author is talking. He visits the cemetery because that is where his own life is connected. But the graves of the dead yield obscure, difficult, and sometimes conflicting messages, and the writer must take his pick from the half-deciphered material to make sense of that past, that place and that time. In this case too, the loss is acknowledged, the mourning experienced. It is the struggle for the realization of the externality that is represented in the narrative.

Notes

1. Translated in English under the title *Amen* (London, New York, San Francisco: Harper & Row 1977, Oxford University Press, 1978).

2. *Baruah hanoraah hazot* (Tel Aviv: Shocken, 1961). Some of these stories were translated into English and published as a collection entitled *The World is a Room* (Philadelphia: Jewish Publication Society, 1984).

3. Boaz Arpaly, *Haperahim vehaagartel*, p. 18.

4. In *Baruah hanoraah hazot*.

5. *Baruah hanoraah hazot*, p. 155.

6. *Mi yitneni malon* (Bitan, 1971).

7. Gershon Shaked, "Hoi dori heatsuv vehamukeh", in *Yehuda Amichai; mivar maamarei bikkoret al yetsirato* (Tel Aviv: Hakibbutz Hameuhad, 1989).

8. Leon Yudkin, *Escape into Siege* (London: Littman Library, 1974), pp. 90–103.

9. Hanna Segal, "Delusion and Artistic Creativity", *International Review of Psychoanalysis* (1974). Republished in *Delusion and Artistic Creativity and other Psychoanalytic Essays* (Free Association Books, 1986).

10. Marcel Proust, *Le Temps Retrouvé. A la Récherche du Temps Perdu*, vol. 6 (Paris: Pleiade Edition), p. 451.

13

Poetic and Dramatic Elements in the Children's Literature of Yehuda Amichai

Menucha Gilboa

My discussion of Yehuda Amichai's books for children, especially their poetic and dramatic aspects, will centre on two books, *The Fat Tail of the Numa*[1] and *The Great Book of the Night*.[2] I shall also touch on the book *What Happened to Roni in New York*.[3]

There is an interesting connection between *The Fat Tail of the Numa* and *The Great Book of the Night*. The former is the story of a young boy who goes to kindergarten for seven nightless days, starting on Sunday (the first day of the week) and ending on Saturday. The latter is the story of the nights of a little girl, Emanuella, as she is about to enter the first grade; the events cover a period of seven nights from Sunday night until Saturday. Both books have a young hero, but there are important differences between the day and the night in a child's life. If the days hold their hints of realism, the nights are another, different world.

The dream which he dreams at night is not governed by the child himself, for subconscious forces are in control. On the other hand, day-dreams are actually the sublimation of desires, and the child directs them. Thus, with the help of the imagination, certain components of reality become a reality that is chosen.

The literary world of dreams may be thought of as a fantasy world, leading the young reader to games in the world of the imagination and the adult reader to the psychological world of the character by means of dream analysis.

At this point I should like to digress in order to call attention to the affinity between children's literature and play or play-acting. Play departs from what is customary and familiar; it is life in another world, in a different world, to be more exact. Play is activity, at times very spirited, and in Amichai's works it becomes drama. It is theatre because its participants act out lives that are different from their real lives. Consider, for example, the concluding poem in *What Happened to Roni in New York,* in which the child recounts his adventures in New York, and another poem which makes a connection between the situation described and dreams or even play:

The Big Bridge

A bridge, grand and stately
Spans the river.
Roni stood and gazed and then crossed over.
For almost two hours he walked and walked
And felt like a king.
The bridge trembles
All the time and wobbles a bit.

The city is encircled by many bridges.
To Roni they are like wings.
One day they will lift
The whole city up into the sky.
It will happen at night.
It won't be during the day
Because it will be like a dream.

Here we have an ostensibly realistic poem which moves out of reality with the help of simile and metaphor, passing into the realm of dream or fantasy which is the game of a child acting out his visit to New York. Here the link between reality and dream is manifest.

Roni Came Home

Roni came home
And told all that had happened
And all he had done and seen.
The guests listened and said: "Ah,
Roni is truly daring and dear,
He saw New York alone
Without fear."

> *But at night, his uncle, whom Roni loves very much,*
> *Said to him: "Roni, sit down.*
> *Were you really*
> *There? Maybe it was only a dream and you were mistaken?"*
> *Roni replied: "I don't lie,*
> *All that I told you is correct."*
> *The two stood beside the window.*
> *"Roni, what happens in a dream*
> *Is not a lie, it is the truth."*
> *Roni sat and remained silent.*
> *Then his uncle said:*
> *"I love you very much.*
> *You are a good and an honest boy*
> *But something strange happened to you:*
> *I know—*
> *Because you are lonely*
> *For your father who is there,*
> *You dreamt that you were there too."*
>
> *After his uncle left, Roni still sat*
> *And sat and thought and thought and thought.*
> *For a long time he sat silently.*
> *"My uncle is almost right",*
> *He thought to himself.*
>
> *The next day daddy came home.*

The poet opens up children's poetry to the essence of acting. Actually, the child here, like every child, lives his life and at the same time acts out the lives of others, in this case the life of his father.

Uri Rapp, discussing the connection between play, mimesis, art, and simulation, notes that Aristotle's statement "art imitates nature" does not appear in his book on poetics but rather in his *Physics*.[4] Mimesis is not false imitation but rather potentially serious simulation. The play-acting of drama may be serious business. Here in the descriptions of New York we have, on the one hand, mimesis or simulation and, on the other, a drama about New York. Many philosophers from Plato on saw play as the essence of mankind and even accorded it religious significance.[5] It is no wonder that such ideas arose and developed in ancient Greece where drama and play-acting had an important place in literature.

This view, however, is not limited to ancient Greece; it is also modern. Schiller (in the eighteenth century) and Herbert Spenser (in the nineteenth century), as well as many of the writers and philosophers of the twentieth century, consider art to be a form of play. If it is true that in acting there is a certain exaggeration, it is repeated and creates its own rhythm and its own variations.[6] The psychologist Eric Erikson makes the connection between play-acting and day-dreaming.[7]

To return to Amichai's works for children: the journey to the world of the imagination is usually a pleasant trip to another world. We have seen this in the poem about Roni. In *The Great Book of the Night* (which is perhaps the most important children's book in Hebrew) the excursion is actually in the form of a play and perhaps a kind of dream: "Have a pleasant trip into the night", says Emanuella. That is the child's new bedtime blessing. "Emanuella knows exactly what she means", the narrator tells us. Every adult in the story comprehends Emanuella's blessing in his or her own way: "Luckily, at least at night we don't need to travel very much, says mother" (p. 46). Here the mother's interpretation of what the daughter has said is realistic or literal or, as Aristotle would describe it, mimesis. In contrast, the perception implicit in the father's interpretation is similar to that of his daughter. While in the case of the daughter it may be imagination, in that of the father it is probably a psychological perception and perhaps even contemplation concerning the nature of life: "And father says: The child is right. Life is one long journey, and even while sleeping, the trip continues" (ibid.). In other words, here we have the philosophical view of the poet Yehuda Amichai, represented in the book by the father speaking of his little girl's expression.

We can say that even the prose passages are anti-prose. The lyrical writing of *The Fat Tail of the Numa*—all poems—and *The Great Book of the Night*—a kind of prose—is full of metaphor and metonymy. In the second book, too, many poems are interwoven. Moreover, there is no on-going plot. Each day or each night is a separate story; that is, there is a multiplicity of narratives. It is difficult to combine them into a single tale, just as it is difficult to make a unified account out of a book of poems. Perhaps we might say that what we have here are "fragments of plot" or a mosaic of narratives. In both books, the conclusions drawn from each day or each night go beyond realism. Realism is different from the imaginary world that both Dadi (David, in *The Fat Tail of Numa*) and Emanuella see.

Through *The Great Book of the Night* runs the unifying thread of Emanuella's repeated meetings with the queen of the night, but each journey is to another world. Thus, here too, it is possible to speak of many imaginary plots which lack continuity, just as Emanuella's play lacks continuity. It is possible to say that almost every story is a play, a drama which occurs in another, imaginary world.

The realistic figures who recur in the two books are the boy or the girl, the mother, and the father. In *The Great Book of the Night* the recurrent figure of the queen of the night is a fantasy character. In this book the girl's imagination and her views on her life and her surroundings are revealed to us in several different ways. Use is made of metaphor and simile, art and thought, play, words and dreams.

Consider the following as an example of art and thought: on one of her journeys with Emanuella, the queen explains about the earth's rotation and about the sun, about far-off stars, and so on. After the queen disappears and the child is about to wake up, she begins "a series of 'games and interventions'" (p. 53). In the course of her thought-games the girl sets rules for herself and then she says that it is possible to change what happens "with the help of the little man in the brain" (p. 53). All this happens just prior to awakening. At night the actions of the "little man in the brain" are completely different. The child takes the information which she has about reality and mingles it with her imaginary world according to her wishes. At night, in her dreams, "the little man in the brain" does not dictate the plot.

As for the metaphors and similes in the books, they are present as in every poem in a book of poetry. Except that, unlike modern poetry, Amichai retains rhyme for the most part, which itself is a linguistic game. It is interesting to note that we are sometimes made aware of a break in the rhymes, like an intermission in a theatre play.

Here are several examples of metaphor and simile: "And it is a great joy to be an infant. Each evening just before bedtime, she is allowed to again be an infant, to whine a little, to complain a little, to whistle and crow and to cuddle and curl up in bed, as if inside a large stomach, as if within a large shell, as though inside a large egg, and to be endlessly pampered" (p. 9). In other words, the passage expresses a desire to return to the foetal state. The pampering takes place only at night when that is possible.

Here we have a deep psychological effect for the perusal of adults and a metaphor for the child's desire for pampering. All these are an expression of longings for infancy which can only be realized at night. Only the night can "pamper without limitations", something which daytime life does not permit. Perhaps only in play is it possible to make dreams come true. Here again we have the interesting philosophical perspective of the narrator "I" reflecting the views of the authorial "I" in the works of Yehuda Amichai.

Or another example of simile:

> *A story no one has heard*
> *Like a room without walls*
> *Like a cake made out of air*
>
> *Like rain without water*
> *Like speech without lips*
> *Like hearing without ears*
>
> *Like dreams without a dreamer*
> *Like a child without a name*
> *Like air without anyone to breathe it*
>
> *Like rain from blue skies*
> *Like a poem without words*
> *Like a letter without stamps*
> *Like basketball without baskets.*

Each of these fascinating similes is an image of the impossible. Here again there is a confrontation with the essence of life. What is impossible in life is possible in play.

We have another interesting comparison when the girl sees herself as perhaps a leader like Moses: "And she is three days and seven hours and forty-three minutes old, and she is still in the maternity ward of the big hospital, an infant inside an *ark* . . . [my emphasis, M. G.]" (p. 28). Here as well we have the impression that the girl needs to be rescued. Moreover, something interesting happens to Emanuella. She is a small child, and yet she already wants to return to the past, to memories, and to leadership.

What the queen and Emanuella say to each other about love employs the richest of metaphors, in keeping with the entire body of Amichai's poetry. Items in "a list of 'the small and sweet articles of love'" include: a red velvet heart inside a small fur basket; scissors with red handles; a blue heart; and a ball of thread, twisted and knotted. The depth of the metaphors is unusual, to the extent that at first, the objects would appear not to have any connection with love and would seem difficult to decode or interpret. Perhaps only in poetry for adults is it possible to deal with such matters. Moreover, the apparent continuity of daily or nightly stories, especially the latter, creates a metaphor of another and different world, which qualitatively is a unique artistic phenomenon.

An example which is both metaphorical and philosophical: in a conversation about Emanuella's brother coming home on leave from the army, the queen of the night says to Emanuella: "At night the entire kingdom of the night is nothing but a huge sleeping bag [borrowed of course from the army]—she zips it up . . . with a zipper as long as the whole world" (p. 73). In other words, the kingdom of the night is closed, isolated from the real, everyday world which is visible and exposed. A connection of analogy is created between the closed kingdom of the night and the army.

Interestingly, it is possible to interpret the discussions and expeditions of the queen of the night and Emanuella as dreams. But there are also dreams as such: perhaps they are a kind of journey within a journey. It may be that the dreams appear as the embodiment of the child's inner world:

> At this point the child awoke from her dream. But she did not know that what she had dreamt would actually happen to her at some future time in some far-distant land. Only the queen of the night knew it. And by the last light of the moon, she again took the dream from the girl, wrapped it, and put it in the storeroom of dreams until the day that this dream would again be removed from the storeroom to become reality. And all that had happened in the dream would come to pass, would really happen. (p. 40)

In contrast to day-dreaming or play-acting, the child does not control the nocturnal dream. As already noted, what influences the nocturnal dream is the unconscious mind. The interpretation of psychologists is the only way, or almost the only way, to reach the unconscious. Since dreams are unconscious, they are not always easily understood, and this holds true for the dreams of *The Great Book of the Night*.

On the other hand, the day-dream (as we have seen in the poem about Roni's visit to New York) is a sublimation of desires. In it too there are elements of both reality and imagination. In the case of the story of the child in New York, the scene and the longings for the father have become the personal sublimation and even the dramatic play-acting of the child in New York, and it is thus easier to interpret.

We have very poetic and lyric elements, dramatic and personal, in Amichai's works for children. The poetics are not uniform. The narrator "I", and behind him the authorial "I", testifies to this abundance of content and of lyric poetics and drama:

> *Good morning*
> *May the day bring only good things*
> *May it be tasty and fragrant*
> *(Here, there would seem to be a reminder of last night's roll).*

> *May it be a relaxed day, calm as water*
> *(Apparently a faint memory of the dream).*

Here the narrator "I" is clearly in evidence, and his words in the poem are set in parentheses, as in modern poetry.

The linguistic element is one of the distinctive and very dominant aspects of Amichai's works for children. Their language is filled with wordplay, especially synonym and rhyme. It may even be said that the word play is musical in nature. Some of it is intended to attract the children to what is being said by the narrator "I"; some of it expresses children's wishes.

It has been observed that "each new word is a discovery and new world for the child".[8] This phenomenon is a result of the child's creative ability, and it links the child to the poet and to the words in his poems.

In the two books the characters of the father and mother are fascinating. Here is a poem about the father from *The Fat Tail of the Numa*:

> *My father is not only a father*
> *He is all sorts of things.*
> *He is a horse for me to sit on his shoulders*
> *And he is a camel to ride*
> *He's a ladder up to the sky*
> *And a diving board beside the swimming pool*
> *He's a chair to sit on at home*
> *And a good boat for sailing.*
>
> (p. 30)

The child's view of the fathers and mothers and his reluctance to allow them to leave the bedside and go out of the bedroom are also common to the two books; in both, the same elements recur.

Both books provide a frame for their stories. We have already noted that *The Fat Tail of the Numa* and *The Great Book of the Night* complement each other in some ways. The subtitle of the former is: *And All the Other Things That Happened Every Day for a Week*. It opens by introducing the child Dadi (David), who is the central character. It then presents the parents, who have thought up many nicknames for the child, such as names of animals: chick, warbler, thrush, and so on. The presentation of the child serves as a kind of background story or frame. Immediately after the child is introduced come the poems of his adventures during the week: going to nursery school with his mother who takes him there, getting dressed, going to sleep, meetings with animals, bathing, and so on. In other words, they tell of everything that happens to the child within his milieu, what happens to him and to those he meets, all in the form of poetry, always rhymed and replete with wordplay and humour, like the poem "Dadi's Wordplay". There is even a philosophical discussion about the nature of time which is perceived differently by adults and children.

Within the frame it is possible to change the order of the poems, since each poem stands on its own and its connection with a particular day is arbitrary—except, of course, for the first poem, and for the last, which ends the book as the house is being prepared for the wonderful Sabbath.

The Great Book of the Night also has its frame, which incidentally has no connection with nights, and is proclaimed by the narrator "I". The opening is an apparently completely realistic story of Emanuella's birth and naming. A rationale is provided for the dreams: "First the dreams! Sometimes they are more interesting than what really happens during the day" (p. 7). The narrator says that he will recount the events of an entire week of nights.

In the poem of the first night there is an attempt to explain why precisely there are dreams and why precisely there are nights:

> *During the day the child is expected*
> *To be grown-up and well-mannered,*
> *Even to travel alone on the bus,*
> *And to be neat,*
> *To behave differently.*
> . . .
> *And without argument or disagreement*
> *"You're not an infant any more!"*
>
> **(pp. 8–9)**

Thus, the poem relates to the psychological difficulty of a little girl confronted by the demand that she be grown-up and well-mannered, governed by everyday rules. This is very interesting, because we have already shown how the girl longs for her childhood, to be an infant again, to be pampered, and even to return to the womb. In other words, the child's difficult real situation is one of the reasons for her longing to be an infant.

In the final chapter, the frame ends with an expression of Emanuella's joy at night and sadness during the day:

> *The child was very sad and was lonesome for the queen [that is,*
> *the queen of the night who had accompanied her in her dreams]* . . .

*Days and weeks passed
And the child began to think that it had all happened in a dream.*
(p. 103)

Finally:

> Emanuella awakened, and here was the new red schoolbag for the first grade hugged tightly in her arms. Her parents stood beside her bed and said: "With that kind of bear hug, you're bound to be a good, successful pupil". (p. 104)

The frame or setting in this book is reality, and the nights and the imagination are the voyages to outside the real, objective world. This suggests an association with *Alice in Wonderland,* because Alice too breaks out of the real and, by shrinking, penetrates other worlds before returning home. But Alice was a young teenager, and the journey from realism for the sake of confronting the social world helped her cope with herself as she grew up. A similar thing happened to Emanuella when she sailed away to other worlds as compensation for her daily life, and perhaps to help her to break away from her infancy.

Emanuella does not become an adult. She departs from early childhood and starts going to school. Therefore it is no wonder that her dream worlds are completely different from those of Alice. And if *Alice in Wonderland* has become a world classic, *The Great Book of the Night* also deserves to become known worldwide, but for a much younger readership.

There is no doubt that children's literature leads the young reader to identify and to internalize, and brings him or her, as does play, reward and compensation. This will surely be true for most of the children who read the works of Yehuda Amichai.

Notes

1. *Hazanav hashamen shel hanumah* (Schocken Press Children's Books, 1978).
2. *Sefer halaylah hagadol* (Schocken Press Children's Books, 1988).
3. *Mah shekarah leroni beNew York* (Tel Aviv: Am Oved, Sifriyat Shafan Hasofer, 1968).
4. Uri Rapp, the "University on the Air" library: *The World of Play, Chapters in the Behavioral Sciences* (Tel Aviv: Ministry of Defense Press, 1980), p. 18. I would call the reader's attention to Rapp's bibliography, p. 86 (in Hebrew).
5. Rapp, p. 10.
6. Rapp, p. 17.
7. Eric H. Erikson, *Childhood and Society* (New York: W. H. Norton & Co., 1950).
8. Rapp, p. 29.

About the Book

Yehuda Amichai is Israel's foremost poet as well as a significant novelist and dramatist. He has received every major Israeli prize for literature, and his poetry has been translated into over twenty languages. Amichai has served as poet-in-residence at major universities across the United States and has been a frequent visitor to the University of Oxford.

In this volume, the world's leading authorities on Amichai explore all the major genres and themes of his work. The result is an important book that is a unique and comprehensive scholarly overview of a major twentieth-century literary figure. It will prove especially valuable to those teaching modern Hebrew literature at English-language universities.

About the Editor and Contributors

Glenda Abramson was born in South Africa and received her Ph.D. from the University of the Witwatersrand in Johannesburg where she taught for eleven years prior to her departure for the United Kingdom in 1978. She has been teaching at the University of Oxford and the Oxford Centre for Hebrew and Jewish Studies since 1981. Among her publications are: *Modern Hebrew Drama* (1979); *The Great Transition* (with Tudor Parfitt, 1985); *The Writing of Yehuda Amichai* (1989); and *Hebrew in Three Months* (Hugo, 1993). She edited *The Blackwell Companion to Jewish Culture* (1989); *Jewish Education and Learning* (with Tudor Parfitt, 1995); *Tradition and Trauma* (with David Patterson, 1995); and *The Oxford Book of Hebrew Short Stories* (1996).

Boaz Arpaly was born in Israel and is now an Associate Professor in the Department of Hebrew Literature at Tel Aviv University. He has been a member of a kibbutz and an officer in the Israeli army. Among his publications (in Hebrew) are the following: *Bonds of Darkness: Nine Chapters on Natan Alterman's Poetry* (1983); *The Flowers and the Urn: Amichai's Poetry 1948–68* (1986); *The Negative Principle: Ideology and Poetics in Y. H. Brenner's Fiction* (1992); and *Saul Tchernichowsky: Studies and Documents* (1994).

Arnold J. Band was born in Boston, Massachusetts, and received his Ph.D. in Classical and Comparative Literature from Harvard. He was Professor of Hebrew Literature at the University of California, Los Angeles, from 1959, and in 1969 he founded the Department of Comparative Literature, serving as its Chair for ten years. Band's distinguished career has included appointments at Harvard, Brandeis, and Hebrew Union College, numerous awards, and three honorary doctorates. Among his many publications is *Nostalgia and Nightmare*, the seminal study of S. J. Agnon.

Risa Domb was born in Israel. She is the first-ever holder of a lectureship in Modern Hebrew at the University of Cambridge; she is also Honorary Director of the Centre for Modern Hebrew Studies in the Faculty of Oriental Studies, and a Fellow of Girton College. She is the author of *The Arab in Hebrew Prose* and *Home Thoughts from Abroad*, as well as the editor of an anthology entitled *New Women's Writings from Israel*.

Ziva Feldman was awarded a doctorate by Bar Ilan University, Israel, in 1993 for her thesis entitled *Yehuda Amichai: Kinetic Transformation From Form to Meaning*.

Menucha Gilboa was born in Jerusalem. She joined the Haganah and took part, as a soldier, in the newly founded IDF in the Israeli War of Independence. Dr Gilboa graduated from the Hebrew University in 1962, received her M.A. in 1969, and her Ph.D. in 1972 at Tel Aviv University. She holds the post of Senior Lecturer in the Department of Hebrew Literature at Tel Aviv University. Her publications include two books of children's short stories, two books of poetry, ten volumes of Hebrew literary research, and over a hundred articles and papers about literature and philosophy. Among them (in Hebrew) are: *Between Realism and Romanticism* (a study of the critical work of David Frieschman); *Constructions and Meanings: Scars of Identity* (studies in Hanoch Bartov's works); and *Hebrew Periodicals in the 18th and 19th Centuries* (a study of Hebrew periodicals and the Hebrew press).

Abd El-Khalik Gobah teaches in the Department of Semitic Languages at Assiut University in Cairo, Egypt.

Nili Scharf Gold is an Associate Professor of Hebrew Literature and Language at Columbia University in New York. She received her B.A. from the Hebrew University of Jerusalem and her M.A. and Ph.D. from the Jewish Theological Seminary of America. Her book *Not Like A Cypress: Transformations of Images and Structures in Yehuda Amichai's Poetry* (in Hebrew), which was published by Schocken Publishing in Israel (1994), won the first-book prize of the Israeli Ministry of Culture.

Masha Itzhaki was born in Tel Aviv. She is a specialist in medieval Hebrew poetry. She teaches in Paris, at the Institut Nationale des Langues et Civilisations Orientales, and is the author of several books in Hebrew: *Ani Hashar* (studies in the Hebrew secular poetry of Spain, 1986); *Hachai gefen vehamavet botzer* (studies in the Spanish Tokhehot, 1987); *Elei ginat arugot* (Garden poetry in Spain, 1988); and *Jardin d'Eden, Jardins d'Espagne—Anthologie de la poésie hébraïque en Espagne et en Provence* (1993).

Gershon Shaked was born in Vienna in 1929. He and his parents immigrated to Palestine in 1939, soon after the Nazis entered Austria. The family lived in the young city of Tel Aviv. After the War of Independence, Shaked studied at the Hebrew University in Jerusalem, and eventually earned his Ph.D. in Hebrew literature. In Switzerland he studied German, English, and French literature as well. Shaked is now Professor of Hebrew and Comparative Literature at the Hebrew University of Jerusalem. He has been Visiting Professor at many American universities, including Berkeley, Hebrew Union College, Columbia, The Jewish Theological Seminary, and Harvard, and has lectured all over the world. Author of more than twenty books of criticism in many languages, Shaked was the winner in 1986 of Israel's prestigious Bialik Literary Prize. He lives in Jerusalem with his wife, Malka Shaked, who is also a scholar of Hebrew literature. They are the parents of two daughters.

Ziva Shamir, born in Tel Aviv, is head of the Katz Institute for Literary Research at Tel Aviv University. Her books (in Hebrew) are: *Poet of Poetry* (folkloristic elements in Bialik's works, 1986); *Not For Adults Only* (children's literature by H. N. Bialik, 1986); *Where Shall Poetry be Found* (*Ars Poetica* in Bialik's works, 1987); *The Vagrant Bard* (*Avant Garde* and Alterman's poetic style, 1989); *Love Unveiled* (Bialik's personal world of ideas, 1991); and *The Origins of Originality* (the poetry of Jonathan Ratosh, 1993).

Gabriella Moscati Steindler graduated from the Istituto Universitario Orientale of Naples (Italy) with the degree of Doctor in Oriental Languages, Literatures and Institutions (Near Eastern section) with a dissertation on Eliezer Ben Yehuda and the Revival of Hebrew (1962). Her early studies were devoted to Hebrew and Semitic Studies. These researches led to the publication of a monograph, *Hayyim Habshush, Immagine dello Yemen* (1976), and some articles. In order to study contemporary Israeli literature and drama Professor Moscati Steindler visited Paris and Israel after having been awarded a fellowship by the Consiglio Nazionale delle Ricerche. In 1980 she was awarded a Fulbright Fellowship for research into the sociology of literature (University of California at Berkeley), where she studied under Robert Alter. In 1984 she was appointed Associate Professor of Hebrew Language and Modern Hebrew Literature at the Istituto Universitario Orientale of Naples. She is the author of a number of critical editions of Israeli plays, such as *Ghetto* by Yehoshua Sobol and *Gan Riki* by David Grosman (1990), and she is the editor of an anthology of Israeli fiction in Italian translation, *Racconti da Israele* (1993).

Leon I. Yudkin, D. Litt., has written eight volumes of literary criticism dealing with modern Jewish and modern Hebrew literature. The most recent, *A Home Within* (1996), addresses the intersection between modernism and Jewishness. He has edited a further five volumes, and directs an annual international workshop for university teachers of Hebrew literature, in Jerusalem. After many years at the University of Manchester, he now teaches at University College London.

Index

Abramson, Glenda, 9, 10, 12–16, 123, 126
Agudat Hasofrim, 97
Akhmatova, Anna, 29
Al Hamishmar(Mishmar), 104, 105, 108
Alterman, Nathan, 11, 17, 18, 26, 72
    influence of, 99–100, 115
Amati-Mehler, Jacqueline, 87
Amichai, Yehuda
    accessibility of, xix–xx
    compared with other poets, 11–12, 15, 31
    critical response to, xviii–xix, 10–12
    education of, xiii, 71
    historical context of, 13
    innovations of, 30–31
    irony of, 44
    love poetry of, 14
    as mannerist, 21
    moderation of, 32, 42–44, 48
    pacifism of, 3–5, 24, 44, 47–48, 114
    periodization of, 10, 13
    and personalization, 71–72
    popularity of poetry, 32, 44–45
    prizes won, xx, 71, 104
    and religion, xiv
    secularity of, 41, 44
    and suffering, 56
    totality of poetry, 9–10
    world view of, 32, 33–35
    Works: "Abu Ghosh," 61, 67–68; "Ahavnu kan" (We loved here), 19, 83, 84, 105–108; *Akhshav baraash* (Now in the noise), xv, 10, 14; *Akhshav uvayamin haaherim* (Now and in other days), xiv, 2, 10, 83, 93; Akhziv cycle, *See* Shaar Akhziv; *Aravim aherim* (Other evenings), 109–111; "Autobiography 1952," 83, 104, 112–115; *Baginah hatziburit* (In the public garden), 2; "Bagivot hanegev," (In the hills of the Negev) 61; *Bamerhak shtei tikvot* (Two hopes apart), xiv, 2, 18, 94; *Baruah honoraah hazot* (In this terrible wind), xiv, 2, 10, 141; "Beheyoti yeled," (When I was a child) 88; *Bemotzaei hahofesh* ("After the vacation"), 94; "Bezavit yesharah" (At right angles), 147; Caesarea cycle, *See* Shaar Kesariya; "Clouds are the first to die, The," (Haananim hem hametim harishonim) 37; "Dangerous land, A," (Eretz mesukenet) 85; "David hatzair" (Young David), 19–20; "Elegy," 38; "El male rahamim" (God full of mercy), 4–5, 25, 61, 79; "Eyes," (Einayim) 84; *Fat Tail of the Numa, The*, 149, 156; "Forever and ever, sweet distortions," (Leolam vaed, serusim metukim) 88; "From man you are and to man you will return," (Meadam ata veel adam tashuv) 85; *Gam haegrof haya paam yad petuhah veetzbaot* (The fist was once an open hand and fingers), xvi, xvii–xviii; *Great Book of the Night, The*, 149, 152–158; "Hagibbor haamiti shel haakedah" (The real hero of the Akedah), 23–24; "Haishah halkhah" (The woman has gone), 21; "Hakrav bagivah" (Battle on the hill), 141; "Halal basadeh," (A casualty in the field) 61; "Haolam hu heder" (The world is a room), 143; *Hayom shebo*

nikbar Martin Buber (The day Martin Buber was buried), 2; "Ibn Gabirol," 51, 54–56, 109; "I'm a poor prophet," (Ani navi ani) xvii–xviii, 72; "Imi meta bashavuot" (My mother died on Shavuot), 22; "I want to die in my bed," (Ani rotze lamut al mitati) 20, 72; "I work in my small garden," (Ani oved baginati haketana) 85; "Language of Images, The," 134–135; "Lemaalah baetz itztrubalim" (Pine cones in the tree), 21; "Letter of recommendation, A," (Mikhtav hamlatza) 89–90; *Lo meakhshav, lo mikan* (Not of This Time, Not of This Place), xiv, 2, 10, 75, 133–140, 141, 143–146; "Love in the season of truth," (Ahava beona shel emet) xv–xvi; *Love Poems,* (Shirei ahava) 2; *Masa leninveh (Journey to Nineveh),* xvi, 123–130; *Mashakhta oti kmo sefinah* (You drew me like a boat), 104, 109; *Masot benyamin haaharon mitudela* (The travels of the last Benjamin of Tudela), xv, 13–14, 36, 38, 40, 138; "Matan Torah" (The revelation on Mt. Sinai), 25–26; "Mayor," (Rosh ir) 66–67; *Meadam ata veeladam tashuv* (From man you are and to man you will return), 2–3, 85; *Meakhorei kol zeh mistater osher gadol,* (Behind all this a great happiness is hiding) 86–87; "Meaz," (Since then) 60, 61; "Memorial service for those who fell at Ramat Yohanan, A," (Tekes zikhron hanoflim beramat yohanan) 62; "Misheloshah o arbaah baheder," (Out of three or four in a room) 21; *Mishirei Tveria* (Poems of Tiberius), 104–108; *Mi yitneni malon (To have a dwelling place),* xv, 141, 144, 146–147; *Moto shel Stalin* (The death of Stalin), 108–109; "My father," (Avi) 83; "My God, the soul," (Elohai, haneshama shenatata bi) 74; "My parents' immigration," (Vehagirat horay) 20; "Not like a cypress," (Lo kabrosh) 31, 84–85; *Paamonim verakavot* (Bells and trains), xiv, 2, 10; "Pegishat anshei hapalmah," (A meeting of members of the *Palmah*) 62–63, 65; "Pegishat hakitah" (Class meeting), 142–143; "Rain on the battlefield," (Geshem bisde hakrav) 60; "Rei anahnu shneinu misparim" (See, we are two numbers), 53–54; "Rosebush hangs over the wall, A," (Siah veradim meal lahoma) 79–84; "Second meeting with my father, A," (Pegisha sheniya im avi) 84; *Selected Poetry,* 83, 104, 112–115; "Seven laments for the war dead," (Kinot al hametim bamilhama) 84, 85; *Shalvah gedolah, sheelot uteshuvot* (Great tranquility— questions and answers), 2; *Sheat hahesed (The hour of grace),* 5, 64; *Shetah shel hefker* (No-man's-land), 2, 73; "Shirei hapahad haribua" (Poems of square fear), 115; *Shirim 1948–1962,* 2, 4–5, 14, 49 *(Poems 1948–1962);* "Shnei shirei Yom Kippur," (Two poems of Yom Kippur) 87; "Shnei shirim al hakravot harishonim," (Two poems on the first battles) 85; "Sonnet habinyanim," (The sonnet of the buildings) 54; "Tel Gat," 60–61, 62; "Therefore I am rich," (Lakhen and akhshav ashir) 86–87; *Time* (*Hazeman*), 86; "Tourists," (Tayarim) 85; "Travel by train," (Nesia barakevet) 83, 85–86; *Velo al menat lizkor* (Not for the sake of remembering), xv, 2, 10; *What Happened to Roni in New York,* 149, 150–152, 155–156; "Yehuda Halevi," 51–54, 109; *Yerushalayim 1967* (Jerusalem 1967), xv; *Yovlot milhamah* (Jubilees of war), 60, 62

Argentieri, Simona, 87
Aristotle, 151
Arpaly, Boaz, xviii, 9, 10–12, 15–16, 79, 139, 142
Atzmon, Tzvi, 68

Auden, W. H., xiii
Autobiography, xvi, 21
　as figuration, 13
　and landscape, 68
　and political significance, 33–34
　as source of poetry, 113–114
Avidan, David, 30, 47

Babel of the Unconscious (Amati-Mehler and Argentieri), 87
Bachelard, Gaston, 136
Bamaalah, 98
Band, Arnold, xx
Barzel, Hillel, 78
Ben Ezer, Ehud, 66
Ben-Shaul, Moshe, 98–99, 115
Bialik, C. N., 26
Bialik Prize, xx
Bible, 63, 123–124, 128
Bion, W., 78
Bordieu, 94

Cahan, Yaakov, 17
Catalogue technique, 11, 39, 51, 111, 139
Children's literature
　day-dreams in, 155–156
　dreams in, 149–150, 155
　and imagination, 152–154
　play in, 149–154
Chomsky, Noam, 87
Cixous, Hélène, 78
Cocteau, Jean: *Orphée,* 127–128
Cognitive dissonance, 20
Cohen, Israel, 97
Cohen, Tova, 58
Collective, 128–129, 136
Collective consciousness, 36–39
Conceit, xiv, xix, 65
　of English Metaphysical poets, 21, 24–25, 26(n1)
　inner logic of, 23–25
　levels of, 26
　as new trend, 17–18
　and wit, 20, 21, 24
Criticism, xviii–xix
　audience for, 12
　deconstruction, 42
　evolution of, 10
　New Criticism, 13
　Russian Formalist tradition, 11–12

Domb, Risa, xiv
Donne, John, 21–22
Dor, Moshe, 98, 100–101, 115, 119 (nn17, 22)
Dor baaretz, xiii, 94–97
Dualism, 72

Egyptian intellectuals, 1–5
Eliot, T. S., xiii
Ellul, Jacques, 58
Eternity, 39–40
Europe, and distance, 134–135

Father, xvii, 152
　as feminine vessel, 82–86, 89–90
　Jacob as, 86
　and language, 85–90
　and timebound commandments, 78, 90(n9)
Feldman, Yael, 86
Feldman, Ziva, xviii
Femininity
　and binary oppositions, 77–78
　and enclosure, 78, 82–86
　and giving, 83
　and marriage, 78
　and nurturing, 78
　and passive voice, 84–85
　and sweetness, 84
Fiction
　lyrical fictions, 74–75
　and new generation, 116
Fisch, Harold, 124–126
Freud, Sigmund, 77–78
Frustration, 107, 142, 143–144

Gardner, Helen, 24
Generations
　Aliyah generations, 94
　indigenous generation (*"dor baaretz"*), xiii, 94–97
Genotype, 93, 94, 105, 111, 115, 118(n9)
　and framework, 107

Gilboa, Amir, 116–117
Gilyonot, 109–110
Gobah, Abd El-Khalik, xviii–xix
God, 25, 56, 79
    filial relationship to, 123, 128
    and individual, 41
Gold, Nili, xix, 9, 10, 14–16, 50(n3), 120(n40)
Goldberg, Leah, 17, 95, 104–105
Golden intersection, 73–74
Greenberg, Uri Zvi, 21
Greenberg Diaspora Teachers' College, 71
Greenson, R. R., 87
Grodensky, Shlomo, 45
Guicharnaud, Jacques, 127
Guri, Haim, 116

Haaretz, 45
Hagalgal, 94
Halevi, Yehuda, 52, 53
Hanagid, Shmuel, xiii
Haperahim vehaargatel: shirat Amichai (Arpaly), 9, 10–12
Hashomer hatzair, 108
Hazman, 65, 66
Hebrew literature
    and impersonal style, 19
    and inside/outside dichotomy, 133–134
    and language, 72–73, 99, 113
    secular poetry, 54
Hero, xvi–xvii
    anti-hero, 19–20, 21, 24, 35, 47, 72
    and exile, 134, 144
    and forbidden goal, 125
    splitting of, xiv, 124–125, 136, 145–146
History
    and crisis of values, 21–22
    and digestive imagery, 38
    and individual, 37–38
    as opposite of life, 37
    and significance, 29–30
Home
    and instability, 146–147
    and journeys, 134–135, 139–140, 144
    and mourning, 147–148
    See also Place; Time
Hrushovski, Binyamin, 96, 100, 102

Humanism, 47

Ibn Gabirol, 55, 56
Imagery, 15
    of darkness, 65, 67–68
    public park, 2, 66
    of rosebush, 80–81, 91(n19)
Individual
    and collective, 136
    and history, 37–38
    as Israeli-Jewish, 49
    and other, 49–50
Individualism, 35
    and Everyman, 46
    and government, 36–38, 43, 48
    and war, 36–37
Instability, 135–136
    and home, 146–147
    and landscape, 64–68
    and persona, 20, 73–75
Interpretation, 11, 16
Israel, 133, 145
    and individual, 49
    landscape of, 57–58
    See also Jerusalem
Israel Academic Centre, 3
Israel Prize, xx, 71

Jerusalem, 44, 81, 136–138
    and collective consciousness, 38–39
Jewish Brigade, xiii
Journeys, 134–135, 139–140, 144
Jung, Carl Gustav, 125

Katznelson, Gideon, 93, 105, 117(n2)
Kinetics, 73
Klein, Melanie, 78, 147
Kol Yisrael, 2, 94
Kraemer, Susan B., 90(n5)
Kristeva, Julie, 88

Lacan, Jacques, 87–88
Lacocque, A., 124
Lacocque, P., 124
Lamdan, Isaac, 17
Landscape, 138
    and autobiography, 68

of Bible, 63
and emotion, 59
and English garden, 57
and events, 68
and historical association, 63
and individual, 109
and instability, 64–68
interiorization of, 58–59
Israeli, 57–58
and love, 63–66
and moral didacticism, 57, 58
and movement, 64–68
pastoral, 60
and place, 58, 59–60
political component of, 58
of Promised Land, 58
as text, 58, 62
and transformation, 66–67
as undefined, 73
Language
and adjectives, 68
diction, 103
and father, 85–90
and frustration, 142, 143–144
Hebrew, 72–73, 99, 113
ideolect, 14, 78–79, 90(n10)
mother-tongue, 87
and new generation, 94–95, 103
passive voice, 84–85
and politics, 37–40
register of, 103, 107–108, 110, 111
segolate words, 99, 101, 107, 115
simplicity of, 4, 17–18, 46
sociolect, 78, 80
syntax, 82
theatrical, 127
Laor, Itzhak, 31
Lean hem holkim ("Where are they heading?") (Katznelson), 93–94
Likrat
  Beshlosha, 100, 103
  early poems, 95–96
  and entry time, 96–98
  and *olim* poets, 96
  and *Pamalia* collection, 97–101
  and Shlonsky, 95
Linguistics, 14–15

and dislocation, 72
and displacement, 65
Literary system, 94
Lo kabrosh: gilgulei imagim vetavniyot beshirato shel Yehuda Amichai (Gold), 9, 14–16
Love, 33
  and darkness, 65
  father's, 86–87, 89–90
  and inner world, 107–108
  and landscape, 59–60, 63–66
  patriarchal concept of, 79
  and revenge, 138
  and time, 142–143

Man, Paul de, 16
Meaning, 28, 32, 39
Memory, xvii, 43–44
  areas of remembering, 59
  and creative process, 64
  and imagination, 58–59
  and memorialization, 59–61, 62
  as national obligation, 61–62
  and nostalgia, 60
  and personal experience, 58–59
  synonyms for, 59
Metaphor, xix, 65
  black and white, 52–53
  in children's literature, 152–154
  of self, 72
Michali, B.Y., 97, 119(n15)
Miron, Dan, 79, 83, 106, 135
Modernism, 20, 55, 71–72
Movement, 64–68, 73–74
Moznayim, 97
Myth, xvi–xvii, 124–127

Narrative stance, 145
New Criticism, 13
Noyes, John, 59

Ofrat, Gideon, 125, 127
Order, 55–56
Orpaz, Yizhak, 135
Otniel, A., 127
Oxymoron, 21, 26, 72

Palmah generation, xiii, 19–20, 61, 62, 99

Paradox, 20–23, 31
Penn, Alexander, 20, 29
Persona
    in children's literature, 155–157
    Everyman, 46, 49
    and experience, 35
    "I," 13–14, 35, 87, 146, 155–157
    and instability, 20, 73–75
    integration of, 146
    lyric, 13–14, 73–74
    and mother-tongue, 87
    and movement, 73–74
    and object, 72–74
    poetic *vs.* speaking, 71
    and split personality, xiv, 124–125, 136, 145–146
    and transformation, 75
Phillips, Adam, 83, 84
Piaget, Jean, 87
Piyyutim, 2
Place, xiv, 58–60, 139–140
Plot, 114, 142
Poetical Works of Yehuda Amichai, The (Gobah), 3
Poetics, 11–12
    biblical references in, 123–124
    external models, 53–54
    love poetry, 14
    meagreness of, 18
    medieval, 51, 53–54, 80
    of Modernism, 20, 55
    1950s, 18
    and political climate, 29
    as system, 31, 32
Politics, xviii
    and autobiography, 33–34
    and individual, 33–39
    and intratextual interpretation, 29–30
    and landscape, 58
    and language, 39–42
    left-wing, 108–109, 120(n33)
    link with literature, 27–28
    and literary community, 30–32
    and popularity, 46
    and reader, 46–50
    and significance, 27–30, 48–50
    and specific circumstances, 28–29
    and subversion, 42–44
Popov, 104
Pratt, Annis, 78
Prooftexts, 14
Prophecy, xix, 1, 40, 81–82, 144
Proust, Marcel, 148

Rabikovitz, Dalia, 31, 47
Rahel, 85
Rapp, Uri, 151
Ratosh, Yonatan, 29, 100, 115
Reader
    act of reading, 10, 21, 24–25, 52, 53
    and familiarization, 30–31, 33
    and intellect, 53, 56
    intimate connection to, 31, 32–33
    and meaning, 32, 39
    and order, 55–56
    and politics, 46–50
    and popularity of Amichai, 44–46
    and pseudo-religiosity, 42
    reception by, xviii, 30
    and scepticism, 48
Reality, 34–35, 39, 41, 47
Religion, xiv
    as performed, 128
    vocabulary of, 39–42
Riffaterre, Michael, 90(n1)
Rilke, Rainer Maria, 59, 104
Romance of the Rose, The, 80
Rubinstein, A., 134

Sabra, 134
Said, Edward, 59
Scepticism, 47–48
Schneur, Zalman, 17
Semiotics of Poetry (Riffaterre), 15
Shaar Akhziv, 64, 65, 66
Shaar Kesariya, 64
Shaked, Gershon, xiii, xx, 45, 123, 134, 137, 145
Shamir, Ziva, xiv
Sheinfeld, Ilan, 69(n14)
Shlonsky, Avraham, 11, 12, 17, 18, 71, 95, 118(n4)
    as patron, 104
    tradition of, 99, 101, 115

Shlonsky Prize, 71, 104
Sifriat Hapoalim, 95
Significance
    and apolitical texts, 29–30
    and experience, 46
    and historical context, 29
    and intratextual interpretation, 15, 29–30
    and political change, 27–28, 48–50
Sivan, Arieh, 98–100, 115
Six-Day War, 66, 144
Sobriety, 47–48
Sociocultural conditions, 21
Song of Songs, 80–81
Soul, 4–41, 52
Spitz, 87
Stalin, Joseph, 108, 120(n32)
Structure, 103–104
    repetition, 110–111, 113
    rhetorical, 39
    rhyme, 99, 106–107, 109, 153
    rhythm, 110, 113

Tchernichowsky, Saul, 58
Ten Commandments, 89–90
Theatre, 2
    ancient Greek, 151–152
    children's play as, 150
    scenic devices, 127
Thomas, Dylan, 21
Time, 73–75
    and childhood, 157
    and love, 142–143
    past, 141–143

Torah, 86–87, 88
Transformation
    and dialogue, 72–73
    of landscape, 66–67
Translations, xx, 3
Turner, Victor, 128
Tzvik, Yehudit, 9

Values, 35, 43

Wallach, Yonah, 15
War of Independence, xix, 19, 59–61, 63, 104
Winnicott, D. W., 78
Writing of Yehuda Amichai: A Thematic Approach, The (Abramson), 9, 12–14
Würzburg, xiv, 71, 73

Yehoshua, A. B., 134
Yehuda Amichai: A Life of Poetry 1948–1994 trans. Harshav, 4–5, 25, 61, 79
Yehuda Amichai: mivhar maamarei bikoret al yetsirato (Tzvik), 9
Yishuv, 58, 66
Yom Kippur, 128–129
Yom Kippur War, 48

Zach, Natan, 11, 12, 18, 29–31, 46–47, 79, 93–94
    on Amichai, 112, 120(n31)
    on journey, 135
    and *Likrat* group, 96, 102–104, 111–112, 115–116
Zionism, 36, 42

The experienced sour : studies in Amicha
892.4 Ami   53264

AKIBA HEBREW ACADEMY LIBRARY

AKIBA HEBREW ACADEMY
223 N. HIGHLAND AVENUE
MERION STATION, PA. 19066